DATE DUE

~~5-99~~			
~~ ~~			
~~ ~~			

DEMCO 38-296

Internet and Intranet Security

For a complete listing of the *Artech House Computer Science Library*,
turn to the back of this book.

Internet and Intranet Security

Rolf Oppliger

Artech House
Boston • London

Data

Internet and intranet security / Rolf Oppliger
    p.   cm.
Includes bibliographical references and index.
ISBN 0-89006-829-1   (alk. paper)
    1. Interent (Computer network)—Security measures.   2. Intranets (Computer
networks)—Security measures.   3. Computers—Access control.   4. TCP/IP (Computer
network protocol)   I.   Title.
    TK5105.875.I57O67   1997
    005.8—dc21   97-42908
                                                                  CIP

British Library Cataloguing in Publication Data
Oppliger, Rolf
    Internet and intranet security. – (Artech House computer science library)
    1. Internet (Computer network) – Security measures   2. Internet (Computer networks) –
Access control   3. Intranets (Computer networks) – Security measures   4. Intranets
(Computer networks) – Access control   I. Title
    005.8

    ISBN 0-89006-829-1

Cover illustration by Jay Gordon

© 1998 ARTECH HOUSE, INC.
685 Canton Street
Norwood, MA 02062

International Standard Book Number: 0-89006-829-1
Library of Congress Catalog Card Number: 97-42908

10 9 8 7 6 5 4 3 2

To my wife Isabelle

Contents

Preface

The emerging use of the transmission control and Internet protocol (TCP/IP) suite has led to a global system of interconnected hosts and networks that is commonly referred to as the Internet.[1] The Internet was created initially to help foster communications among government-sponsored researchers and grew steadily to include educational institutions, commercial organizations, and government agencies as well. During the last decade, the Internet has experienced a triumphant advance. Today, it is the world's largest computer network and has been doubling in size each year since 1988. With this phenomenal growth, the Internet's size is increasing faster than any other network ever created, including even the public switched telephone network (PSTN). Projections based on its current rate of growth suggest that there will be over one million networks presumably connected to the Internet and well over one billion users by the end of the century. The Internet is commonly seen as the basis and first incarnation of an information superhighway, or national information infrastructure (NII) as, for example, promoted by the U.S. government.

But in spite of this exacting role, the initial, research-oriented Internet and its communications protocol suite were designed for a more benign environment than now exists. It could, perhaps, best be described as a collegial environment, where the users were mutually trusting each other and interested in a free and open exchange of information. In this environment, the people on the Internet were the

---

[1]Note the definite article and the capital letter "I" in the term "the Internet." More generally, the term "internet" is used to refer to any TCP/IP-based internetwork.

people who actually built the Internet. Later on, when the Internet became more useful and reliable, these people were joined by others. With fewer common goals and more people, the Internet steadily twisted away from its original intent.

Today, the Internet environment is much less collegial and trustworthy. It contains all the dangerous situations, nasty people, and risks that one can find in society as a whole. Along with the well-intentioned and honest users of the Internet, there are always people who intentionally try to break into systems connected to it. The Internet is plagued with the kind of delinquents who enjoy the electronic equivalent of writing on other people's walls with spray paint, tearing off mailboxes, or sitting in the street blowing their car horns. In this new environment, the openness of the Internet has turned out to be a double-edged sword. Since its very beginning, but especially since its opening in the early 1990s and its ongoing commercialization, the Internet has become a popular target to attack. The number of security breaches has in fact escalated more than in proportion to the growth of the Internet as a whole.

Many security problems with networks in general and the Internet in particular have received public attention, and the media have carried stories of high-profile malicious attacks via the Internet against government, business, and academic sites. Perhaps the first and most significant incident was the Internet Worm, launched by Robert T. Morris, Jr. on November 2, 1988 [1,2]. The Internet Worm flooded thousands of hosts connected to the Internet and woke up the Internet community accordingly. Since then, reports of network-based attacks, such as password sniffing, IP spoofing, session hijacking, flooding, and other denial of service attacks, as well as exploitations of well-known bugs and design limitations, have grown dramatically [3 – 5]. In addition, the use and wide deployment of executable content, such as provided by Java applets and ActiveX controls, for example, has also provided new possibilities to attack hosts or entire sites.[2]

The Internet Worm gained a lot of publicity and led to increased awareness of security issues on the Internet. The Computer Emergency Response Team (CERT[3]) that is operated by the Software Engineering Institute at Carnegie Mellon University was created in the aftermath of the Internet Worm, and other CERTs have been founded in various countries around the world. Today, the CERT at Carnegie Mellon University serves as CERT coordination center (CERT/CC). The CERT/CC receives an average of three to four new computer security incident reports each day. Many Internet breaches are publicized and attract the attention of the Internet

---

[2]Contact the WWW home page of DigiCrime at URL http://www.digicrime.com to convince yourself that executable content is in fact dangerous.

[3]http://cert.org

community, while numerous incidents go unnoticed. For example, early in 1994, thousands of passwords were captured by sniffer programs that had been remotely installed on compromised hosts on various university networks connected to the Internet. At the end of the same year, sequence number attacks were successfully launched by Kevin Mitnick against several computer centers, including Tsutomu Shimomura's San Diego Center for Supercomputing [6]. This story actually shocked the world when it became *New York Times* headline news on January 23, 1995. In 1996, several forms of denial of service attacks were launched, such as e-mail bombing and TCP SYN flooding. In spite of the fact that unscrupulous people make press headlines with various types of attacks, the vulnerabilities they exploit are usually well known. For example, security experts have warned against passwords transmitted in the clear since the very beginning of (inter)networking, and Robert T. Morris, Jr. described sequence number attacks for BSD UNIX version 4.2 when he was with AT&T Bell Laboratories in 1985 [7,8].

Some of the problems related to Internet security are a result of inherent vulnerabilities in the TCP/IP protocols and services, while others are a result of host configuration and access controls that are poorly implemented or overly complex to administer. Additionally, the role and importance of system management is often short-changed in job descriptions, resulting in many administrators being, at best, part-time and poorly prepared. This is further aggravated by the tremendous growth of the Internet and how the Internet is used. Today, individuals, commercial organizations, and government agencies depend on the Internet for communications and research, and thus have much more to lose if their sites are attacked. As a matter of fact, virtually everyone on the Internet is vulnerable, and the Internet's security problems are the center of attention, generating much fear throughout both the computer and communications industries. Concerns about security problems have already begun to chill the overheated expectations about the Internet's readiness for full commercial activity, possibly delaying or preventing it from becoming a mass medium for the NII, or even the global information infrastructure (GII).

Several studies have independently shown that many individuals and companies are abstaining from joining the Internet simply because of security concerns. At the same time, analysts are warning companies about the dangers of not being connected to the Internet. In this conflicting situation, almost everyone agrees that the Internet needs more and better security. In a workshop held by the Internet Architecture Board (IAB) in February 1994, scaling and security were nominated as the two most important problem areas for the Internet architecture as a whole [9]. This has not changed so far and is not likely to change in the foreseeable future. For example, in November and December 1996, Dan Farmer conducted a security survey of approximately 2,200 computing systems on the Internet.[4] What he found was indeed surprising: almost two-thirds of the more interesting sites had serious security problems that could have been exploited by determined attackers.

But security in general and Internet security in particular are vague terms that may mean various things to different people. Security is a property that is not provable by nature. The best we can show is resistance against a certain set of attacks we know and are familiar with. There is nothing in the world that can protect us against new types of attack. For example, timing attacks in cryptanalysis and differential fault analysis (DFA) attacks against hardware devices that have been designed to securely store secret keys have gained a lot of attention in the recent past. In this book, we are not going to give a formal definition of what exactly is security. Instead, we focus on techniques and mechanisms that are available today and that can be used to provide network security in terms of access control and communication security services. The assumption is that if a network is able to provide these classes of security services, there are at least some obstacles to overcome in order to successfully launch an attack. If the security services are well designed and properly implemented, the resulting obstacles are far too big to be overcome by occasional intruders.

Obviously, the same techniques and mechanisms that are used to secure the Internet as a whole can also be used to secure parts of the Internet. As the term "intranet" refers to a TCP/IP-based corporate or enterprise network, any book that focuses on TCP/IP and Internet security automatically addresses intranet security as well. As a matter of fact, the title "intranet security" better reflects the scope of any book on TCP/IP and Internet security, since it is usually not the Internet as a whole that must be protected, but well-defined parts of it, and these parts are usually an intranet or a set of interconnected but logically separated intranets. Consequently, *Internet and Intranet Security* has been chosen as a title for this book. This title reflects our interest in both standardized security techniques for the entire Internet, as well as security techniques and mechanisms that can be used and deployed within intranet environments.

When I started to work on Internet and intranet security, the situation was comparably simple. There were some authentication and key distribution systems available that made people believe the Internet would become secure if only these systems were used and widely deployed. It was at this time I wrote *Authentication Systems for Secure Networks*, a companion book also published by Artech House [10]. As its title suggests, *Authentication Systems for Secure Networks* gives a com-

---

[4]http://www.trouble.org/survey/

prehensive overview about the authentication and key distribution systems that were available at that time, including Kerberos, NetSP, SPX, TESS, SESAME, and OSF DCE. But after having written the book, I realized that alternative techniques and mechanisms had been developed to provide Internet and intranet security. For example, firewalls started their triumphal march that has continued until today. Also, cryptographic security protocols for the Internet, transport, and application layer had been developed, proposed, and partly implemented. Consequently, I realized that the use of authentication systems is just one possibility to address Internet security, and that there are other possibilities as well. In this situation, I decided to write *Internet and Intranet Security* as a companion book to *Authentication Systems for Secure Networks*. In particular, *Internet and Intranet Security* enlarges the scope of *Authentication Systems for Secure Networks* and tries to give a more comprehensive overview about currently available Internet and intranet security techniques and mechanisms. Due to their close relationship, some parts of *Authentication Systems for Secure Networks* are included in *Internet and Intranet Security* in a slightly modified form. For example, Chapter 1 of *Authentication Systems for Secure Networks* is extended and divided up into several chapters that together consitute the first part of *Internet and Intranet Security*.

Internet and Intranet Security has been written to serve the needs of computer and network professionals that have interest in understanding, establishing, and supporting secure TCP/IP-based networks. I also hope that the book provides sufficient background to help security professionals propose approaches to secure commercial applications for the Internet. The book is tutorial in nature but still requires some familiarity with the fundamentals of computer networks and distributed systems, as well as cryptography and the use of cryptographic protocols in networked and distributed systems. Many of the references cited throughout the book are also tutorial and may be used to obtain additional background information. In particular, I recommend [11 – 14] for an introduction to computer networks and distributed systems. With regard to cryptography I recommend [15 – 22], and with regard to the use of cryptographic protocols in networked and distributed environments I recommend [23 – 30]. Historical notes on cryptography can be found in [31,32]. A good source for contemporary information are various information pages offered in the World Wide Web (WWW) by companies that are actively working in the field, as well as the frequently asked questions (FAQs) periodically posted to the corresponding USENET newsgroups.

In short, *Internet and Intranet Security* introduces and discusses security techniques and mechanisms that are available today to provide Internet and intranet security in terms of access control and communication security services. As such, it does not cover issues related the security of the underlying operating systems. There are many books, mainly on computer security, that address these issues [33 – 35]. *Internet and Intranet Security* is organized in four parts:

- Part 1, *Fundamentals*, introduces the fundamentals that are necessary to understand the rest of the book.

- Part 2, *Access Control*, addresses the firewall technology that can be used to provide access control services to corporate intranets connected either to other intranets or to the Internet.

- Part 3, *Communication Security*, addresses security protocols that have been proposed, specified, and partially implemented for the Internet, transport, and application layer.

- Part 4, *Discussion*, concludes with some final remarks on electronic commerce and security tools.

The book also includes a glossary that defines major terms, as well as a list of abbreviations and acronyms. References are included at the end of each chapter. At the end of the book, an About the Author page is appended to tell you a little bit about me, and there is an index to help you find particular terms.

Internet and intranet security is such a fast-moving field that I have to reserve the right to be out of date or simply wrong. While time brings new technologies and outdates current technologies, I have attempted to focus primarily on the conceptual approaches for Internet and intranet security. By the time this book is published, several of my comments will probably have moved from the future to the present, and from the present to the past.

Due to the nature of this book, it is also necessary to mention some company, product, and service names. It is, however, only fair to mention that the presence or absence of a specific name neither implies any criticism or endorsement, nor does it imply that the corresponding company, product, or service is necessarily the best available. For a more comprehensive products overview we recommend the annually published *Computer Security Products Buyers Guide* from the Computer Security Institute (CSI) based in San Francisco.

Whenever possible, I have added uniform resource locators (URLs) as footnotes to the text. The URLs point to corresponding information pages provided in the WWW. While care has been taken to ensure that the URLs are valid now, unfortunately, due to the dynamic nature of the WWW, I cannot guarantee that these

URLs as well as their contents remain valid forever. With regard to these URLs, I apologize for any information page that may have been removed or replaced since the writing and publishing of this book.

I would like to take the opportunity to invite you as a reader of this book to let me know your opinions and thoughts. If you have something to correct or add, please let me know. If I haven't expressed myself clearly please let me know that, too. I appreciate and sincerely welcome any comment or suggestion, in order to update the book periodically. The best way to reach me is to send electronic mail to `oppligerr@acm.org` or `oppliger@computer.org`. You can also visit my WWW home page and drop a message there. This page can be found by following the URL `http://iamwww.unibe.ch/~oppliger`.

REFERENCES

[1] E.H. Spafford, "The Internet Worm: Crisis and Aftermath," *Communications of the ACM*, Vol. 32, 1989, pp. 678 – 688.

[2] J.A. Rochlis, and M.W. Eichin, "With Microscope and Tweezers: The Worm from MIT's Perspective," *Communications of the ACM*, Vol. 32, 1989, pp. 689 – 703.

[3] P.J. Denning, *Computers under Attack: Intruders, Worms, and Viruses*, ACM Press/ Addison-Wesley, New York, NY, 1990.

[4] P.G. Neumann, *Computer-Related Risks*, ACM Press/Addison-Wesley, New York, NY, 1995.

[5] J.D. Howard, *An Analysis Of Security Incidents On The Internet 1989 – 1995*, Ph.D. Thesis, Carnegie Mellon University, April 1997.

[6] T. Shimomura with J. Markoff, *Takedown*, Hyperion, New York, NY, 1996.

[7] R.T. Morris, "A weakness in the 4.2BSD UNIX TCP/IP Software," Computer Science Technical Report No. 117, AT&T Bell Laboratories, Murray Hill, NJ, February 1985.

[8] S.M. Bellovin, "Security Problems in the TCP/IP Protocol Suite," *ACM Computer Communication Review*, Vol. 19, No. 2, 1989, pp. 32 – 48.

[9] R. Braden, D. Clark, S. Crocker, and C. Huitema, "Report of the IAB Workshop on Security in the Internet Architecture (February 8 – 10, 1994)," Request for Comments 1636, June 1994.

[10] R. Oppliger, *Authentication Systems for Secure Networks*, Artech House, Norwood, MA, 1996.

[11] D. Comer, *Internetworking with TCP/IP: Principles, Protocols, and Architecture*, Prentice-Hall, Englewood Cliffs, NJ, 1988.

[12] A.S. Tanenbaum, *Computer Networks*, Prentice-Hall, Englewood Cliffs, NJ, 1988.

[13] S. Carl-Mitchell, and J.S. Quaterman, *Practical Internetworking with TCP/IP and UNIX*, Addison-Wesley, Reading, MA, 1993.

[14] D. Piscitello, and A.L. Chapin, *Open Systems Networking: TCP/IP and OSI*, Addison-Wesley, Reading, MA, 1993.

[15] A.G. Konheim, *Cryptography: A Primer*, John Wiley & Sons, New York, NY, 1981.

[16] C.H. Meyer, and S.M. Matias, *Cryptography: A New Dimension in Computer Data Security*, John Wiley & Sons, New York, NY, 1982.

[17] D.E. Denning, *Cryptography and Data Security*, Addison-Wesley, Reading, MA, 1982.

[18] G. Brassard, *Modern Cryptology*, Springer-Verlag, Berlin, Germany, 1988.

[19] M.Y. Rhee, *Cryptography and Secure Communications*, McGraw-Hill, New York, NY, 1994.

[20] D. Stinson, *Cryptography Theory and Practice*, CRC Press, Boca Raton, FL, 1995.

[21] B. Schneier, *Applied Cryptography: Protocols, Algorithms, and Source Code in C*, 2nd Edition, John Wiley & Sons, New York, NY, 1996.

[22] A. Menezes, P. van Oorschot, and S. Vanstone, *Handbook of Applied Cryptography*, CRC Press, Boca Raton, FL, 1996.

[23] D.W. Davies, and W.L. Price, *Security for Computer Networks*, John Wiley & Sons, Chichester, UK, 1984.

[24] S. Muftic, *Security Mechanisms for Computer Networks*, Ellis Horwood, Chichester, UK, 1989.

[25] S. Muftic, A. Patel, P. Sanders, R. Colon, J. Heijnsdijk, and U. Pulkkinen, *Security Architecture for Open Distributed Systems*, John Wiley & Sons, Chichester, UK, 1993.

[26] M. Purser, *Secure Data Networking*, Artech House, Norwood, MA, 1993.

[27] M. Devargas, *Network Security*, NCC Blackwell, Oxford, UK, 1993.

[28] W. Ford, *Computer Communications Security: Principles, Standard Protocols and Techniques*, Prentice Hall, Englewood Cliffs, NJ, 1994.

[29] W. Stallings, *Network and Internetwork Security*, Prentice-Hall, Englewood Cliffs, NJ, 1994.

[30] C. Kaufman, R. Perlman, and M. Speciner, *Network Security: Private Communication in a Public World*, Prentice Hall, Englewood Cliffs, NJ, 1995.

[31] D. Kahn, *Sezing the Enigma*, Houghton Mifflin, Boston, MA, 1991.

[32] D. Kahn, *The Codebreakers*, Revised Edition, Scribner, New York, NY, 1996.

[33] R.H. Baker, *Computer Security Handbook*, McGraw-Hill, New York, NY, 1991.

[34] E. Amoroso, *Fundamentals of Computer Security Technology*, Prentice-Hall, Englewood Cliffs, NJ, 1994.

[35] R. Oppliger, *IT-Sicherheit: Grundlagen und Umsetzung in der Praxis*, DuD-Fachbeiträge, Vieweg-Verlag, Wiesbaden, Germany, 1997.

Acknowledgments

One of the more pleasurable tasks of being an author is to thank all the people who have contributed to and been involved in the writing and publishing of a book. First of all, I'd like to sincerely thank Kurt Bauknecht from the University of Zürich, Switzerland, for his ongoing interest, encouragement, and support. The book has also gained a lot from discussions with and information provided by Andres Albanese, Daniel Bleichenbacher, Domenico Ferrari, Marcel Frauenknecht, Andreas Greulich, Dieter Hogrefe, Phil Karn, Hansjürg Mey, Jean-Luc Nottaris, Günther Pernul, Basie von Solms, and Peter Trachsel. In spite of all their help, remaining ambiguities, errors, and difficult-to-read passages are caused by myself and are not their fault. I'd also like to thank Artech House for publishing the book, Kate Hawes, Susanna Taggart, Judi Stone, Kat Schott, and Dennis Weaver for making the publishing process most convenient to me, Jennifer Stuart for designing the book cover, and Michael Purser for reviewing the manuscript and always providing useful comments and suggestions. It has been a pleasure to work with all of them. A special thanks is due to my wife Isabelle for always offering complete cooperation to my unconventional working hours during nights, weekends, and holidays. Without her love, patience, and support this book would not have been possible.

Acknowledgments

Part I

FUNDAMENTALS

Chapter 1

Introduction

The field of computer science is filled with ill-defined terminology used by different authors in conflicting and contradictory ways. This is especially true in the field of computer and communication security. Hence, we sacrifice the first chapter of this book to work against this tradition, and to introduce and define some of the major terms that are used in the rest of this book. Specialists in computer networks and distributed systems are invited to skip the chapter. For the reasons explained in the Preface, this is also true for the readers of [1].

According to *Webster's Dictionary*, the term *information* refers to "knowledge communicated or received concerning a particular fact or circumstance" in general, and "data that can be coded for processing by a computer or similar device" in computer science. This definition is fairly broad and not too precise. However, it is sufficient for our purposes. Anybody who is interested in a more precise and formal definition and treatment of information is referred to Claude E. Shannon's communication or information theory [2,3].

In accordance with the definition of information given above, we use the term *information technology* (IT) to refer to any kind of technology that deals with information. In particular, IT focuses on the question(s) of how to effectively store, process, and transmit data that encodes information. Similarly, we use the term *IT security* to refer to the special field of IT that deals with security-related issues. IT security comprises both computer and communication security:

- The aim of *computer security* is to preserve computing resources against unauthorized use and abuse, as well as to protect data that encode information from accidental or deliberate damage, disclosure, and modification.

- The aim of *communication security* is to protect data that encode information during its transmission in computer networks and distributed systems.

According to Tanenbaum, the term *computer network* refers to an interconnected collection of autonomous computer systems [4]. Two computer systems are interconnected if they are able to exchange data. The systems are autonomous if there doesn't exist a clear master/slave relationship between them. For example, a system with one control unit and several slaves is not a network; nor is a large computer with remote card readers, printers, and terminals.

There is considerable confusion in the literature about what exactly distinguishes a distributed system from a computer network. Referring to Leslie Lamport, a *distributed system* consists of a collection of distinct processes that are spatially separated and that communicate with each other by exchanging messages.[1] In addition to that, Lamport refers to a system as a distributed system if the message transmission delay is not negligible compared to the time between events in a single process [5]. Note that this definition is particularly well suited to discuss time, clocks, and temporal ordering of events in distributed environments.

Again referring to Tanenbaum, the key distinction between a computer network and a distributed system is that in a distributed system, the existence of multiple autonomous computer systems is transparent, and not necessarily visible to the user. In principle, the user can type a command to run a program, and it runs. It is up to the operating system to select the best processor available for the program to run, to find and transport all input data to that processor, and to put the results as output data in the appropriate place. In other words, the user of a distributed system should not necessarily be aware that there are multiple processors involved; to the user, the distributed system looks like a virtual uniprocessor. Note that in this example, a distributed system can be seen as a special case of a computer network, namely one whose software gives it a very high degree of cohesiveness and transparency. Thus the distinction between a computer network and a distributed system lies within the software in general and the operating system in particular, rather than within the hardware.

---

[1]In a more humorous note, Lamport has also defined a distributed system as a "system that stops you from getting work done when a machine you've never seen crashes."

In accordance with the security frameworks being developed by the Joint Technical Committee 1 (JTC1) of the International Organization for Standardization (ISO) and the International Electrotechnical Committee (IEC) [6], we use the term *principal* to refer to a human or system entity that is registered in and authenticatable to a computer network or distributed system. Users, hosts, and processes are commonly considered as principals:

- A *user* is an entity made accountable and ultimately responsible for his or her activities within a computer network or distributed system.

- A *host* is an addressable entity within a computer network or distributed system. The entity is typically addressed either by its name or by its network address.

- A *process* is an instantiation of a program running on a particular host. It is common to use the *client/server model* to distinguish between client and server processes:

  - A *client process* (client) is a process that requests (and eventually also obtains and uses) a network service.
  - A *server process* (server) is a process that provides a network service. In this terminology, a service refers to a coherent set of abstract functionality, and a server is typically a continuously running background program (a so-called *daemon*) that is specialized in providing the functionality.

Note that sometimes a process can act either as client or server. For example, in a UNIX system a print server is usually created by and associated with the superuser. On the one hand, the print server acts as a server for printing requests by clients; on the other hand, the print server acts as a client when the server requests files to print from a file server. Also note that a client and a server use specific protocols to communicate with each other.

The client/server model provides an attractive paradigm for designing and implementing distributed systems and applications. In the simplest case, a service is implemented by just one server. But sometimes it is more convenient to have two or even more servers working cooperatively to provide a specific service. One point is that a single server may become overloaded or may not be sufficiently close to all users in a networked or distributed environment. Another point is availability. If a service is replicated, it does not matter if some of the replicas are down or unavailable. Often, the fact that a service is replicated is transparent to the user, meaning that the user does not know whether there's a single copy of the service or there are replicas. The study and development of techniques to securely replicate services has become a new and fast growing area of research [7,8] that is beyond the scope of this book.

The ISO uses the term *standard* to refer to a documented agreement containing technical specifications or other precise criteria to be used consistently as rules, guidelines, or definitions of characteristics to ensure that materials, products, processes and services are fit for their purpose. Consequently, an *open system standard* is a standard that specifies an open system and allows manufacturers to build corresponding interoperable products, whereas an *open system* is a system that conforms to open system standards.

A computer network in general, and a distributed system in particular, is a complex collection of cooperating software and hardware. To aid in the understanding of these systems, network practitioners have developed some standard ways to model networked and distributed systems, and to break them down into simpler pieces. A reference model is a model used to explain how the various components of a system fit together and explains what the common interface specifications are between the various components. A basic feature of a reference model is the division of the overall functionality into layers, done in an attempt to reduce complexity.

Table 1.1
Layers of the OSI Reference Model

Layer 7	Application layer
Layer 6	Presentation layer
Layer 5	Session layer
Layer 4	Transport layer
Layer 3	Network layer
Layer 2	Data link layer
Layer 1	Physical layer

In 1978 the ISO/IEC JTC1 proposed a *Reference Model for Open Systems Interconnection* (OSI-RM) as a preeminent model for structuring and understanding communication functions within open systems. The OSI-RM follows the widely accepted structuring technique of layering, and the communication functions are partitioned into a hierarchical set of layers accordingly. In OSI terminology, there is a strong distinction between services and protocols:

- A *service* refers to something an application program or a higher-layer protocol makes use of;

- A *protocol* refers to a set of rules and messages to actually provide a service.

Protocols can be characterized according to the services they provide. A protocol layer provides a broad characterization of the services of protocols that fit in that layer.

The OSI-RM specifies seven layers of communications system functionality, from the physical layer at the bottom to the application layer at the top. The layers are overviewed in Table 1.1 and also illustrated on the left side of Figure 2.3. Refer to the books cited in the Preface for a more comprehensive description of the OSI-RM and the OSI layers. The OSI-RM is useful because it provides a commonly used terminology and defines a structure for data communication standards. It was approved as an international standard (IS) in 1982 [9]. Two years later, the Telecommunication Standardization Sector of the International Telecommunication Union (ITU-T[2]) adopted the OSI-RM in its recommendation X.200.

The use of open system standards and open systems that conform to these standards has many advantages, and we are not going to discuss them in this book. However, we want to point out that the current trend towards open systems may also negatively influence security. A corresponding report from Bell Communications Research (Bellcore) has shown that "intruders were assisted in their endeavors by the openness and standardization that the telecommunications industry has undergone in the last decade" [10]. Security is thus a vital concern in open systems, and the apparent contradiction between openness and security is deceptive. In fact, it has often seduced people to buy proprietary systems instead of open systems. The assumption that has led to this purchase behavior is our strong belief in "security through obscurity." We think that to hide information about the design of a system is the best way to prevent potential attackers from learning something about the system's own vulnerabilities. Network security techniques, if well designed and properly implemented, can be used to solve the contradiction between openness and security, and it is one of the main goals of this book to provide a basic understanding for the proper design and implementation of these techniques.

A *protocol suite* is a set of protocols that work together and fit into a common protocol model. However, there might be more protocols in a protocol suite than are practical for use with a particular application. Therefore a *protocol stack* is a selection of protocols from a protocol suite that is selected to support a particular application or class of applications. In the OSI world, various national and international standarization bodies specify profiles for stacks of OSI protocols. In the

---

[2]The ITU-T was formerly known as Consultative Committee on International Telegraphy and Telephony (CCITT).

United States, for example, the National Institute of Standards and Technology (NIST) specifies such stacks in the Government OSI Profile (GOSIP).

This book is entitled *Internet and Intranet Security*. As such, it focuses on the security of special computer networks and distributed systems, namely such that are based on the TCP/IP communications protocol suite. The fundamentals of TCP/IP networking are introduced in the following chapter. However, we still want to point out that many things that are said in this book are equally true for other data networks as well, especially if they use packet switching as their basic enabling technique.

Input/Output (i.e. UNIX getty)

Operating System (i.e. UNIX)

Figure 1.1   Accessibility of a stand-alone computer system.

In general, a *vulnerability* refers to a weakness that can be exploited by an intruder to violate a system or the information it contains. In a computer network or distributed system, passwords transmitted in the clear often represent a major vulnerability. The passwords are exposed to passive eavesdropping and corresponding sniffing attacks. Similarly, the ability of a network host to boot with a network address that has originally been assigned to another host refers to another vulnerability that can be used to spoof that particular host and to masquerade accordingly.

A *threat* refers to a circumstance, condition, or event with the potential to either violate the security of a system or to cause harm to system resources. Computer networks and distributed systems are susceptible to a wide variety of possible threats that may be mounted either by intruders[3] or legitimate users. As a matter of fact, legitimate users are more powerful adversaries, since they possess internal information that is not usually available to intruders.

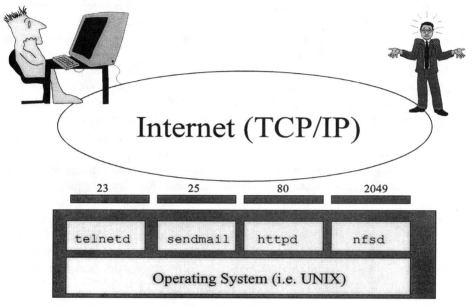

Figure 1.2 Accessibility of a networked computer system.

In order to better understand the vulnerabilities of networked computer systems, it is useful and worthwhile to have a closer look at the accessibility of a stand-alone computer system as illustrated in Figure 1.1. In this case, the situation is comparatively simple. The computer system runs an operating system (i.e., UNIX) with some input/output processes (i.e., UNIX `getty` processes). Any legitimate user who is able to physically access the computer system can now log in by providing his or her user name and password to a login prompt. In Figure 1.1, the legitimate user is illustrated on the left side of the computer system. Note that any intruder who wants to gain illegitimate access to the computer system must not only have physical access to the system, but must also be able to impersonate a legitimate user by providing this user's proper name and password to the login prompt. In

---

[3]The term *hacker* is often used to describe computer vandals that break into computer systems. These vandals call themselves hackers, and that is how they got the name, but in my opinion, they don't deserve it. In this book, we use the terms *intruder* and *attacker* instead.

Figure 1.1, the intruder who wants to gain illegitimate access by impersonating a legitimate user is illustrated on the right side of the computer system.

From the intruder's point of view, the situation is much simpler in the case of a networked computer system as illustrated in Figure 1.2. In this case, the computer system makes available some basic network services that are typically provided at well-known ports. For example, the remote terminal access service (`telnetd`) is provided at port 23, the electronic mail service (`sendmail`) at port 25, the WWW service (`httpd`) at port 80, and the network file service (`nsfd`) at port 2049. In reality, a computer system would provide a large number of other network services as well. Similar to Figure 1.1, the legitimate user is illustrated on the left side and the intruder is illustrated on the right side of the computer system. It is important to note that in the case of a networked computer system, an intruder must not necessarily have physical access to the system in order to log in, but can use any TCP/IP service that is offered by the system instead. To make things worse, the intruder is not only able to attack the communications that may take place between the legitimate user and the computer system, but can attack each of the system's network services and corresponding ports as well. There is software running on each of these ports, and if the software is buggy or contains trapdoors the intruder may be able to illegitimately access the system. In general, there are at least three reasons why networked computer systems are more vulnerable than their stand-alone counterparts:

- First and foremost, more points exist from which an attack can be launched. Someone who is not able to physically access or connect to a computer system cannot attack it. Consequently, by adding more network connections for legitimate users, more vulnerabilities are automatically added as well.

- Second, the physical perimeter of a system is artificially extended by having it connect to a computer network. This extension usually leads beyond what is controllable by system administrators.

- Third, networked computer systems typically run software that is inherently more complex and errorprone. There are many network software packages that are known to be buggy, and more often than not, intruders learn about these bugs before system administrators do. To make things even worse, intruders must know and be able to exploit just one single bug, whereas system administrators usually must know and be able to fix each of them.

With respect to possible threats in computer networks and distributed systems, it is common to distinguish between host and communication compromises.

- A *host compromise* is the result of a subversion of an individual host within a computer network or distributed system. Various degrees of subversion are possible, ranging from the relatively benign case of corrupting process state information to the extreme case of assuming total control of the host.

- A *communication compromise* is the result of a subversion of a communication line within a computer network or distributed system.

An attack is an exploitation by an intruder of a vulnerability. In general, there are two types of attacks to be distinguished, namely passive and active attacks.

A *passive attack* threatens the confidentiality of data being transmitted. The situation is illustrated in Figure 1.3. The data transmitted from the sender (on the right side) to the receiver (on the left side) are observed by the intruder (in the middle). With respect to the intruder's possibilities to interpret the information that the transmitted data encodes, passive wiretapping and traffic analysis attacks must be distinguished:

- In a *passive wiretapping attack*, the intruder is able to interpret the data and to extract the information accordingly.

- In a *traffic analysis attack*, the intruder is not able to do so. Consequently, traffic analysis refers to the inference of information from the observation of external traffic characteristics. For example, if we observe that two companies — one financially strong, the other financially weak — begin to trade a large number of messages, we may infer that they are discussing a merger. Other examples occur in military environments.

Figure 1.3   A passive attack threatens the confidentiality of data being transmitted.

Note that the feasibility of a passive attack primarily depends on the physical transmission media in use and its physical accessibility for intruders. For example, mobile communications is by its very nature easy to tap, whereas metallic transmission media at least require some sort of physical access. Lightwave conductors can also be tapped, but this is quite expensive. Also note that the use of concentrating and multiplexing techniques, in general, makes it more difficult to passively attack a communications line. However, it is only fair to mention that a passive attacker doesn't necessarily have to tap a physical communications line. Most local area network interfaces can operate in the so-called promiscuous mode. In this mode, they are usually able to capture all frames on a local area network they are connected to, rather than just those frames addressed to the machines they are part of. This capability has useful purposes for network analysis, testing, and debugging (e.g., by utilities such as `etherfind` and `tcpdump` in the case of the UNIX operating system). Unfortunately, this capability can also be used by attackers to snoop on all traffic on a particular network segment. Today, several software packages are available for monitoring network traffic, primarily for the purpose of network management. These software packages are dual-use, meaning they can, for example, be effective at eavesdropping and capturing passwords as they are transmitted over communications lines. A widely used software package of this kind is LANWatch from FTP Software. With regard to TCP/IP networking, it is important to note that when a user connects to his or her account on a remote host, using Telnet or FTP, for example, his or her password travels in the clear and is exposed to passive eavesdropping accordingly. Another possibility to grab passwords without tapping a communications line is to make use of the X Window system. If the system is not correctly configured it is sometimes possible for an attacker to open windows on other systems and read keystrokes that could eventually contain some passwords or other sensitive information.

Figure 1.4   An active attack threatens the integrity or availability of data being transmitted.

An *active attack* threatens the integrity or availability of data being transmitted. The situation is illustrated in Figure 1.4. In this case, the intruder is able to observe and fully control the data that is flowing by. In general, the intruder can modify, extend, delete, and replay data units. The intruder can also influence or modify the routing tables of the systems to redirect traffic. In addition to that, he or she can also flood a receiver and cause a denial of service. In short, a denial of service refers to the prevention of authorized access to resources or the delaying of time-critical operations. Consequently, a denial of service attack prevents resources from functioning according to their intended purposes. It may range from a lack of available memory or disk space to a partial shutdown of the entire network. Typically, a denial of service attack leaves one or more hosts incapable of serving their users [11]. E-mail bombing is an example of an increasingly popular denial of service attack. It takes three forms. The first form is to write a script that constantly bombards an e-mail account with messages that may contain very long binary attachments. The second form is to post something offensive to a USENET newsgroup with a forged return address. The third form is to send an e-mail with a forged originator address and a subscribe request to large listservers such as cypherpunks that generate in excess of a hundred messages a day. Another example of a denial of service attack is TCP SYN flooding as discussed later in this book.

Very often, passive and active attacks are used together to effectively intrude on a corporate intranet environment. For example, a passive wiretapping attack can be used to grab some authentication information transmitted in the clear, and this authentication information can then be used to launch a replay attack. Referring to the example given above, where a user connects to his or her account on a remote host with an unencrypted password, it is fairly obvious that the password can be eavesdropped and replayed to launch an identity spoofing attack, also referred to as a masquerade. Thus, another method for breaking into systems is to monitor TCP/IP traffic for bearing valid usernames and passwords, and then using them on a system to log in normally. If a captured password is to an administrator account, then the job of obtaining privileged access is made much easier. Having this possibility in mind, it is obvious that password-based authentication is not sufficiently secure in a networked or distributed environment today. Again, we will come back to this particular problem later in this book.

A *countermeasure* is a feature or function that reduces or eliminates a vulnerability. For example, the use of strong authentication techniques reduces the vulnerability of passwords transmitted in the clear. Similarly, the use of cryptographic authentication at the network layer effectively eliminates attacks based on machines spoofing other machines' IP addresses. In essence, this book is about countermeasures that can be used and deployed to provide Internet and intranet security.

REFERENCES

[1] R. Oppliger, *Authentication Systems for Secure Networks*, Artech House, Norwood, MA, 1996.

[2] C.E. Shannon, "A Mathematical Theory of Communication," *Bell System Technical Journal*, Vol. 27, No. 3/4, July/October 1948, pp. 379 – 423/623 – 656.

[3] C.E. Shannon, "Communication Theory of Secrecy Systems," *The Bell System Technical Journal*, Vol. 28, No. 4, October 1949, pp. 656 – 715.

[4] A.S. Tanenbaum, *Computer Networks*, Prentice-Hall, Englewood Cliffs, NJ, 1988.

[5] L. Lamport, "Time, Clocks, and the Ordering of Events in a Distributed System," *Communications of the ACM*, Vol. 21, 1978, pp. 558 – 565.

[6] ISO/IEC 10181, Information technology – Security frameworks in open systems, 1993.

[7] L. Gong, "Increasing Availability and Security of an Authentication Service," *IEEE Journal on Selected Areas in Communications*, Vol. 11, 1993, pp. 657 – 662.

[8] M.K. Reiter, and K.P. Birman, "How to Securely Replicate Services," *ACM Transactions on Programming Languages and Systems*, Vol. 16, 1994, pp. 986 – 1009.

[9] ISO/IEC 7498, Information Processing Systems — Open Systems Interconnection Reference Model, 1982.

[10] H.M. Kluepfel, "A Systems Engineering Approach to Security Baselines for SS7," Technical Report TM-STS-020882, Bellcore, Murray Hill, NJ, 1992.

[11] R.M. Needham, "Denial of Service: An Example," *Communications of the ACM*, Vol. 37, No. 11, November 1994, pp. 42 – 46.

Chapter 2

TCP/IP Networking

The term TCP/IP is often used to refer to an entire suite of data communications protocols[1] that gets its name from two of its major protocols, namely the transmission control protocol (TCP) and the internet protocol (IP). IP provides a connectionless and unreliable packet-switching service, whereas TCP provides a connection-oriented and reliable data transport service on top of IP. In this chapter, we overview and briefly discuss the fundamentals of TCP/IP networking. In particular, we describe the development of the TCP/IP protocols in Section 2.1, explain how Internet standardization works in Section 2.2, and introduce the Internet model with its four layers in Section 2.3.

2.1 DEVELOPMENT

The predecessor of the Internet was called the ARPANET. As a matter of fact, the Internet has evolved from the ARPANET and sometimes people still confuse the ARPANET with the Internet. This confusion mainly results because the ARPANET

---

[1] Some people dispute whether the TCP/IP protocols should be referred to as protocols or services. It could be argued, for example, that Telnet is a protocol, a service, or even a command. Where it makes obvious sense, this book follows the protocol view.

was the first backbone network of the early Internet and remained a part of it until it was finally retired in 1990.

The ARPANET was originally created by the Advanced Research Projects Agency (ARPA[2]) of the U.S. Department of Defense (DoD). The aim of the ARPANET was to develop and to come up with network technologies and topologies that would provide reliability even in the case of node and circuit failures. Packet switching was considered to be the right network technology to provide this kind of functionality. In packet switching, messages to be sent over the network are divided into discrete parts, each of which is called a packet. Each packet is routed from one computer to the next across the network until it reaches its final destination. Dedicated computers called routers are used to route the packets through the network. Routers are connected to each other by physical data connections that are also called links. Each networked computer is called a host. A host is connected to a network in the same way as a router. The main difference between a host and a router is that a host usually has a single link to one network, whereas a router may have several links typically to more than just one network.

The first ARPANET nodes were installed in 1969 at the UC Los Angeles, the Stanford Research Institute (SRI), the UC Santa Barbara, and the University of Utah. The protocols that were used at that time were not TCP/IP, but rather the network control protocol (NCP) and BBN 1822, which was named after the technical report that actually specified it. The name Internet was first applied to a research program in 1973, with the first workable system deployed in 1977. This first implementation of an internet involved four networks: a packet satellite network, a packet radio network, the ARPANET, and an Ethernet at the XEROX Palo Alto Research Center (PARC). By 1983, the ARPANET had become so successful that ARPA no longer considered it experimental and passed operational control of it to the Defense Communications Agency (DCA), now known as Defense Information Systems Agency (DISA). A nonexperimental internetwork, known as the ARPA Internet, started in January 1983, when DCA required all nodes to use the more sophisticated TCP/IP protocols instead of NCP and BBN 1822. Simultaneously, DCA mandated the split of the original ARPANET into two networks: ARPANET for continued research and MILNET for military operations.

Much of the early popularity of the TCP/IP protocols is due to their implementation in the 4.2BSD version of the UNIX operating system. The 4.2BSD was developed at the University of California at Berkeley (UCB) by the Computer Systems Research Group (CSRG). Again, the development was partly funded by

---

[2]The ARPA was previously called Defense Advanced Research Projects Agency (DARPA).

ARPA. Because of the source of its funding, 4.2BSD was made publicly available at the cost of its distribution and so its use spread quickly. Coincidentally, the 4.2BSD implementation became available at the same time as some inexpensive micropro- cessors, such as the Motorola 680x0 and the Intel 80x86 chip series. Startup and established companies took advantage of the combination to build systems, mainly workstations, incorporating both the newly available microprocessors and 4.2BSD UNIX. Notably the most prominent startup company of this kind is Sun Microsys- tems, Inc. From now on, the development of the UNIX operating system and the TCP/IP protocols became intimately intertwined. Nevertheless, it is important to note that the Internet is not a UNIX network and that the TCP/IP protocols have also been implemented on other operating systems.

ARPANET and MILNET were the two early transcontinental national backbone networks in the developing internetwork, with others added by government agencies such as the National Aeronautics and Space Agency (NASA). As the participation of other government agencies increased, the name of this composite internetwork changed, from ARPA Internet to the Federal Research Internet to TCP/IP Internet and finally to its current name of just the Internet. In 1984, the National Science Foundation (NSF) established an office for networking and implemented several versions of its NSFNET national backbone network. In addition to that, the NSF also provided seed money for the NSFNET midlevel networks, which are also known as NSFNET regionals. These regional networks provided extensive connectivity for campus networks at educational institutions, government agencies, and commercial businesses. Today, most of these regionals are self-supporting and most of the other networks that have been deployed during the development of the Internet, such as CSNET, BITNET, UUCP, USENET, and FidoNet, have been absorbed by the Internet.

The TCP/IP communications protocol suite and the Internet are mostly associ- ated with the U.S. research community. However, the research has not been limited to just the United States. For example, Norway and the United Kingdom (U.K.) were connected from the earliest days of TCP/IP development, and considerable technical input for both IP and TCP came from France and the U.K.

Today, the Internet is growing exponentially and diversifying rapidly, hence the exact form of its future is unpredictable. Beginning about 1988, the size of the Internet has been more than doubling every year and promises to continue doing so. Projections based on its current rate of growth suggest that there will be over one million computer networks presumably connected to the Internet and well over one billion users by the end of the century. In October 1995, the Federal Networking Council unanimously passed a resolution defining the term *Internet*. According to this resolution, the term refers to the global information system that

- Is logically linked together by a globally unique address space based on IP or its subsequent extensions/follow-ons;

- Is able to support communications using the TCP/IP protocol suite or its subsequent extensions/follow-ons, and/or other IP-compatible protocols;

- Provides, uses, or makes accessible, either publicly or privately, high-level services layered on the communications and related infrastructure.

As this definition is neither sufficiently simple nor very precise, we are not going to use it in this book. Instead we use the term *Internet* to refer to the global internet(work) based on the TCP/IP communications protocol suite, and the term *intranet* to refer to a TCP/IP-based corporate or enterprise network. We have already discussed in the Preface that the Internet is seen as the basis and first incarnation of an information superhighway or national information infrastructure (NII) as promoted by the U.S. government. We have also seen that virtually everyone on the Internet is vulnerable, and that the Internet's security problems are the center of attention, generating much fear throughout both the computer and communications industries.

In spite of the fact that UNIX is still the predominant operating system used for Internet hosts, many other types of operating systems are used to connect to the Internet as well, including mainframe operating systems, such as IBM MVS or DEC VMS, and personal computer operating systems, such as MS-DOS/Windows, Windows 95, or MacOS. Although personal computer systems often provide only client services, increasingly powerful personal computers are also beginning to provide, at low cost, the same services as large systems. Versions of UNIX for the personal computer, including Linux, FreeBSD, and BSDi, and some other operating systems, most notably Windows NT, can provide the same services and applications that were, until recently, found only on large systems. The ramifications of this are that more people are able to utilize a wider array of TCP/IP services than ever before. While this is good in that the benefits of networking are more available, it has also some negative consequences in that there is more potential for harm from intruders. The latest trend in making TCP/IP networking widely available is the concept of thin clients and network computers currently being promoted by computer manufacturers and vendors.

2.2   INTERNET STANDARDIZATION

In this section, we overview the technical bodies that are engaged in Internet standardization, the documentation series that are officially published, as well as the Internet standards process. Refer to [1] for a critical and more contemporary discussion of Internet standardization and governance.

2.2.1   Technical Bodies

The technical bodies that are engaged in Internet standardization are overviewed in Figure 2.1. On the top level, there is the Internet Society (ISOC), which is an international nonprofit membership organization formed in 1992 to promote the use of the Internet for research and scholarly communication and collaboration. Its members include individuals, who can vote for ISOC Trustees, and several classes of institutional members, who can't vote. Acitivities of the ISOC include education about how to use the Internet and exploration of new applications. The ISOC holds an annual meeting and periodically publishes a newsletter.

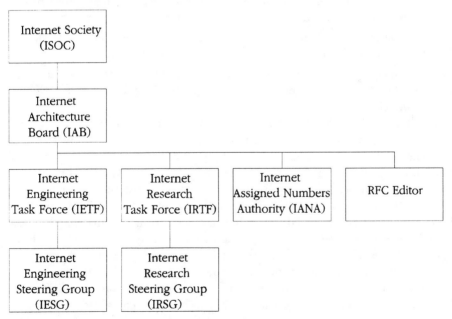

Figure 2.1   The technical bodies that are engaged in Internet standardization.

On the next level is the Internet Architecture Board (IAB[3]) which is an appointed group that assists in the management of the Internet standards process operating under the auspices of the ISOC. In short, the IAB is responsible for the design, engineering, and management of the TCP/IP protocols. It does not attempt to manage the daily operation of the Internet. Rather, it limits itself to providing a forum for communication and collaboration among network operators, as well as to specify and recommend policies and technologies. The IAB doesn't require anybody to do anything. It does issue standards, but these are adhered to voluntarily. Any participant network organization could presumably issue its own mandatory operational standards, but it is not known of any that have done so. The IAB has the following two task forces:

- The Internet Research Task Force (IRTF) is responsible for topics that are oriented more toward research than toward operational engineering. The mission of the IRTF is "to promote research of importance to the evolution of the future Internet by creating focused, long-term and small Research Groups working on topics related to Internet protocols, applications, architecture and technology." There are currently three IRTF research groups, namely an End-to-End Research Group, an Information Infrastructure Architecture Research Group, and a Privacy and Security Research Group.

- The Internet Engineering Task Force (IETF), which does detailed work on the TCP/IP protocols and specifications for standardization.

Both the IRTF and the IETF have steering groups associated with them. They are called the Internet Research Steering Group (IRSG) and the Internet Engineering Steering Group (IESG).

The IETF is organized in technical areas, each of which has a director responsible for coordinating the activities in that particular area. The area directors plus a chair, executive director, and secretary form the IESG. The chair of the IESG is also the chair of the IETF and as such also a member of the IAB. The IESG recommends actions on standardization to the IAB, which makes most actual decisions.

Table 2.1 overviews the IETF technical areas as of March 1997 (in alphabetical order). Note that this book addresses Internet and intranet security, and therefore primarily focuses on the work being done in the security area. Each IETF technical area has working groups (WGs) that handle specific design and specification projects. Every WG has a charter with projected milestones. Participation in the WGs is by individuals and not by representatives of organizations. The IETF meets three times a year. In addition to meetings of each WG, there is also a plenary of all

---

[3]Until June 1992, the acronym IAB was used to refer to "Internet Activities Board."

Table 2.1
IETF Technical Areas

Application area
General area
Internet area
Operational Requirements area
Routing area
Security area
Transport area
User Services area

attendees. WGs may meet outside the IETF meetings, and they regularly discuss drafts of documents and other issues using electronic mail. Table 2.2 overviews the active IETF security area WGs (again in alphabetical order).

Table 2.2
Active IETF Security Area WGs

Name	Acronym
Authenticated Firewall Traversal	AFT
Common Authentication Technology	CAT
Domain Name System Security	DNSsec
IP Security Protocol	IPsec
One Time Password Authentication	OTP
Public Key Infrastructure (X.509)	PKIX
Secure Shell	SECSH
Simple Public Key Infrastructure	SPKI
Transport Layer Security	TLS
Web Transaction Security	WTS

The AFT WG addresses the issue of application-layer support for firewall traversal. The work of this WG is addressed in Section 7.3 when we talk about the SOCKS circuit-level gateway. The CAT WG seeks to specify distributed security services to a variety of protocol callers in a manner that insulates the callers from the specifics of the underlying security mechanisms. The main achievement of this WG is the generic security service application programming interface (GSS-API) to which most authentication and key distribution systems in use today conform to. The DNSsec WG ensures security enhancements and extensions to the domain name system (DNS). As discussed in Chapter 9, the IPsec WG standardizes security protocols for the Internet layer. The OTP WG addresses technologies that are deployed by one-time password systems. The goal of the PKIX WG is to specify and set up a public key infrastructure (PKI) based on the ITU-T recommendation X.509, whereas the complementary SPKI WG was chartered recently to define a simpler PKI. The SECSH WG seeks to update and standardize the Secure Shell (SSH) protocol, whereas the TLS WG develops a more general security protocol for the transport layer. We will address the work of the SECSH and TLS WGs in Chapter 10. And last but not least, the WTS WG develops requirements and specifications for WWW transaction security. This work will be addressed in Chapter 11. Throughout the rest of this book we describe and further discuss some activities that are being done by these IETF security area WGs.

As indicated in Figure 2.1, there are also two additional bodies involved in Internet standardization: the Internet Assigned Numbers Authority (IANA) which assigns and reserves numbers,[4] and the RFC Editor who is responsible for the publishing of the documentation series described next.

2.2.2   Documentation Series

A key to the rapid growth of the Internet has been the free and open access to basic documents, especially the specifications of the TCP/IP protocols. There are two major series of documents related to Internet standardization: Internet Drafts and Requests for Comments.

Internet Drafts

Internet Drafts are working documents of the IETF, its technical areas' WGs, and some related groups. During the development of a specification, Internet Drafts are made publicly available for informal review and comment by placing them in the IETF Internet Drafts directory. The directory is replicated on a number of sites, such as ds.internic.net for the U.S. East Coast, ftp.isi.edu for the U.S. West Coast, nic.nordu.net for Europe, munnari.oz.au for the Pacific Region, and ftp.is.co.za for Africa. This replication makes an evolving document readily available to a wide audience, facilitating the process of public review and revision.

Internet Drafts are valid for a maximum of six months and may be updated, replaced, and obsoleted by other documents at any time. An Internet Draft that is published as an RFC, or that has remained unchanged in the Internet Drafts

---

[4]ftp://ftp.isi.edu/in-notes/iana/assignments/

directory for more than six months without being recommended by the IESG for publication as an RFC is silently discarded and removed from the IETF Internet Drafts directory. To learn the current status of a particular Internet Draft, the `1id-abstract.txt` listing available in the Internet Drafts directory can be checked. Due to their transient nature, it is inappropriate to use Internet Drafts as reference material or to cite them other than as works in progress. Following this rule, the number of references related to Internet Drafts is comparably small in this book. Where appropriate, Internet Drafts are appended as footnotes to the text.

Requests for Comments

The beginnings of the ARPANET and the Internet in the university research community promoted the academic tradition of open publication of ideas and results. However, the normal cycle of academic publication was considered to be too formal and too slow for the dynamic exchange of ideas essential to creating contemporary networks. In 1969, a key step was therefore taken in establishing the Request for Comments (RFC) series of documents. The RFC series were intended to be an informal fast-distribution way to share ideas with other network researchers. Today, the RFC series is the official publication channel for Internet standards and other publications for the Internet community. It covers a wide range of topics in addition to Internet standards, from early discussion of new research topics and concepts to status memos about the Internet as a whole. RFC publication is in the direct responsibility of the RFC Editor, under the general direction of the IAB. RFCs are numbered and usually referred to by their appropriate numbers. They can be obtained from many Internet sites that serve as RFC archives.

The rules for formatting and submitting RFCs are defined in [2]. In short, every RFC must be available in ASCII text format and may additionally be available in other formats, too. In this case, the other versions of the RFC may contain additional material such as diagrams, figures, and illustrations not present in the ASCII text version, and it may be formatted differently. For Internet standards track specifications, however, the ASCII text version is considered as the definitive reference. As such, it must be a complete and accurate specification of the standard, including all necessary diagrams, figures, and illustrations.

Some RFCs document Internet standards. These RFCs form the STD subseries of the RFC series of documents. When a specification has been adopted as an Internet standard, it is given an additional STD label, but it also keeps its original RFC number and its place in the RFC series is unchanged. An STD number generally refers to a protocol rather than a specification, so an STD number can apply to several RFCs that specify different versions of the protocol. STD-1 is the authoritative source for references on Internet standards.

Historically Internet standards have been concerned with the technical specifications for hardware and software required for computer communication across interconnected networks. However, since the Internet itself is composed of networks operated by a great variety of organizations with diverse goals and rules, good user service also requires that the operators and administrators of the Internet follow some common guidelines for policy and operation. While these guidelines are usually different in scope and style from protocol standards, their establishment needs a similar process for consensus building. Therefore, some RFCs document the results of community deliberations about statements of principle or conclusions about what is the best way to perform some specific operations or IETF process function. These RFCs form the Best Current Practice (BCP) subseries of the RFC series. As such they are given additional BCP labels, but again keep their original RFC numbers and their place in the RFC series unchanged.

As we will see later in this chapter, not all specifications of protocols or services for the Internet should or will become Internet standards or BCPs. Such nonstandards track specifications are not subject to the general rules for Internet standardization. Nonstandards track specifications may be published directly as experimental or informational RFCs at the discretion of the RFC Editor in consultation with the IESG [3].

2.2.3   Internet Standards Process

In the past, TCP/IP protocols were often specified and implemented ad hoc with little formality, and this informality was considered to be a major factor in their success. This situation has changed. Today, there are many people involved in specifying TCP/IP protocols and even more people involved in implementing and using these protocols. In this new environment, the need has arisen for a more formal, or at least more codified, Internet standards process.

In essence, an Internet standard is a specification that is stable and well understood, is technically competent, has multiple, independent, and interoperable implementations with substantial operational experience, enjoys significant public support, and is recognizably useful in some or all parts of the Internet. In theory, the process of creating an Internet standard is simple and straightforward. A specification undergoes a period of development and several iterations of review by the Internet community and revision based upon experience, is adopted as an Internet standard by the appropriate body, and is finally published in an appropriate format. In practice, however, the process is more complicated, due to the difficulty of creating specifications of high technical quality, the need to consider the interests of all affected parties, the importance of establishing widespread community consensus, and the difficulty of evaluating the utility of a particular specification for the Internet community.

The Internet standards process is an activity of the ISOC that is organized and managed on behalf of the Internet community by the IAB and IESG [4]. It is concerned with all protocols, procedures, and conventions that are used in or by the Internet, whether or not they are part of the TCP/IP communications protocol suite. As such, it resembles many other standards processes, such as that of the ISO, which has the states committee draft (CD), draft international standard (DIS), and international standard (IS).

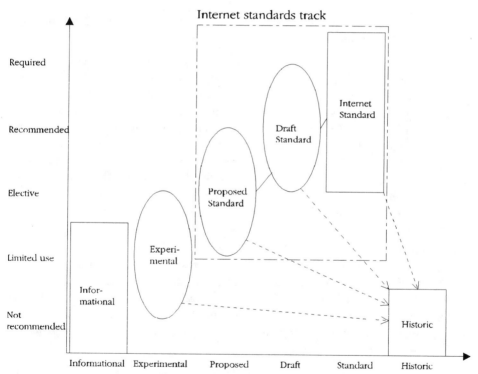

Figure 2.2   The Internet standards process.

In the Internet standards process, a specification flows from being a proposed standard to a draft standard to an Internet standard. But the Internet standards track also has an applicability status or requirement level in addition to a maturity level of the standardization state dimension. This leads to a two-dimensional standards track, as illustrated in Figure 2.2. In this figure, the requirement levels are indicated on the vertical axis, whereas the maturity levels are indicated on the horizontal axis. We are going to overview the specification categories first, before we further address the requirement and maturity levels and the standardization process as a whole.

Specification Categories

The specifications that are subject to the Internet standards process fall into one of two categories: technical specifications or applicability statements.

- A *technical specification* (TS) is a description of a protocol, service, procedure, convention, or format that either completely describes all of its relevant aspects or leaves one or more parameters or options unspecified. Consequently, a TS may be completely self-contained, or it may incorporate material from other specifications by reference to other documents. A TS must include a statement of its scope and the general intent for its use. Thus, a TS that is inherently specific to a particular context shall contain a statement to that effect. However, a TS does not specify requirements for its use within the Internet; these requirements, which depend on the particular context in which the TS is incorporated by different system configurations, are defined by an applicability statement (AS).

- An *applicability statement* (AS) specifies how, and under what circumstances, one or more TSs may be applied to support a particular Internet capability. An AS identifies the relevant TSs and the specific way in which they are to be combined, and may also specify particular values or ranges of TS parameters or subfunctions of a TS protocol that must be implemented. An AS may also specify the circumstances in which the use of a particular TS is required, recommended, or elective.

An AS may not have a higher maturity level in the standards track than any standards track TS on which the AS relies. For example, a TS at draft standard level may be referenced by an AS at the proposed standard or draft standard level, but not by an AS at the Internet standard level.

Requirement Levels

An AS shall apply one of the following requirement levels to each of the TSs to which it refers:

- *Required:* Implementation of the referenced TS, as specified by the AS, is required to achieve minimal conformance.

- *Recommended:* Implementation of the referenced TS is not required for minimal conformance, but experience or generally accepted technical wisdom suggest its desirability in the domain of applicability of the AS. Vendors are strongly encouraged to include the functions, features, and protocols of recommended TSs in their products, and should omit them only if the omission is justified by some special circumstance.

- *Elective:* Implementation of the referenced TS is optional within the domain of applicability of the AS. Consequently, the AS creates no explicit necessity to apply the TS. However, a particular vendor may decide to implement it, or a particular user may decide that it is a necessity in a specific environment.

For example, IP and ICMP are both required and must be implemented by all Internet hosts using the TCP/IP protocols. In addition to that, the Telnet protocol is recommended and should be implemented by all hosts that would benefit from remote terminal access, whereas the DECnet management information base (MIB) is elective and could be seen as valuable only in environments where DECnet protocols are still in use.

There are also TSs that are not subject to the Internet standards track or that have been retired from it. These TSs are not required, recommended, or elective. The following two requirement-level designations are available for them:

- *Limited use:* The referenced TS is considered to be appropriate for use only in limited or unique circumstances.

- *Not recommended:* The referenced TS is considered to be inappropriate for general use. This may be because of its limited functionality, specialized nature, or historic status.

Although TSs and ASs are conceptually separate, in practice an Internet standards track document may combine an AS and one or more related TSs. For example, TSs that are developed specifically and exclusively for some particular domain of applicability, such as for e-mail servers, often contain within a single specification all of the relevant AS and TS information. In such cases, no useful purpose would be served by deliberately distributing the information among several documents just to preserve the formal AS/TS distinction. However, a TS that is likely to apply to more than one domain of applicability should be developed in a modular fashion to facilitate its incorporation by multiple ASs.

Maturity Levels

Each protocol enters the Internet standards track with the goal of becoming an Internet standard and being widely used and deployed within the Internet. For this reason, Internet standardization has a strong emphasis on implementation and testing by actual interoperation with other implementations, preferably on existing networks, where feasible. Internet specifications that are intended to become Internet standards go through stages of development, testing, and acceptance. Within the Internet standards process, these stages are formally labeled maturity levels. A specific action by the IESG is required to move a protocol specification onto the Internet standards track at the proposed standard level. Afterwards, the specification may move forward to the draft standard level and eventually to the Internet standard level, where it may stay indefinitely until it is either superseded by a later protocol or otherwise retired.

- *Proposed Standard:* A specification that is generally stable, has resolved known design choices, is believed to be well understood, has received significant community review, and appears to enjoy enough community interest to be considered valuable. However, further experience might result in a change or retraction of the specification before it advances. Usually, neither implementation nor operational experience is required for the designation of a specification as a proposed standard. However, such experience is highly desirable and will usually represent a strong argument in favor of a proposed standard designation. As a matter of fact, the IESG may require implementation or operational experience prior to granting proposed standard status to a specification that materially affects the core Internet protocols or that specifies behavior that may have significant operational impact on the Internet. Implementors should treat proposed standards as immature specifications. It is desirable to implement them in order to gain experience and to validate, test, and clarify the specification. However, since the content of proposed standards may be changed if problems are found or better solutions are identified, deploying implementations of such standards into a disruption-sensitive environment is not recommended. A specification must remain at the proposed standard level for at least six months.

- *Draft Standard:* A specification from which at least two independent and interoperable implementations from different code bases have been developed, and for which sufficient successful operational experience has been obtained, may be elevated to the draft standard level. The corresponding WG chair is responsible for documenting the specific implementations that qualify the specification for draft or Internet standard status along with documentation about testing of the interoperation of these implementations. The documentation must include information about the support of each of the individual options and features. This documentation should be submitted to the responsible IETF area director with the protocol action request. In general, elevation to draft standard is a major advance in status, indicating a strong belief that the specification is mature and will be useful. A draft standard is normally considered to be a final specification, and changes are likely to be made only to solve specific problems encountered. In most circumstances, it is reasonable for vendors to deploy implementations of draft standards into a disruption-sensitive environment. A specification must remain at the draft standard level for at least four months, or until at least one IETF meeting has occurred, whichever comes later.

- *Internet Standard:* A specification for which significant implementation and successful operational experience has been obtained may be elevated to the Internet standard level. An Internet standard is characterized by a high degree of technical maturity and by a generally held belief that the specified protocol or service provides significant benefit to the Internet community. A specification that reaches the status of an Internet standard is assigned a number in the STD subseries while retaining its RFC number.

Not every specification is on the Internet standards track. A specification may not be intended to be an Internet standard, or it may be intended for eventual standardization but not yet ready to enter the standards track. A specification may have been superseded by a more recent Internet standard, or have otherwise fallen into disuse or disfavor. Specifications that are not on the Internet standards track are typically labeled with one of three off-track maturity levels, and the documents bearing these labels are not Internet standards in any sense. There are currently three off-track maturity levels:

- *Experimental:* A specification that is part of some research or development effort. Such a specification is published for the general information of the Internet community and as an archival record of the work, subject only to editorial considerations and to verification that there has been adequate coordination with the standards process.

- *Informational:* A specification that is published for the general information of the Internet community and does not represent an Internet community consensus or recommendation.

- *Historic:* A specification that has been superseded by a more recent specification or is for any other reason considered to be obsolete.[5]

The informational, Internet standard, and historic states are permanent, or at least there is no limit on how long a protocol may stay in one of those states. That's the reason why they are shown as rectangles in Figure 2.2. The other states are all temporary and shown as ellipses.

Standardization Process

The mechanics of the Internet standardization process involve decisions of the IESG concerning the elevation of a specification onto the standards track or the movement of a standards track specification from one maturity level to another. Although a number of reasonably objective criteria are available to guide the IESG in making a decision to move a protocol specification onto, along, or off the standards track, there is no guarantee of elevation to or progression along the standards track for any specification. The experienced collective judgment of the IESG concerning the technical quality of a specification is an essential component of the decision-making process.

A specification that is intended to enter or advance in the Internet standards track must be posted as an Internet draft unless it has not changed since publication as an RFC. It shall remain as an Internet draft for a period of time, not less than two weeks, that permits useful community review, after which a recommendation for action may be initiated. A standards action is initiated by a recommendation by the IETF WG responsible for a specification to its area director, copied to the IETF secretariat or, in the case of a specification not associated with a WG, a recommendation by an individual to the IESG. The IESG then determines whether or not the specification submitted to it satisfies the applicable criteria for the recommended action, and must also determine whether or not the technical quality and clarity of the specification is consistent with that expected for the maturity level to which the specification is recommended. The IESG sends notice to the IETF of the pending IESG consideration of the document(s) to permit a final review by the Internet community. This last-call notification shall be via electronic mail to the IETF announce mailing list. Comments shall be accepted from anyone, and should be sent as directed in the last-call announcement. The last-call period shall be no shorter than two weeks except in those cases where the proposed standards action was not initiated by an IETF WG, in which case the last-call period shall

---

[5]Some people have suggested that the correct word for "historic" should be "historical;" however, the use of "historic" is historical.

be no shorter than four weeks. If the IESG believes that the community interest would be served by allowing more time for comment, it may decide on a longer last-call period or to explicitly lengthen a period. In a timely fashion after the expiration of the last-call period, the IESG shall make its final determination of whether or not to approve the standards action, and shall notify the IETF of its decision again via electronic mail to the IETF announce mailing list. If a standards action is approved, notification is sent to the RFC Editor and copied to the IETF with instructions to publish the specification as an RFC. The specification shall at that point be removed from the Internet drafts directory.

An official summary of standards actions completed and pending appears in each issue of the ISOC newsletter. In addition to that, the RFC Editor also publishes periodically an "Internet Official Protocol Standards" RFC, summarizing the current status of all Internet protocol and service specifications. This RFC is reissued frequently as a new RFC with a new number.

Note that the minimum time for a protocol specification to reach Internet standard status is ten months (six months for the Proposed standard status and another four months for the draft standard status). These minimum periods are intended to ensure adequate opportunity for community review without severely impacting timeliness. When a standards track specification has not reached the Internet standard level but has remained at the same maturity level for 24 months, and every 12 months thereafter until the status is changed, the IESG shall review the viability of the standardization effort responsible for that specification and the usefulness of the technology. Following each such review, the IESG shall approve termination or continuation of the development effort. At the same time the IESG shall also decide to maintain the specification at the same maturity level or to move it to historic status. This provision is not intended to threaten a legitimate and active WG effort, but to provide an administrative mechanism for terminating a moribund effort.

A new version of an established Internet standard must progress through the full Internet standardization process as if it were a completely new specification. As technology changes and matures, it is possible and even likely that the new Internet standard specification is so clearly superior technically that one or more existing standards track specifications for the same function should be retired. In this case, or when it is felt for some other reason that an existing standards track specification should be retired, the IESG shall approve a change of status of the old specification(s) to historic. This recommendation shall be issued with the same last-call and notification procedures used for any other standards action. A request to retire an existing standard can originate from a WG, an area director, or some other interested party. In other cases, both versions may remain Internet standards to honor the requirements of an installed base. In this situation, the relationship between the previous and the new versions must be explicitly stated in the text of the new version or in another appropriate document.

Disputes are possible and likely to appear at various stages during the Internet standards process. As much as possible, the process is designed so that compromises can be made and genuine consensus achieved. However, there are times when even the most reasonable and knowledgeable people are unable to agree. Such conflict must be resolved by a process of open review and discussion. RFC 2026 specifies the procedures that shall be followed to deal with Internet standards issues that cannot be resolved through the normal processes whereby IETF WGs and other Internet standards process participants ordinarily reach consensus.

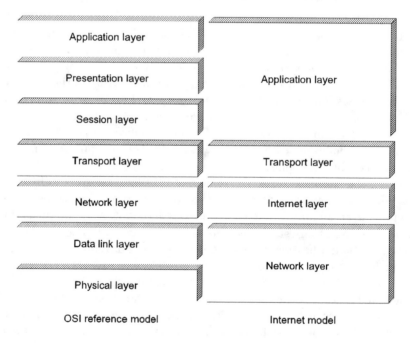

Figure 2.3   The OSI reference model and the Internet model.

2.3   INTERNET MODEL

In this section, we introduce and briefly overview the Internet model. As illustrated on the right side of Figure 2.3, the Internet model consists of four layers, namely the network (or network access) layer, the Internet layer, the transport layer, and the application layer. This is somehow contradictory to the OSI reference model (OSI-RM) in which the Internet application layer is divided into three distinct OSI layers (application, presentation, and session layer), and the Internet network access layer is further divided into two OSI layers (data link, and physical layer). The fact that the Internet model uses another layering structure than the OSI-RM should not be overemphasized and is mainly due to the fact that the Internet model was designed before the OSI-RM. In the following subsections we are going to briefly overview and discuss the four layers of the Internet model.

2.3.1   Network Access Layer

Part of the popularity of the TCP/IP communications protocol suite is due to its ability to be implemented on top of various network technologies and corresponding network access layer protocols, such as Ethernet, IEEE 802.3, IEEE 802.4 (Token Bus), and IEEE 802.5 (Token Ring). The predominant strategy today is to use Ethernet for local area networking, and to connect the Ethernet via a T1 line to a regional TCP/IP backbone network that connects to the Internet. This is also the strategy an organization new to TCP/IP networking is likely to use, if for no other reason than because all major vendors of UNIX workstations sell their systems with a built-in Ethernet interface. Modem speeds are increasing as new communications standards are being approved, thus versions of TCP/IP that operate over the PSTN are becoming more popular each day. Many sites and individuals use the point-to-point protocol (PPP) or the serial line IP (SLIP) to connect their hosts to a TCP/IP network using the PSTN. In this case, they can use either the password authentication protocol (PAP) or the challenge-response authentication protocol (CHAP) to authenticate themselves. As their names suggest, PAP refers to a password-based authentication protocol, whereas CHAP refers to an authentication protocol that makes use of a challenge-response mechanism. In short, CHAP requires the claimant and the verifier to share a secret key. The verifier then challenges the claimant with a random number that serves as nonce, and the claimant has to respond with a proper keyed one-way hash value for that nonce. CHAP suggests the use of MD5 as a one-way hash function.

TCP/IP networking is an internetworking technology. As such, its primary focus is on the Internet, transport, and application layers, rather than on the network access layer. Therefore, we are not going to further discuss the details of the network access layer in this book.

2.3.2   Internet Layer

In this subsection, we are going to overview and briefly discuss the protocols for the Internet layer, namely the Internet protocol (IP) and some routing and support protocols.

Internet Protocol

IP is the key protocol for the TCP/IP communications protocol suite. Much like the center of an hourglass, the IP funnels data to and from the protocols above and below it. It lets an internetwork use many different network access layer protocols and allows applications to employ different transport layer protocols. In essence, the IP provides an internetwork address space, routing, and some other services across various underlying networks and network technologies. In the internetwork address space that the IP provides, each host network interface must be configured with a unique IP address. If a host has more than one network interface, each interface must have a separate IP address. Network practitioners often refer to a host address when they really mean the host's network interface address. But keep in mind that hosts do not have IP addresses; network interfaces do. Unfortunately, the protocols specified in various RFCs often use the term host address instead of network interface address, so, this nomenclature is followed in this book, although it is somehow misleading.

The current version of IP is IP version 4, or IPv4 in short. Its address space is 4 bytes wide. The corresponding IP addresses are usually written in dotted-decimal notation, where each byte appears as a decimal number separated by periods, arranged from high-order byte to low-order byte. Primarily to simplify routing, an IP address is divided into a network number and a host number. For all machines to communicate successfully, every network interface on the same physical network segment must have the same network number and a unique host number. Originally, IP used the high-order byte as the network number and the lower-order 3 bytes as the host number. But soon after IP was specified in this manner, it became obvious that there would be more than just 254 interconnected networks. A specific encoding of the high-order bits in the high-order byte of the IP address lets the network number be 1, 2, or 3 bytes long, with the remaining byte(s) used for the host number. This encoding scheme divides the IP address space into five address classes, A through E. Table 2.3 summarizes the five IP address classes and their corresponding bit encodings. Class A through class C are the most commonly used address classes. Class D is reserved for multicast addresses, and class E is still unused and reserved for future use except for one address. This address (255.255.255.255) refers to "any host on this network." It can be used only as a destination address, and an IP packet with this address will be broadcast only to hosts on the same physical network segment as the sender of the packet.

Table 2.3
IP Address Classes

Class	Bit Encoding	Network Range	Host Range
A	0	0.0.0.0 to 127.0.0.0	0.0.0 to 255.255.255
B	10	128.0.0.0 to 191.255.0.0	0.0 to 255.255
C	110	192.0.0.0 to 223.255.255.0	0 to 255
D	1110	224.0.0.0 to 239.255.255.255	—
E	1111	240.0.0.0 to 255.255.255.255	—

When an IP address is written in dotted-decimal notation, it is fairly simple and straightforward to determine the class of the address from the bit encoding simply by referring to the value of the highest-order byte. Addresses in each class are numerically contiguous. IP allows the host number to be further subdivided by using subnets. IP subnetting makes it possible to logically partition an IP address space, and to use each partition as if it belonged to a distinct IP network number. IP uses a network mask to determine which bits in the host number are to be used as subnet number. The IP address space allows to construct large internetworks concatenated from many different networks. Each network access layer protocol has its own addressing scheme and has no knowledge of IP addressing.

IP packetizes a message by creating an IP packet for each message it receives from a transport layer protocol module. Each packet consists of an IP header, followed by a payload that may contain transport layer protocol data. As far as IP is concerned, the payload is simply a sequence of data bytes. Figure 2.4 illustrates the format of an IPv4 header. It consists of the following fields:

- The 4-bit *Version* field is used to indicate the IP version number. The current version is 4, although the next version of IP (IP version 6) is already specified and being deployed.

- The 4-bit *Header Length* field is used to indicate the length of the IP header. The minimum, and typical, size of an IP header is 20 bytes. Since the header length is always indicated in 32-bit words, the number 5 is specified in this case.

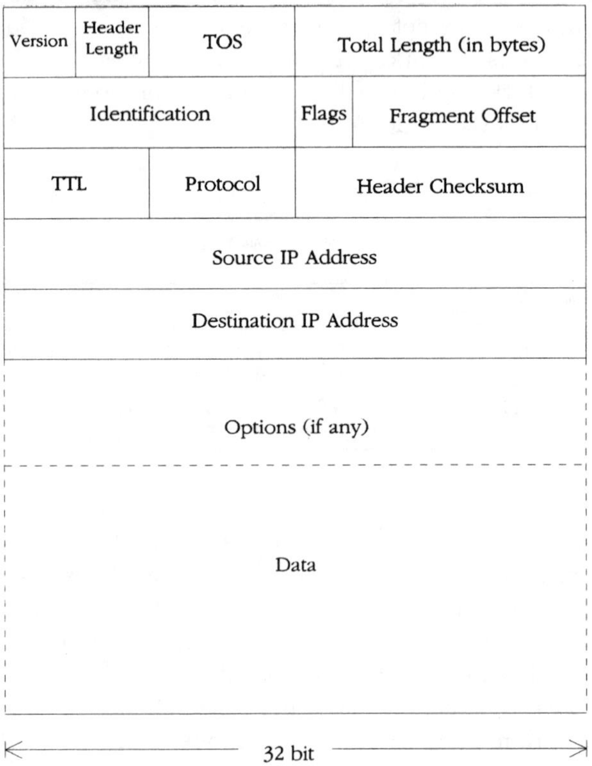

Version	Header Length	TOS	Total Length (in bytes)	
Identification			Flags	Fragment Offset
TTL		Protocol	Header Checksum	
Source IP Address				
Destination IP Address				
Options (if any)				
Data				

$\longleftarrow$ 32 bit $\longrightarrow$

Figure 2.4   The IPv4 header format.

- The 8-bit *TOS* field is used to indicate a type of service (TOS) or priority for the IP packet. Type of service processing is not used often today, so this field is almost always set to the default value of 0.

- The 16-bit *Total Length* field is used to indicate the total length of the IP packet (including the header) in bytes. Note, however, that the total length does not include the header and trailer of the network access layer protocol such as Ethernet frames.

- The 16-bit *Identification*, 3-bit *Flags*, and 13-bit *Fragment Offset* fields are used to fragment and properly reassemble IP packets.

- The 8-bit *TTL* field is used to indicate a time to live (TTL). The TTL value specifies the time in seconds that an IP packet may exist. The value is decremented by at least 1 each time the IP header is processed by a router or host. Unless the packet is queued in a buffer for a long period of time, the TTL value actually indicates the maximum number of intermediate routers a packet may cross before it is dropped. Whenever the TTL reaches 0, IP must drop the packet unconditionally. This feature prevents a packet from looping around an internetwork forever because of a routing error.

- The 8-bit *Protocol* field is used to indicate the protocol data that is encapsulated in the IP packet. For example, this value is 1 for ICMP, 6 for TCP, and 17 for UDP. These are not the only possible values, and other protocols use different values for the protocol field.

- The 16-bit *Header Checksum* field is used for error detection. It carries the 16-bit 1's complement sum of all 16-bit words in the IP header, and checks for transmission errors that may have occured accordingly. It is important to note that the header checksum covers the IP header only, and that the upper-layer protocols must handle error control for the encapsulated data themselves. For example, a packet can be lost on its route to the destination because of transmission errors or a router might deliberately drop a packet because of buffer space shortage. Also, IP may deliver a packet more than once. It is up to the protocols that compose the encapsulated payload to be aware of these problems and to take appropriate steps. IP simply moves packets through the internetwork using a best-effort algorithm.

- The 32-bit *Source IP Address* field is used to carry the IP address of the host or network interface from which the packet originated.

- The 32-bit *Destination IP Address* field is used to carry the IP address of the packet's final destination host or network interface, regardless of the number of intermediate routers the packet may pass through. Note that because each IP packet header contains a source and destination IP address, it is self-contained and may be routed independently to its destination.

- The *Options* field can be used to indicate the following options:
  - Source routing (enables an IP packet's route to be explicitly controlled);
  - Route recording (records the route of the packet);
  - Timestamping (adds a timestamp by each intermediate router);
  - Security (includes security options);

  – Padding (pads the IP packet header to an even 4-bye boundary).

From a security point of view, the IP source routing and security options are of primary interest. In short, IP source routing can be used to specify a direct route to a destination and return path back to the origin. The route could involve the use of other routers or hosts that normally would not be used to forward the packet to its destination. As source routing can be used to launch sophisticated attacks, it should be normally disabled on a firewall system. The IP security options are mainly used in environments that provide support for multilevel security, such as military applications [5]. IP security options can also be used to constrain routing decisions or to control cryptographic transformations.

IP is not finished when it creates a packet. It also has to determine which network interface to use and then pass enough information to the network access layer protocol output module so it can properly encapsulate the IP packet in a corresponding frame. Frame formats are specific to each network access layer protocol. For example, when sending a packet on an Ethernet, IP passes to the output module the Ethernet destination address, the Ethernet-type field value that indicates that the encapsulated packet is an IP packet, and the IP packet itself. The Ethernet output module, in turn, sets the source Ethernet address to the Ethernet address of the network interface it uses to transmit the frame, calculates an Ethernet checksum, and generates a corresponding frame with header and trailer.

Since different transport protocols layered on top of IP can send messages that are larger than the frame size of the underlying network hardware, IP also does fragmentation of packets when they are transmitted on a network that can't accomodate the original packet size or reassembly of the pieces of a previously fragmented packet. The process of packetizing, framing, fragmenting, and reassembling are fundamental IP operations. They give IP the flexibility to operate with many different physical network media and transport layer protocols.

IP next generation (IPng) or IP version 6 (IPv6[6]) is a new version of IP that builds upon the architecture that made IPv4 successful, and is designed to solve the growth problems the Internet is encountering. This includes the direct issues of addressing and routing, as well as dealing with long-term growth issues such as security, autoconfiguration, real-time services, and transition. The development of IPv6 is briefly overviewed in [6] and fully described in [7,8]. It was approved as a

---

[6]The new IP became IP version 6, following version 4 that is currently in use. The number 5 could not be used for IPng because it had been allocated to ST, an experimental "stream" protocol designed to carry real-time services in parallel with IP.

proposed standard by the IESG in November 1994 and specified in a corresponding RFC in December 1995 [9]. The main change from IPv4 to IPv6 is the increase in IP address size from 32 to 128 bits. In addition, some IPv4 header fields have been dropped or made optional to reduce the common-case processing cost of packet handling and to limit the bandwidth cost of the IPv6 header accordingly. Figure 2.5 illustrates the format of a basic IPv6 header. It consists of the following fields:

- The 4-bit *Version* field has remained unchanged from IPv4. It is still used to indicate the version number of IP.

- The 4-bit *Priority* field is used to indicate the priority of an IP packet relative to other packets traveling across the network.

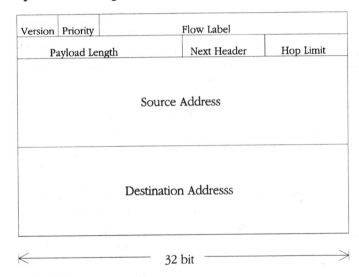

Figure 2.5   The IPv6 header format.

- The 24-bit *Flow Label* field remains somehow experimental for IPv6. The flow label value, together with the source IP address, identifies a particular traffic flow in the network. Establishing flow labels is the responsibility of protocols other than IP such as the Resource Reservation Protocol (RSVP).

- The 16-bit *Payload Length* field is used to indicate the length of the IP packet payload data in bytes (i.e., the rest of the packet following the IPv6 header). Since this field is 16 bits in size, it normally limits IP packets to 65,535 bytes or less.

- The 8-bit *Next Header* field identifies the type of header immediately following the basic IPv6 header. This field uses the same values as the IPv4 protocol field.

- The 8-bit *Hop Limit* field is used to indicate a hop limit value. The value is decremented by 1 each node that forwards the IP packet. The packet is discarded if the value is decremented to zero. In short, the hop limit value determines how far a datagram will travel and is conceptually similar to the TTL field in IPv4.

- The 128-bit *Source Address* field identifies the IP address of the originator of the IP packet.

- The 128-bit *Destination Address* field identifies the IP address of the intended receiver of the IP packet.

In IPv6, optional Internet layer information may be encoded in separate extension headers that are placed between the IPv6 basic header and the upper-layer protocol header. There is a relatively small number of extension headers, each identified by a distinct next header value. There are extension headers defined for Hop-by-Hop Options, Routing, Fragment, Destination Options, Authentication, and Encapsulating Security Payload. With the exception of the last two, we are not going to further address IPv6 extension headers in this book.

Routing Protocols

The purpose of a routing protocol is to enable routing decisions to be made at the Internet layer. As such, the routing protocol must manage and periodically update the routing tables that are stored at each router. An Internet router may be part of an autonomous system, which is basically a collection of routers that are under a single administration. These routers run the same routing protocol, usually called an interior gateway protocol (IGP). There are several IGPs is use today, but all routers within an autonomous system normally run the same one. To communicate with another autonomous system, however, a router usually uses an exterior gateway protocol (EGP). The EGP doesn't know details of routing within another domain. To take an analogy, an IGP is like a local telephone exchange, whereas an EGP is more like a long-distance operator.

Today, a wide variety of routing protocols are used on the Internet. These routing protocols generally fall into two categories: reachability and distance vector protocols:

- A reachability protocol tells whether a path exists to a distant network.

- A distance vector protocol calculates a distance metric to this network. The distance metric can be just the number of routers between the source and destination network or it can include more information about each link, such as bandwidth and load.

In general, IGPs are distance vector protocols and EGPs are reachability protocols.

Support Protocols

Support protocols for the IP handle specific tasks, such as routing redirects, error messages, and mappings between IP addresses and physical network access layer addresses. They do not make routing decisions at the Internet layer, although they can be used by protocols that do make such decisions.

- The Internet control message protocol (ICMP) is a required protocol that must be implemented in conjunction with IP. Its aim is to send information and control messages between hosts, such as error messages upon attempts to send packets to an unreachable host or network and other unrecoverable routing errors. ICMP messages are sent like transport layer protocol data, that is, they are encapsulated in IP packets. These messages set the protocol field in the IP headers to 1.

- Given an IP address, the purpose of the address resolution protocol (ARP) is to find the corresponding network access layer address by broadcasting on the local network segment a message that contains the IP address and then waiting for a response. Once an ARP response has been seen for an IP address, that pair of addresses is cached so there is no need to broadcast a request again, at least for some time. ARP is commonly used over network access layer protocols such as Ethernet that support broadcasting.

- Given a physical network access layer address, the purpose of the reverse address resolution protocol (RARP) is to find the corresponding IP address. RARP is particularly useful for diskless workstations that need to find an IP address on startup time.

Support protocols are essential for the overall security of a TCP/IP implementation. For example, ICMP redirect messages can be used to fake routes and hosts acting as routers into using false routes. These false routes would aid in directing traffic to an attacker's system instead of a legitimate trusted system.

2.3.3   Transport Layer

The two major transport layer protocols, TCP and UDP, compose messages received from application processes and deliver them using IP's packet delivery service. Because IP delivers packets only to hosts, the transport layer protocols must add information to allow addressing to individual application processes.

Transmission Control Protocol

The transmission control protocol (TCP) is by far the most commonly used transport layer protocol on the Internet. It provides a connection-oriented, reliable, and bidirectional transport service, thus eliminating duplicate packets, handling retransmissions of lost packets, and ensuring data are delivered in order. Providing a connection-oriented transport service, TCP implements virtual circuits between communicating peers.

The TCP module on the sending side of a connection processes a byte stream from an application process and divides it into distinct messages that are sent to the TCP module on the receiving side of the connection. The receiving TCP module, in turn, collects the messages, recreates the original byte stream and passes it on to the corresponding application process. Figure 2.6 illustrates the format of a TCP message header.

- Along with the source and destination IP addresses found in a packet's IP header, the 16-bit *Source Port Number* and the 16-bit *Destination Port Number* uniquely identify the two application processes associated with the TCP/IP connection.

- The 32-bit *Sequence Number* field is used to indicate the relative byte offset of the first byte in the current message. The sequence number starts at an arbitrary 32-bit number that is negotiated when a TCP/IP connection is established. The field is examined only when the SYN bit is set (see the discussion of the flags below.)

- The 32-bit *Acknowledgment Number* field is used to acknowledge received data. In particular, its value indicates the relative byte position of the last byte successfully acknowledged. The field is examined only when the ACK bit is set (again see the discussion of the flags below.)

- The 4-bit *Header Length* field is used to indicate the number of 32-bit words in the TCP header, or the offset to the beginning of the *Data* field from the beginning of the header respectively.

- The 6-bit *Reserved* field is reserved for future use. It is always set to zero.

- The 6-bit *Flags* field is used to indicate 1-bit values for the flags summarized in Table 2.4.

- The 16-bit *Window Size* field is used to indicate the number of data bytes that the sender of a message is willing to accept. TCP uses this field for flow control and buffer management, which is very important in an internetwork with links of varying speed.

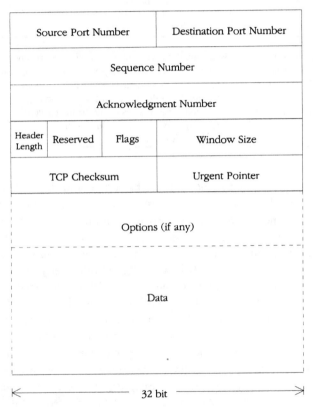

Figure 2.6   The TCP header format.

- The 16-bit *TCP Checksum* field is used for error detection. It usually carries the 16-bit 1's complement sum of each 16 bits in the header and data portion of the message.

- The 16-bit *Urgent Pointer* field is used to indicate the byte position of data in the message that should be processed first.

- The *Options* field may be used to specify various TCP options. These options, however, are very seldomly used today.

- Finally, the *Data* field contains the payload data of the TCP message up to a maximum of 65,535 bytes.

Table 2.4
TCP Flags

Flag	Description
URG	This flag is used to send out data without waiting for the receiver to process data already in the stream. When the flag is set, the urgent pointer field is valid.
ACK	When the flag is set, the acknowledgment number field is valid.
PSH	The flag tells the TCP module to deliver data for this message immediately.
RST	When the flag is set, the connection is reset due to unrecoverable errors.
SYN	When the flag is set, the sequence number field is valid.
FIN	This flag is used to terminate a connection.

It should be noted at this point that the source and destination port numbers uniquely identify the application processes that send and receive messages. Port numbers are assigned to each client process running on a host; therefore no two clients on the same host use the same port number for a TCP/IP connection. Client port assignments are enforced by the local host operating system. On the other side, well-known port numbers are assigned to server processes depending on the service they provide. For example, an SMTP server usually uses TCP port 25, a Telnet server TCP port 23, and an FTP server TCP port 21 for the control connection and TCP port 20 for the data connection. A server port number must be well known because it, along with the destination IP address, needs to be used when initiating a TCP/IP connection to a particular host and service. There is a general rule that only privileged server processes (i.e., those processes that operate with UNIX superuser privileges) can use port numbers less than 1,024. These port numbers are referred to as privileged ports. Servers mostly use privileged ports, whereas clients generally request unprivileged port numbers from the local operating system. Although this rule is not firm and is not required in the TCP/IP specifications, BSD-based UNIX systems generally adhere to it.

Because client port assignments are unique for each host and servers use well-known ports, a unique address for each connection is the concatenation of the server IP address, the server port number, the client IP address, the client port number, and the transport layer protocol in use, such as TCP or UDP. To illustrate, suppose a Telnet server listens on port 23 on a host with IP address 130.92.64.29 using TCP as a transport layer protocol. A client on a host with IP address 130.92.64.25 wants to establish a TCP/IP connection with this server and so obtains a unique and unused port number (for example 1,758) for its end of the connection. It therefore initiates a connection to port 23 with IP address 130.92.64.29. When the connection is established, it is identified by the unique 5-tuple <130.92.64.29,23,130.92.64.25,1758,TCP> which is often written with each IP address and the port number concatenated together, that is <130.92.64.29.23,130.92.64.25.1758,TCP>. Also the tuple is written with the local system IP address and port number first. Therefore on the client side, the tuple is <130.92.64.25.1758,130.92.64.29.23,TCP>, which is a unique identifier for the processes on both the client and server side of the connection.

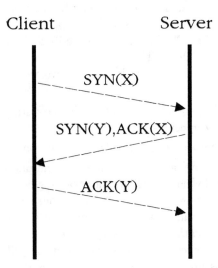

Figure 2.7 The TCP/IP three-way handshake connection establishment protocol.

TCP uses a three-way handshake protocol to establish a connection, and to set the initial sequence numbers for each side of the connection accordingly. Referring to Figure 2.7, we assume the client on the left side wishes to establish a TCP/IP connection to the server on the right side. Therefore, the client begins by sending a SYN message to the server. The SYN message is basically a TCP message with the SYN flag set and the client's initial sequence number X contained in the sequence number field. The server acknowledges the SYN message by sending a SYN-ACK message back to the client. The SYN-ACK message is a TCP message with both the SYN and ACK flags set, and containing the client's sequence number X in the acknowledgment number field and the server's sequence number Y in the sequence number field.[7] The client finishes establishing the TCP/IP connection by responding with an ACK message. This is a TCP message with the ACK flag set and the server's sequence number Y contained in the acknowledgment number field. From that moment on, the TCP/IP connection between the client and server is established and can be used for data transmission. None of the three messages contains any data; all information passed is conveyed in the TCP headers. Also note that the closing of the connection is handled by a two-way handshake protocol. When one side the connection has finished sending data, it sends a message with the FIN flag set. Because the connection is full duplex, the other side can continue to send data until it also sends a message with the FIN flag set.

The TCP three-way handshake connection establishment protocol lends itself to the so-called sequence number or IP spoofing attack. We have already mentioned in the Preface that Robert T. Morris, Jr. described the feasibility of the attack in a technical report in 1985. The same attack was also reported in a CERT advisory in January 1995. The attack exploits two weaknesses in most TCP/IP implementations:

- A TCP/IP host, in general, does not verify the authenticity of the source IP address in packets it receives;
- Initial sequence numbers, in general, are not randomly generated.

The first weakness allows an attacking host to send packets on behalf of another host, whereas the second weakness allows the attacking host to guess initial sequence numbers that must be known to successfully establish a TCP/IP connection. In spite of the fact that initial sequence numbers are intended to be more or less random, the TCP specification proposes to increment a 32-bit counter by 1 in the low-order position about every 4 microseconds, and the BSD-derived UNIX kernels increment it by a constant every second, and by another constant for each new connection. In both cases, the resulting initial sequence numbers are not randomly generated and can be guessed with a high degree of confidence.

Let's assume that host A trusts host B in an intranet setting, and that an attacker C wants to make use of this trust relationship to launch a sequence number attack. Therefore, C generates a TCP message that looks like a connection establishment or SYN message originated by B. The message has its source IP address set to B and includes an initial sequence number X that C chooses on B's behalf. C initiates the three-way handshake by sending the message to A. A, in turn, ac-

---

[7]For simplicity, we omit the fact that the server acknowledges X+1 instead of X at this point.

knowledges the receipt of the message by sending a SYN-ACK message to B. This message includes both the acknowledged sequence number X and a newly generated sequence number Y. C will not be able to receive the message, but if he's able to correctly guess the value of Y, he can create the ACK message and finish the three-way handshake accordingly. In the positive case, C has established a TCP/IP connection with A and can now use the connection to launch arbitrary commands to exploit system vulnerabilities accordingly. But what happens if B receives the SYN-ACK message that A sends out in step two of the three-way handshake? In this case, B would send a RST packet back to A and finish the handshake accordingly. Thus, in order to successfully launch a sequence number attack, C has to make sure that B doesn't receive A's SYN-ACK message. C can therefore launch a TCP SYN flooding attack against B, before he starts the sequence number attack against A, or simply wait until B is out of service or taken off the intranet.

Any system connected to the Internet and providing TCP/IP network services is potentially subject to the TCP SYN flooding attack [10]. The potential for this attack arises at the point where the server has returned a SYN-ACK message to the client but has not yet received a corresponding ACK message. This situation refers to a half-open connection on the server side. As a matter of fact, the server has built in its system memory a data structure describing all pending connections. This data structure is of finite size and it can be made to overflow by intentionally creating too many half-open connections. Consequently, TCP SYN flooding can be used to launch a denial of service attack. The attacking system simply sends SYN messages to the victim server. The messages appear to be legitimate but in fact reference a client that is unable to respond to the SYN-ACK messages generated by the server. This means that the final ACK message will never be sent to the server and that the half-open connection data structures on the server will eventually fill. At that moment, however, the server will be unable to accept any new incoming connection establishment requests until the table is emptied out. Normally, there is a time-out associated with a pending connection, so the half-open connections will eventually expire and the server will recover. However, the attacking system can simply continue sending packets requesting new connections faster than the victim server expires pending connections. In most cases, the victim of a TCP SYN flooding attack will have difficulty in accepting any new incoming network connection. In these cases, the attack does not affect existing incoming connections nor the ability to originate outgoing connections. However, in some cases, the system may exhaust memory, crash, or be rendered otherwise inoperative. Note that the location of the attacking system is typically obscured because the source IP addresses of the SYN messages can be set to arbitrary values. When the messages arrive at the victim server, there is no way to determine their true IP source addresses. Since the network forwards packets based on the IP destination address, the only way to somehow validate the source of a packet is to use packet filtering on inbound interfaces.

More recently, two underground magazines have published code to automatically launch TCP SYN flooding attacks. One can therefore reasonably expect that future attacks will make heavy use of TCP SYN flooding and related denial of service attacks.

There are certain precautions to address sequence number and TCP SYN flooding attacks. With regard to sequence number attacks, cryptographical authentication is obviously the right long-term solution. As this requires each host to change its TCP/IP software, however, a more practical and short-term solution is to generate sequence numbers that are randomly selected [11]. In addition, a firewall configuration can be adapted to resist some attacks of this sort. This is because, in most cases, the attacking host will be from the Internet, but it will send packets on behalf of a system that claims to be inside the firewall. To resist such an attack, a firewall can be configured so that if an IP packet arrives from the Internet with the source address of an inside host, the firewall discards and drops the packet. With regard to TCP SYN flooding attacks, we will discuss some countermeasures in the second part of this book.

User Datagram Protocol

The user datagram protocol (UDP) is similar to TCP in several ways. Each UDP message (or UDP segment) is encapsulated in an IP packet and UDP has the same notion of ports as TCP. Consequently, the *Destination Port Number* and the *Source Port Number* fields serve the same purposes as they do for TCP. Furthermore, a UDP message also includes a *UDP Length* field that indicates the length of the message, as well as a *Checksum* field that contains a checksum for the entire UDP header and message. Figure 2.8 illustrates the format of a UDP header.

Unlike TCP, UDP is an unreliable datagram protocol and is deliberately rudimentary. With UDP, delivery is on a best-effort basis; there is no error correction, retransmission, or lost, duplicated, and reordered packet detection. Even error detection is optional with UDP. An application using UDP sees discrete messages that are exactly the size of the UDP payload. It has no acknowledgment strategy or guarantee of reliable delivery. In principle, UDP just adds port numbers to the basic IP best-effort delivery paradigm. It doesn't ensure packets datagrams in order, unduplicated, or at all. Messages can be lost or arrive out of sequence, and it becomes the job of the application using UDP as a transport protocol to handle these situations.

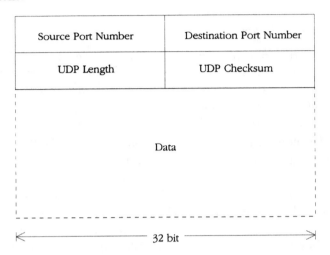

Figure 2.8 The UDP header format.

UDP is a connectionless protocol, and as such it does not have a connection setup procedure. Because sequence numbers and window sizes need not be exchanged, neither the initial three-way handshake nor the closing two-way handshake are needed. A server process using UDP can simply receive datagrams from any client that sends the message to the server's port address. A UDP-based server's ability to receive UDP datagrams from any number of clients contrasts sharply with the TCP paradigm of having each server only receive messages from a single client. In general, there is a higher risk associated with UDP-based services than with TCP-based services. The reason for that is due to the fact that it is much easier to spoof UDP packets than TCP packets, since there are no handshakes or sequence numbers. Extreme caution is therefore indicated when using the IP source address from any such packet. Applications that care must make their own arrangements with regard to proper message authentication.

From an application developer's point of view, it would be inconvenient for every application to deal directly with TCP or UDP. The construction of TCP messages, as well as the details of TCP flow control, need not and should not be a part of an application program. To facilitate dealings with TCP and UDP, several programming interfaces have been developed for programming at the transport layer. Examples are the Berkeley sockets and the Transport Layer Interface (TLI) found on System V UNIX systems. Most commonly, IP applications that run under UNIX are written for one of these interfaces.

2.3.4 Application Layer

There is a wide variety of application protocols and services layered on top of TCP and UDP. The aim of this section is to briefly overview this variety without going into detail with each of these protocols and services. Probably the most important and most commonly used applications are

- Remote terminal access, implemented by the Telnet remote login protocol;
- File transfer, implemented by the file transfer protocol (FTP);
- Electronic mail (e-mail), implemented by the simple mail transfer protocol (SMTP).

These application protocols are layered on top of TCP and are required for all Internet hosts. FTP is somehow special, since it requires two TCP connections to be estabished between the client and server (a control connection and a data connection). Beyond that, there are some other application protocols that are layered on top of TCP:

- The network news transfer protocol (NNTP) can be used to deliver and access USENET news over the Internet.
- The network time protocol (NTP) can be used to arrange for hosts to keep the same time of day.
- The simple network management protocol (SNMP) can be used to manage diverse components in an intranet or Internet environment.
- The X11 protocol can be used to manage X Window sessions between X servers and clients.

In addition to these TCP-based application protocols, there are also several protocols that are layered on UDP:

- The remote procedure sall (RPC) protocol can be used to have procedures executed on remote hosts. Secure RPC extends RPC to support cryptographic authentication. All RPC calls are authenticated using a shared secret key that is distributed using the Diffie-Hellman key exchange. Unfortunately, Sun's version of Secure RPC is not strong enough to resist more sophisticated cryptanalytical attacks [12]. We will come to that later in this book.
- The network file system (NFS) uses RPC to provide transparent file access over a network. To the extent that it is available, NFS can also make use of Secure RPC.

- Similarly, the network information system (NIS) uses RPC to allow multiple systems to share data (e.g., the password file) for centralized management. NIS$^+$ is an enhancement made to NIS primarily to handle large system configurations and to secure exchange of critical information.

Most TCP/IP services and corresponding application protocols require some form of mapping between textual domain and host names and their numeric IP addresses. The Domain Name Service (DNS) provides this functionality for the Internet. For example, DNS maps host names, such as `mogli.unibe.ch`, to IP addresses, such as `130.92.64.29`. It is the most widely distributed service in the Internet today. The DNS namespace is partitioned hierarchically into a tree structure with a single root node. Each node is owned by a naming authority, and it is up to this naming authority to create any number of child nodes. The term domain is used to denote any node with all of its descendant nodes. A DNS server supports the DNS architecture. The most commonly used DNS server is provided by the Berkeley Internet Name Daemon (BIND), which is part of most UNIX systems today.

Last but not least, there are several resource discovery and information services in use today. Examples are Gopher (or the Gopher server index Veronica), the Wide Area Information Service (WAIS), and the Word Wide Web (WWW). The term WWW actually refers to a superset of FTP, Gopher, WAIS, and some other information services, implemented by the Hypertext Transfer Protocol (HTTP).

REFERENCES

[1] W.A. Foster, A.M. Rutkowski, and S.E. Goodman, "Who Governs the Internet?," *Communications of the ACM*, Vol. 40, No. 8, August 1997, pp. 15 – 20.

[2] J. Postel, "Instructions to RFCs Authors," Request for Comments 1543, October 1993.

[3] C. Huitema, J. Postel, and S. Crocker, "Not All RFCs are Standards," Request for Comments 1796, April 1995.

[4] S. Bradner, "The Internet Standards Process – Revision 3," Request for Comments 2026, October 1996.

[5] S. Kent, "Security Options for the Internet Protocol," Request for Comments 1108, November 1991.

[6] R.M. Hinden, "IP Next Generation Overview," *Communications of the ACM*, Vol. 39, No. 6, June 1996, pp. 61 – 71.

[7] C. Huitema, *IPv6: The New Internet Protocol*, Prentice Hall, Englewood Cliffs, NJ, 1996.

[8] S.A. Thomas, *IPng and the TCP/IP Protocols: Implementing the Next Generation Internet*, John Wiley & Sons, New York, NY, 1996.

[9] S. Deering, and R.M. Hinden, "Internet Protocol, Version 6 (IPv6) Specification," Request for Comments 1883, December 1995.

[10] C.L. Schuba, I.V. Krsuland, M.G. Kuhn, E.H. Spafford, A. Sundaram, and D. Zambon, "Analysis of a Denial of Service Attack on TCP," *Proceedings of IEEE Symposium on Security and Privacy*, May 1997.

[11] S. Bellovin, "Defending Against Sequence Number Attacks," Request for Comments 1948, May 1996.

[12] B.A. LaMacchia, and A.M. Odlyzko "Computation of discrete logarithms in prime fields," *Designs, Codes, and Cryptography*, Vol. 1, 1991, pp. 46 – 62.

Chapter 3

OSI Security Architecture

In order to extend the field of application of the OSI-RM, the ISO/IEC JTC1 appended a security architecture as part two of ISO/IEC 7498 in 1989 [1]. Since its publication, the OSI security architecture has turned out to be a primary reference for network security professionals. In 1991, the ITU-T adopted the OSI security architecture in Recommendation X.800 [2], and in the early 1990s the IRTF Privacy and Security Research Group (PSRG) adapted the OSI security architecture in a corresponding Internet security architecture published as an Internet draft. In essence, ISO/IEC 7498-2, ITU-T X.800, and the Internet security architecture all describe the very same security architecture, and in this book we are going to use the term OSI security architecture to refer to all of them.

The OSI security architecture provides a general description of security services and related mechanisms, and discusses their interrelationships. It also shows how the security services map onto a given network architecture, and briefly discusses their appropriate placement within the OSI-RM. In this chapter, we introduce and overview the security services that are enumerated in the OSI security architecture in Section 3.1, and the corresponding security mechanisms in Section 3.2. Security management is briefly addressed in Section 3.3. Again, for the readers of [3] this chapter is repetitive and may be skipped accordingly.

Table 3.1
Classes of OSI Security Services

1	Peer entity authentication service
	Data origin authentication service
2	Access control service
3	Connection confidentiality service
	Connectionless confidentiality service
	Selected field confidentiality service
	Traffic flow confidentiality service
4	Connection integrity service with recovery
	Connection integrity service without recovery
	Selected field connection integrity service
	Connectionless integrity service
	Selected field connectionless integrity service
5	Non-repudiation with proof of origin
	Non-repudiation with proof of delivery

3.1   SECURITY SERVICES

As shown in Table 3.1, the OSI security architecture distinguishes between five classes of security services. These classes comprise authentication, access control, data confidentiality, data integrity, and non-repudiation services. Just as layers define functionality in the OSI-RM, so do services in the OSI security architecture. The services may be placed at appropriate layers in the OSI-RM.

1. *Authentication services* are to provide for the authentication of communicating peer entities or for the authentication of data origins:

   - A *peer entity authentication service* is to provide the ability to verify that a peer entity in an association is the one it claims to be. In particular, a peer entity authentication service provides assurance that an entity is not attempting to masquerade or perform an unauthorized replay of some previous association. Peer entity authentication is typically performed either during a connection establishment phase or, occasionally, during a data transfer phase.

   - A *data origin authentication service* is to allow the sources of data received to be verified to be as claimed. A data origin authentication service, however, cannot provide protection against the duplication or modification of data units. In this case, a data integrity service must be used in conjunction with a data origin authentication service. Data origin authentication is typically provided during a data transfer phase.

Authentication services are important because they are a prerequisite for proper authorization, access control, and accountability. Authorization refers to the process of granting rights, which includes the granting of access based on access rights. Access control refers to the process of enforcing access rights, and accountability the property that ensures that the actions of a principal may be traced uniquely to this particular principal.

2. *Access control services* are to provide for the protection of system resources against unauthorized use. As mentioned above, access control services are closely tied to authentication services: a user or a process acting on a user's behalf must be properly authenticated before an access control service can effectively mediate access to system resources. In general, access control services are the most commonly thought of services in both computer and communication security.

3. Data confidentiality refers to the property that information is not made available or disclosed to unauthorized individuals, entities, or processes. Thus, *data confidentiality services* are to provide for the protection of data from unauthorized disclosure:

- A *connection confidentiality service* is to provide confidentiality of all data transmitted in a connection.

- A *connectionless confidentiality service* is to provide confidentiality of single data units.

- A *selective field confidentiality service* is to provide confidentiality of only certain fields within the data during a connection or in a single data unit.

- A *traffic flow confidentiality service* is to provide protection of information that may otherwise be compromised or indirectly derived from a traffic analysis.

We will see later that the provision of a traffic flow confidentiality service requires fundamentally different security mechanisms than the other data confidentiality services mentioned above.

4. Data integrity refers to the property that information is not altered or destroyed in an unauthorized way. Thus, *data integrity services* are to provide for the protection of data from unauthorized modifications:

- A *connection integrity service with recovery* is to provide integrity of data in a connection. The loss of integrity is recovered, if possible.

- A *connection integrity service without recovery* is to provide integrity of data in a connection. In this case, however, the loss of integrity is not recovered.

- A *selected field connection integrity service* is to provide integrity of specific fields within the data during a connection.

- A *connectionless integrity service* is to provide integrity of single data units.

- A *selected field connectionless integrity service* is to provide integrity of specific fields within single data units.

Note that on a connection, the use of a peer entity authentication service at the start of the connection and a connection integrity service during the connection can jointly provide for the corroboration of the source of all data units transferred on the connection, the integrity of those data units, and may additionally provide for the detection of duplication of data units, for example by using sequence numbers.

5. *Non-repudiation services* are to prevent that one of the entities involved in a communication later denies having participated in all or part of the communication. Consequently, they have to provide some sort of protection against the originator of a message or action denying that he has originated the message or the action, as well as against the recipient of a message denying that he has received the message. Consequently, there are two non-repudiation services to be distinguished:

- A *non-repudiation service with proof of origin* is to provide the recipient of a message with a proof of origin.

- A *non-repudiation service with proof of delivery* is to provide the sender of a message with a proof of delivery.

Non-repudiation services are becoming increasingly important in the context of electronic commerce on the Internet. This importance can be best illustrated through an example. An investor decides to sell a large number of shares, and sends the request to a stockbroker who sells the stocks. Now the stock price rises sharply, and the investor denies ever sending the order to sell the stocks. Conversely, it is possible that under reverse circumstances, the stockbroker may deny receiving the order to sell the stock. In this type of situation, it is easy to see that non-repudiation services are essential and critical for transacting securely over the Internet. We will see later that non-repudiation services with proof of delivery are more difficult to provide than non-repudiation services with proof of origin [4].

3.2 SECURITY MECHANISMS

The OSI security architecture distinguishes between specific security mechanisms and pervasive security mechanisms, and we are going to follow this distinction in this section, too.

3.2.1 Specific Security Mechanisms

Specific security mechanisms may be incorporated into an appropriate layer to provide some of the security services mentioned above. As shown in Table 3.2, the OSI security architecture enumerates eight specific security mechanisms.

Table 3.2
OSI Specific Security Mechanisms

1	Encipherment
2	Digital signature mechanisms
3	Access control mechanisms
4	Data integrity mechanisms
5	Authentication exchange mechanisms
6	Traffic padding mechanisms
7	Routing control mechanisms
8	Notarization mechanisms

1. *Encipherment* is used either to protect the confidentiality of data units and traffic flow information, or to support or complement other security mechanisms.

The cryptographic techniques that are used for encipherment are overviewed in Chapter 4.

2. *Digital signature mechanisms* are used to provide an electronic analog of handwritten signatures for electronic documents. Like handwritten signatures, digital signatures must not be forgeable; a recipient must be able to verify it, and the signer must not be able to repudiate it later. But unlike handwritten signatures, digital signatures incorporate the data (or the hash of the data) that are signed. Different data therefore result in different signatures even if the signatory is unchanged. Again, we postpone the discussion of digital signatures mechanisms to Chapter 4.

3. *Access control mechanisms* use the authenticated identities of principals, information about these principals, or capabilities to determine and enforce access rights. If a principal attempts to use an unauthorized resource, or an authorized resource with an improper type of access, the access control function rejects the attempt and may additionally report the incident for the purposes of generating an alarm and recording it as part of a security audit trail.

Access control mechanisms and the distinction between discretionary access control and mandatory access control have been extensively discussed in the computer security literature referenced in the Preface. They are usually described in terms of subjects, objects, and access rights. A subject is an entity that can access objects. It can be a host, a user, or an application. As such, it is a synonym for the term "principal". An object is a resource to which access should be controlled. An object can range from a single data field in a file to a large program. Access rights specify the level of authority for a subject to access an object, so access rights are defined for each subject-object-pair. Examples of UNIX access rights include read, write, and execute.

4. *Data integrity mechanisms* are used to protect the integrity of either single data units and fields within these data units or sequences of data units and fields within these sequences of data units. Note that data integrity mechanisms, in general, don't protect against replay attacks that work by recording and replaying previously sent valid messages. Also, protecting the integrity of a sequence of data units and fields within these data units generally requires some form of explicit ordering, such as sequence numbering, timestamping, or cryptographic chaining.

5. *Authentication exchange mechanisms* are used to verify the claimed identities of principals. In accordance with ITU-T Recommendation X.509 [5], we use the term strong to refer to an authentication exchange mechanism that uses cryptographic techniques to protect the messages that are exchanged, and weak to refer to an authentication exchange mechanism that doesn't do so. In general, weak authentication exchange mechanisms are vulnerable to passive wiretapping and replay attacks.

6. *Traffic padding mechanisms* are used to protect against traffic analysis attacks. Traffic padding refers to the generation of spurious instances of communication, spurious data units, and spurious data within data units. The aim is not to reveal if data that are being transmitted actually represent and encode information. Consequently, traffic padding mechanisms can only be effective if they are protected by some sort of a data confidentiality service.

More recently, onion routing has been proposed as an alternative approach to protect against traffic analysis attacks in a packet-switched data network such as the Internet [6,7]. Instead of making a TCP/IP connection directly to a destination machine, an application sets up a connection to an onion routing proxy on a particular machine. The onion routing proxy, in turn, uses cryptographic technqiues to build an anonymous connection through several onion routers to the destination machine. In short, packets are encrypted with a temporary key that is digitally enveloped with the public keys of each onion router on the selected route to the destination machine. As the digital envelopes are layered like the peels of an onion around the packets, this routing technique has been named onion routing. Each onion router can only decrypt its digital envelope to see where to route the packets next. Consequently, it can only identify adjacent onion routers along the route of each packet. This considerably limits the impacts of traffic analysis attacks.

7. *Routing control mechanisms* can be used to either dynamically or by prearrangement choose specific routes for data transmission. Communicating systems may, on detection of persistent passive or active attacks, wish to instruct the network service provider to establish a connection via a different route. Similarly, data carrying certain security labels may be forbidden by a security policy to pass through certain networks or links.

8. *Notarization mechanisms* can be used to assure certain properties of the data communicated between two or more entities, such as its integrity, origin, time,

or destination. The assurance is provided by a trusted third party (TTP) in a testifiable manner.

Table 3.3
OSI Pervasive Security Mechanisms

1	Trusted functionality
2	Security labels
3	Event detection
4	Security audit trail
5	Security recovery

3.2.2   Pervasive Security Mechanisms

Pervasive security mechanisms are not specific to any particular security service and are in general directly related to the level of security required. Some of these mechanisms can also be regarded as aspects of security management. As shown in Table 3.3, the OSI security architecture enumerates five pervasive security mechanisms.

1. The general concept of *trusted functionality* can be used either to extend the scope or to establish the effectiveness of other security mechanisms. Any functionality that directly provides, or provides access to, security mechanisms, should be trustworthy.

2. System resources may have *security labels* associated with them, for example, to indicate sensitivity levels. It is often necessary to convey the appropriate security label with data in transit. A security label may be additional data associated with the data transferred or may be implicit (e.g., implied by the use of a specific key to encipher data or implied by the context of the data such as the source address or route).

3. Security-relevant *event detection* can be used to detect apparent violations of security.

4. A security audit refers to an independent review and examination of system records and activities in order to test for adequacy of system controls, to ensure compliance with established policy and operational procedures, to detect

breaches in security, and to recommend any indicated changes in control, policy, and procedures. Consequently, a *security audit trail* refers to data collected and potentially used to facilitate a security audit.

5. *Security recovery* deals with requests from mechanisms such as event handling and management functions, and takes recovery actions as the result of applying a set of rules.

Table 3.4
Areas of Security Management

1	System security management
2	Security service management
3	Security mechanism management

3.3   SECURITY MANAGEMENT

Security of all system and network management functions and the communication of all management information is important. As shown in Table 3.4, the OSI security architecture enumerates three areas of security management.

1. *System security management* addresses the management of the overall distributed computing environment.

2. *Security service management* addresses the management of security services. This service provides for the invocation of specific security mechanisms using appropriate security mechanism management functions.

3. *Security mechanism management* addresses the management of security mechanisms.

In short, a *network management station* is a system that supports a network management protocol and the applications necessary for it to process and access information from managed entities on the network. Examples of network management protocols include the simple network management protocol (SNMP) and the common management information protocol (CMIP). Today, SNMP is by far the most widely used network management protocol on the Internet.

Remember that the OSI security architecture hasn't been developed to solve a particular network security problem, but to provide the network security community with a terminology that can be commonly used to describe and discuss security-related problems and corresponding solutions. We are going to use the terminology to further describe solutions for specific Internet and intranet security problems.

REFERENCES

[1] ISO/IEC 7498-2, Information Processing Systems — Open Systems Interconnection Reference Model — Part 2: Security Architecture, 1989.

[2] ITU X.800, Security Architecture for Open Systems Interconnection for CCITT Applications, 1991.

[3] R. Oppliger, *Authentication Systems for Secure Networks*, Artech House, Norwood, MA, 1996.

[4] N. Zhang, and Q. Shi, "Security Issues in an EDI Environment," *Proceedings of 12th Computer Security Applications Conference*, December 1996, pp. 129 – 136.

[5] ITU-T X.509, The Directory — Authentication Framework, November 1987.

[6] M.G. Reed, P.F. Syverson, and D.M. Goldschlag, "Proxies for Anonymous Routing," *Proceedings of 12th Computer Security Applications Conference*, December 1996, pp. 95 – 104.

[7] P.F. Syverson, D.M. Goldschlag, and M.G. Reed, "Anonymous Connections and Onion Routing," *Proceedings of IEEE Symposium on Security and Privacy*, May 1997.

Chapter 4

Cryptographic Techniques

In this chapter, we introduce and briefly overview the cryptographic techniques that are used and referred to in the rest of this book. In particular, we address one-way hash functions in Section 4.1, secret key cryptography in Section 4.2, public key cryptography in Section 4.3, and legal considerations that surround the use of cryptography in Section 4.4. We further address authentication and key distribution in Sections 4.5 and 4.6, and introduce a notation to describe cryptographic protocols in Section 4.7. In order to keep this chapter sufficiently small, we again refer to the books on cryptography and cryptographic protocols that are referenced in the Preface.

4.1 ONE-WAY HASH FUNCTIONS

Mainly because of their efficiency, one-way functions are of central importance in cryptology. As described later, one-way functions are used, for example, for encrypting secrets, as well as for generating and verifying digital signatures. Informally speaking, a *one-way function* is easy to compute, but hard to invert. More formally speaking, a function $f : X \longrightarrow Y$ is one-way if

- $f(x)$ is easy to compute for all $x \in X$;

- But it is computationally infeasible when given $y \in f(X) = Y$ to find an $x \in X$ such that $f(x) = y$.

This definition is still not precise in a mathematically strong sense, because it doesn't resolve what the terms "easy" and "computationally infeasible" actually mean. However, we still want to use this definition in this book. It is important to note that the existence of one-way functions is still an unproven assumption and that, until today, no function has been shown to be one-way. Obviously, a sufficiently large domain prohibiting an exhaustive search is a necessary but not sufficient condition for a function to be one-way.

In general, it is not required that a one-way function be invertible, and distinct input values may be mapped to the same output. A one-way function $h : X \longrightarrow Y$ for which $| \, Y \, | \ll | \, X \, |$ is called a *one-way hash function*. If, in addition to the conditions for a one-way hash function, it is also computationally infeasible to find distinct input values $x_1, x_2 \in X$ such that $h(x_1) = h(x_2)$, then h is called a *collision-resistant* one-way hash function. We will see that collision resistance is important, for example, to thwart theft of a digital signature from one message for attachment to another.

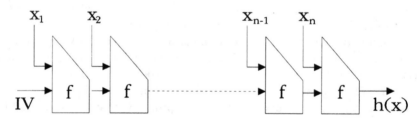

Figure 4.1   An iterative one-way hash function.

Most collision-resistant one-way hash functions in use today are iterative. In short, a one-way hash function is iterative if data is hashed by iterating a basic compression function on subsequent blocks of data. The idea is illustrated in Figure 4.1. A message x is decomposed into n blocks of data $x_1, \ldots, x_n$. A basic compression function f is then applied to each block and the result of the compression function of the previous block. This continues until the result of the last compression step is interpreted as output $h(x)$. Examples of iterative one-way hash functions are MD2 [1], MD4 [2], MD5 [3], and SHA-1 [4]. MD2, MD4, and MD5 produce 128-bit hash values, whereas SHA-1 produces 160-bit hash values. RIPEMD is another example of an iterative one-way hash function. It was developed as part of a European research project and is basically a variation of MD4. RIPEMD-160 is a strengthened version of RIPEMD producing another 160-bit hash value [5].

As of this writing, MD5 and SHA-1 are by far the most widely deployed one-way hash functions. MD5 takes as input a string of arbitrary length and produces as output a 128-bit hash value. In theory, one would need 2^{128} (in the worst case) or 2^{127} (in the average case) trials before finding a collision and hence a new message that results in the same MD5 hash value. Even if each trial only lasted a nanosecond, this would still require some billions of billions of centuries in computing time. However, recent results in cryptographic research have shown that one can take advantage of the particularities of the one-way hash function algorithm to speed up the search process. According to Paul van Oorschot and Michael Wiener, you can actually build a machine able to find messages that hash to an arbitrary value [6]. What this means is that cryptanalysis is catching up and that a 128-bit hash value may fairly soon be insufficient. In addition to that, Hans Dobbertin has shown that MD5 is vulnerable to specific collision search attacks [7]. Taking this into account, SHA-1 and RIPEMD-160 appear to be a cryptographically stronger one-way hash function than MD5. In any case, implementors and users of one-way hash functions should be aware of possible cryptanalytic developments regarding any of these functions, and the eventual need to replace them accordingly.

4.2   SECRET KEY CRYPTOGRAPHY

In *secret key cryptography*, a secret key is established and shared between communicating peers, and this key is used to encrypt and decrypt messages on either side. Because of its symmetry, secret key cryptography is often referred to as *symmetric cryptography*.

The use of a secret key cryptosystem is overviewed in Figure 4.2. Let's assume that A(lice) wants to send a confidential message to B(ob). A therefore shares a secret key K with B. This key may be preconfigured manually or distributed by a key distribution center (KDC). Note that during its distribution, K must be secured in terms of confidentiality, integrity, and authenticity. This has usually been done by having the KDC encrypt K with secret keys that it shares with A and B, respectively. A encrypts a plaintext message P by applying an encryption function E and the key K, and sends the resulting ciphertext $C = E_K(P)$ to B. On the other side, B decrypts C by applying the decryption function D and the key K. He therefore computes $P = D_K(C) = D_K(E_K(P))$.

Secret key cryptography has been in use for thousands of years in a variety of forms. Modern implementations usually take the form of algorithms, which are executed efficiently by computer systems either in hardware, firmware, or software.

In theory,designing a secret key cryptosystem is possible without having a deep understanding of mathematics and cryptology. By combining a set of more or less complex transformations, such as permutations and transpositions, one can usually create a cryptosystem that appears to be too difficult to cryptanalyze even for a powerful enemy. The history of cryptographical failures is long and rich, and most of the failures were either due to the fact that the number and complexity of the transformations were severely limited in the precomputer age, or that too much structure was introduced for the sake of analyzability, which in turn allowed an enemy to successfully cryptanalyze the corresponding cryptosystem.

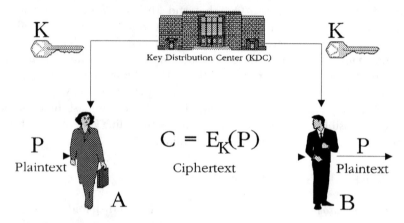

Figure 4.2   A secret key cryptosystem.

Examples of secret key cryptosystems that are in widespread use today are the Data Encryption Standard (DES) [8], two-key and three-key Triple-DES, the International Data Encryption Algorithm (IDEA) [9], Blowfish [10], SAFER (K-64 or K-128) [11], CAST, RC2, RC4, and RC5, as well as the upcoming Advanced Encryption Standard (AES) that is being standardized by the U.S. National Institute of Standards and Technology (NIST) to replace the DES.

4.3   PUBLIC KEY CRYPTOGRAPHY

The idea of having one-way functions with trapdoors has led to the invention of *public key cryptography* or *asymmetric cryptography* [12]. From a practical point of view, a public key cryptosystem is just a cryptosystem in which a user has a pair of mathematically related keys:

- A *public key* that can be published without doing any harm to the system's security;

- A *private key* that is assumed to never leave the possession of its owner.

For both the public and the private key it is computationally infeasible to derive one from the other. The use of a public key cryptosystem is overviewed in Figure 4.3. A(lice) and B(ob) each have a public key pair (k_A, k_A^{-1}) and (k_B, k_B^{-1}). The private keys k_A^{-1} and k_B^{-1} are kept secret, whereas the public keys k_A and k_B are publicly available in certified form. If A wants to protect the confidentiality of a plaintext message P, she uses the public key of B, which is k_B, encrypts P with this key, and sends the resulting ciphertext $C = E_B(P)$ to B. On the other side, B uses his private key k_B^{-1} to successfully decrypt $P = D_B(C) = D_B(E_B(P))$.

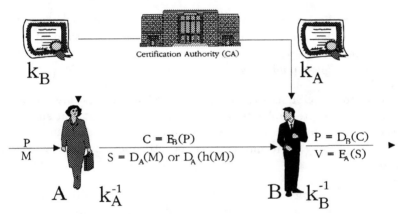

Figure 4.3 A public key cryptosystem.

Note that a public key cryptosystem can not only be used to protect the confidentiality of a message, but to protect its authenticity and integrity as well. If A wants to protect the authenticity and integrity of a message M, she computes a digital signature S for M. It has already been mentioned in Chapter 3 that digital signatures provide an electronic analog of handwritten signatures for electronic documents, and that, similar to handwritten signatures, digital signatures must not be forgeable, recipients must be able to verify them, and the signers must not be able to repudiate them later. However, a major difference between a handwritten signature and a digital signature is that the digital signature can't be constant, but must be a function of the entire document on which it appears. If this were not the case, then a digital signature, due to its electronic nature, could be copied and attached to any document.

Arbitrated digital signature schemes are based on secret key cryptography. In principle, a trusted third party (TTP) validates the signature and forwards it on the signer's behalf. True digital signature schemes, however, should come along without TTPs taking an active role. They usually require the use of public key cryptography: signed messages are sent directly from signers to recipients. A comprehensive study of digital signature schemes is given in [13]. In short, a *digital signature scheme* consists of

- A key-generation algorithm that randomly selects a public key pair;

- A signature algorithm that takes as input a message and a private key, and that generates as output a digital signature for the message;

- A signature verification algorithm that takes as input a digital signature and a public key, and that generates as output an information bit according to whether the signature is consistent with some valid message for the private key corresponding to the given public key.

According to the OSI security architecture, a digital signature refers to data appended to, or a cryptographic transformation of, a data unit that allows a recipient of the data unit to prove the source and integrity of the data unit and protect against forgery (e.g., by the recipient). Consequently, there are two classes of digital signatures:

- A *digital signature giving message recovery* refers to the situation in which a cryptographic transformation is applied to a data unit. In this case, the data are automatically recovered if the recipient verifies the signature.

- In contrast, a *digital signature with appendix* refers to the situation in which some cryptographically protected data are appended to the data unit. In fact, the data represent a digital signature and can be decoupled from the data unit that it signs.

In the case of digital signatures with appendix, the bandwidth limitation of public key cryptography is unimportant due to the use of one-way hash functions as auxiliaries. Again referring to Figure 4.3, A can use her private key k_A^{-1} to compute a digital signature $S = D_A(M)$ or $S = D_A(h(M))$ for message M. In the second case, h refers to a collision-resistant one-way hash function that is applied to M prior to generating the digital signature. Anybody who knows the public key of A can verify the digital signature by decrypting it with k_A and comparing the result with another hash value that is recomputed for the same message with the same one-way hash function.

A topic of current interest that is not addressed in this book is the legality of digital signatures. Note that there are few places, such as Utah in the United States, that already have laws addressing the use of digital signatures. Many places, such as Germany, have draft proposals available that are subject to some heated political discussions. One can reasonably expect that most places will pass laws that address the use of digital signatures in the next decade.

The most widely used public key cryptosystem is RSA, invented by Ron Rivest, Adi Shamir, and Len Adleman at the Massachusetts Institute of Technology (MIT) in 1977 [14]. The RSA cryptosystem gets its security from the difficulty and intractability of the factorization problem. What this means is that it is fairly simple to multiply two large prime numbers, but very difficult to compute the prime factors of a large number. One of the nice properties of RSA is that the same algorithm can be used for both message encryption and digital signature generation and verification. This is not the case for most other public key cryptosystems. For example, the ElGamal cryptosystem uses different algorithms for message encryption and digital signature generation and verification [15,16]. The ElGamal cryptosystem gets its security from the intractability of the discrete logarithm problem in a finite field. What this basically means is that, in general, the inverse operation of the exponentiation function is the logarithm function. There are efficient algorithms for computing logarithms in infinite fields. However, one does not know any efficient algorithm for computing discrete logarithms in finite fields. The digital signature standard (DSS) proposed by the NIST refers to an optimized modification of the ElGamal cryptosystem that can be used only for digital signature generation and verification [17].

Historically the first public key cryptosystem was proposed by Whitfield Diffie and Martin Hellman in their landmark paper in 1976 [12]. They proposed a protocol that two parties can use to exchange and agree on a session key. The resulting protocol is known as the Diffie-Hellman key exchange. Similar to the ElGamal cryptosystem, the Diffie-Hellman key exchange gets its security from the intractability of the discrete logarithm problem in a finite field. In the original version of the protocol, A and B both agree on a large prime number p and a generator g in $GF(p)$. A picks a random number x_a, computes $y_a = g^{x_a}(\bmod\ p)$, and transmits y_a to B. B, in turn, picks another random number x_b, computes $y_b = g^{x_b}(\bmod\ p)$, and transmits y_b to A. At this point, A knows y_b and x_a, and B knows y_a and x_b. A can compute

$K_{ab} = y_b{}^{x_a} = g^{x_b x_a}(\bmod\ p)$, and B can compute $K_{ab} = y_a{}^{x_b} = g^{x_a x_b}(\bmod\ p)$. Obviously, A and B end up computing the same value K_{ab}, and this value can be used as a session key to secure communications between A and B.

The use of the Diffie-Hellman key exchange is attractive because keys are only computed when needed. There is no need to keep secret values for long periods of time. This is a good property, since experience shows that it is usually difficult to keep secret keys in a computer system, and since the Diffie-Hellman key exchange does not require a public key infrastructure (PKI) to exist. Nevertheless, the Diffie-Hellman key exchange also has a well-known set of weaknesses. For example, it does not provide information about the identities of the parties involved in a key exchange. Consequently, the Diffie-Hellman key exchange is subject to the man-in-the-middle attack, in which an attacker C postures as B for A and A for B. In this case, A and B end up negotiating secret keys with C who can then passively or actively attack communications between them. Another disadvantage of the Diffie-Hellman key exchange is that it involves some heavy computation. This heavy computation load can be used in a clogging attack, in which an attacker requests a high number of keys in order to overload the victim. As a matter of fact, the victim may end up spending all of its computing power to do some useless exponentiation instead of real work. We will discuss mechanisms to thwart the man-in-the-middle and clogging attacks in Chapter 9.

The application of public key cryptography usually requires an authentication framework that binds public keys to user identities. A public key *certificate* is a certified proof of such binding vouched for by a *trusted third party* (TTP) or *certification authority* (CA). The use of a CA alleviates the responsibility of individual users to verify directly the correctness of other users' public keys. The ITU-T Recommendation X.509 specifies both a commonly used format for public key certificates, as well as a certificate distribution scheme [18]. X.509 is part of the ITU-T X.500 series of recommendations that specify a directory service. It has been approved by the ISO/IEC JTC1 [19]. In short, an X.509 public key certificate is a data structure that includes the following field entries:

- A *version* that specifies to which version of the ITU-T Recommendation X.509 the certificate's format conforms to. X.509 versions 1, 2, and 3 have been defined so far.

- A *serial number* assigned by the certificate issuing CA. This number should be unique within all certificates issued by the CA.

- An *algorithm identifier* that specifies the algorithm used for the digital signature of the certificate.

- An *issuer* that identifies the CA that issued and digitally signed the certificate.

- A *period of validity* that typically includes two dates. The certificate is not valid before the first date or after the second date.

- A *subject* that defines the name and other identifiers of the user for whom the certificate has been issued. For example, the subject field may include the user name and address.

- Some *public key information* that typically includes the user's public key and the algorithms for which the key is intended to be used.

- A *signature* that comprises the digital signature for the certificate.

Since version 3, it is also possible to define and further use application-specific extension fields in ITU-T X.509 certificates.

In practice, certificates will be issued by several organizations for different purposes. For example, a company may issue certificates to its employees, a university may issue certificates to its students, and a city may issue certificates to its citizens. The criteria to issue certificates may also vary with different CAs. Some CAs may issue a certificate based on the name and address. Others may require proof of date of birth, fingerprints, and so on. Finally, some institutions, such as courts, may accept only notarized certificates.

It is possible and very likely that there will be more than just one CA involved in issuing certificates. It is also possible and very likely that a user may possess more than one certificate, just as we carry more than one proof of identity today, such as credit cards and driver licenses. In fact, X.509 specifies the use of certificate chains and hierarchies. Different CAs may mutually certify their public keys, resulting in a connected graph of CAs. The initial point of trust for a particular user is the CA that registered him or her. For reasons of simplicity, the graph is often looked upon as a tree with optional additional connections. This tree refers to a directory information tree (DIT) in X.500 terminology. If A and B both have certificates from the same CA Z, B can obtain A's public key by first obtaining A's certificate from any source and then checking the authenticity of the certificate with the public key of Z. If A and B are certified by different CAs X and Y, B has to construct a certification path or chain. In essence, this is a sequence of certificates starting with a certificate issued by Y and ending with X's certificate for A, where each certificate in the path contains the public key to check the following certificate.

Certificate revocation refers to the announcement that a public key pair has been revoked and should no longer be used. There are several reasons that may require certificate revocation. For example, a user's or CA's private key may be compromised, or a user may no longer be registered and certified by a particular CA. In general, there are three approaches to address certificate revocation:

- The first approach is to use time-outs and renewals of certificates. Part of the signed message that represents a certificate may be a time after which the certificate should not be valid anymore. Periodically, a CA would renew certificates by signing one with a later time-out. If a key were compromised, a new key would be generated and a new certificate signed. The old certificate would only be valid until its time-out. Time-outs are not perfect revocation mechanisms because they provide only slow revocation and depend on servers having an accurate clock. Someone who can trick a server into turning back its clock can still use expired certificates.

- The second approach is to list all nonrevoked certificates in a directory and to believe only certificates that are found there. The advantage of this method is that it is almost immediate. The disadvantages are that the availability of authentication is only as good as the availability of the directory service, and that the security of the certificate revocation mechanism as a whole is only as good as the security of the directory service.

- The third approach is to have CAs periodically issue certificate revocation lists (CRLs) that itemize certificates that have been revoked and should no longer be used.

The ITU-T Recommendation X.509 follows the third approach. In fact, it recommends that each CA issue a CRL that itemizes all certificates that have been revoked and should no longer be used. Whenever a user receives a certificate, he or she must first check in the issuing CA's CRL whether the certificate has been revoked. The fact that users usually cache CRLs for efficiency reasons should be considered with care in this context. Also, there may be need for archiving certificates for being able to verify messages that are signed with a private key that belongs to a certificate that has been revoked.

There are many companies that provide CA products and services to Internet and intranet users. Examples include VeriSign, Entrust, and GTE CyberTrust in the United States and Canada, as well as Baltimore Technologies in Europe. To further develop and possibly enhance the technology, the European Union (EU) has launched a research and development program called ETS, an acronym derived from European trusted third party services. In addition to that, many software packages, such as the Netscape Navigator or the Microsoft Internet Explorer, are distributed with a set of preconfigured CAs that the users accept and trust by default if they don't explicitly disable them.

The ITU-T Recommendation X.509 has been around for many years and is widely accepted itoday. Looking at current efforts to further extend the functionality of X.509 certificates, two different approaches can be distinguished:

- On the one side, X.509 version 3 extension fields are being used to bind arbitrary attributes to public keys. This approach is being followed by the IETF public key infrastructure (PKIX) WG. It is also pursued by the recently published secure electronic transaction (SET) protocol specification discussed later in this book. SET uses X.509 extension fields in order to associate additional information, such as credit card numbers and merchant identifies, with public keys. Note that in this case, the purpose of the X.509 certificate is not only to identify its owner, but to authorize the owner to perform certain transactions as well.

- On the other side, new concepts are currently under development that reject the further use of X.509 certificates and propose new certificate encoding schemes and key acquisition mechanisms from scratch. Two examples of this kind are the simple distributed security infrastructure (SDSI) developed by Ron Rivest and Butler Lampson, and the simple public key infrastructure (SPKI) currently defined in the corresponding IETF WG.

In summary, public key certificate technology is evolving towards a more flexible mechanism using certificates that have meanings only in a local context. The aim is to use certificates not only for authentication, but for access control decisions as well.

4.4   LEGAL CONSIDERATIONS

There are some legal considerations that should be kept in mind when using cryptography. In particular, there are patent claims and regulations for the import, export, and use of cryptography.

4.4.1   Patent Claims

Patents applied to computer programs are called software patents. In the U.S. computer industry, software patents are still the subject of ongoing controversy. Some of the earliest and most important software patents granted by the U.S. Patent and Trademark Office were in the field of cryptography. These software patents go back to the late 1960s and early 1970s. Although computer algorithms were widely thought to be unpatentable at the time, the cryptography patents were granted because they were written as patents on encryption devices that were built in hardware. Indeed, most early encryption devices were built in hardware because general-purpose computers at the time simply could not execute the encryption algorithms fast enough in software. For example, IBM obtained several patents in the early 1970s on its Lucifer algorithm, which went on to become the DES. Today, many secret key cryptosystems are covered by patent claims. For example, DES is patented but royalty free, whereas IDEA is patented and royalty free for non-commercial use, but requires a license for commercial use. Later in the 1970s, all of the pioneers in the field of public key cryptography filed for and obtained patents on their work. Today, the field of public key cryptography is largely governed by a couple of patents, overviewed in Table 4.1. The patents 4,200,700, 4,218,582, and 4,424,414 were officially assigned to Stanford University, whereas the patent 4,405,829 was assigned to the Massachusetts Institute of Technology (MIT).

Table 4.1
The Major Public Key Cryptography Patents

Inventors	Patent Title and Number	Expiration date
M.E. Hellman, B.W. Diffie, and R.C. Merkle	Cryptographic Apparatus and Method (4,200,700)	April 29, 1997
M.E. Hellman and R.C. Merkle	Public Key Cryptographic Apparatus and Method (4,218,582)	August 19, 1997
R.L. Rivest, A. Shamir, and L.M. Adleman	Cryptographic Communication System and Method (4,405,829)	September 20, 2000
M.E. Hellman and S.C. Pohlig	Exponentiation Cryptographic Apparatus and Method (4,424,414)	January 3, 2001
C.P. Schnorr	Method for Identifying Subscribers and for Generating and Verifying Electronic Signatures in a Data Exchange System (4,995,082)	February 19, 2008

Throughout most of the 1980s, the Stanford patents were exclusively licensed to Cylink, and the MIT patent was held by RSA Data Security, Inc. In 1989, Cylink and RSA Data Security, Inc. created a new company for administering the patent rights, called Public Key Partners. During the early 1990s, Cylink became increasingly dissatisfied with this arrangement. In June 1994, Cylink filed suit against RSA Data Security, Inc. in federal court, claiming that it had new evidence proving that the MIT patent was in fact invalid. Later in 1994, Cylink also filed papers in California to have the Public Key Partners partnership forcibly dissolved. Eventually, the partnership was dissolved by an arbitrator who decreed that the MIT patent would be returned to RSA Data Security, Inc., and the Stanford patents would be returned to Cylink.

Outside the United States, the patent situation is quite different. For example, patent law in Europe and Japan differs from U.S. patent law in one very important fashion. In the United States, an inventor has a grace period of one year between the first public disclosure of an invention and the last day on which a patent application can be filed. In Europe and Japan, there is no grace period. Any public disclosure instantly forfeits all patent rights. Because the inventions contained in the Stanford and MIT patents were publicly disclosed before patent applications were filed, these algorithms were never patentable in Europe and Japan. Also because these algorithms were not covered by patent claims, public key technology has been more widely adopted in the corresponding countries.

Under the United States patent law, patent infringement is not a criminal offense, and the penalties and damages are the jurisdiction of the civil courts. It is the responsibility of the user of a particular cryptographic algorithm or technique to make sure that correct licenses have been obtained from the corresponding patent holders. If these licenses did not exist, the patent holders could fight the user in court. Therefore, most products that make use of cryptographic algorithms or techniques come along with the licenses required to use them. With regard to the Internet standards process, for example, a written statement from the patent holder is required that a license will be made available to applicants under reasonable terms and conditions prior to approving a protocol specification as a proposed, draft, or Internet standard.

4.4.2   Regulations

In the United States, certain cryptographic systems and technical data regarding them are deemed to be defense articles and are subject to federal government export controls accordingly. If a U.S. company wants to sell cryptographic systems and technical data to other countries, it therefore has to have export approval. Exports must be licensed either by the Offices of Defense Trade Controls and Munitions Control of the Department of State (DoS) or the Office of Export Administration of the Department of Commerce (DoC). In general, the DoS is responsible for licensing cryptographic systems and technical data that are used for data encryption, whereas the DoC is responsible for licensing cryptographic systems and technical data that are used for authentication and access control, as well as proprietary hardware devices and software. In spite of this general distinction, the export control laws around encryption are not too clear, and their interpretation changes over time. Sometimes companies get so discouraged that they leave encryption out of their products altogether. Sometimes they generate products that, when sold overseas, have encryption mechanisms seriously weakened or removed. It is usually possible to get export approval for encryption if the key lengths are shortened. So, sometimes companies use short keys or cryptosystems with varying key lengths. Probably the most widely deployed example of this kind is the Netscape Navigator that comes in two versions: the U.S. domestic version that uses strong encryption with 128-bit RC4 session keys, and the international version of the same product that uses encryption with only 40-bit RC4 session keys. It took UC Berkeley graduate student Ian Goldberg only three and a half hours to crack a 40-bit RC4 key. The interconnection of 250 idle workstations at UC Berkeley allowed him to test hundreds of billions of possible keys per hour. It seems to be obvious today that 40-bit keys are far too weak to be used in any serious application [20]. In August 1996, the IAB and IESG published a corresponding statement on cryptographic technology and the Internet in RFC 1984.

In October 1996, the Administration announced a plan to make it easier for U.S. companies to use strong encryption to protect their privacy, intellectual property, and other valuable information. The plan envisions a worldwide key management infrastructure with the use of key escrow and key recovery technologies to promote electronic commerce and secure communications while claiming to protect national security and public safety. To provide for a transition period for the development of this key management infrastructure, the rule permits the export and reexport of 56-bit key length DES or equivalent strength encryption items under the authority of a license exception, if an exporter makes satisfactory commitments to build or market recoverable encryption items and to help build the corresponding key management infrastructure. Once the exporter has implemented the corresponding key recovery mechanisms, he or she will be able to ship products with keys of any length. Several major U.S. companies have formed a Key Recovery Alliance to further support this strategy.

The United States is a country that has been regulating the export of cryptographic systems and technical data regarding them for quite a long time. These regulations go far beyond the Wassenaar Arrangement on export controls for conventional arms and dual-use goods and technologies. The Wassenaar Arrangement is a treaty negotiated in July 1996 and signed by 31 countries to restrict the export of dual-use goods and technologies to specific countries that are considered to be dangerous. The countries that have signed the Wassenaar Arrangement include the former COCOM[1] member and cooperating countries, as well as some new countries such as Russia. In addition to export regulations, there are also countries that regulate either the import or use of cryptographic systems and technical data regarding them [21]. For example, India and South Korea regulate the import, whereas France and Russia regulate the use of cryptography. Many countries have just begun to study the impact of publicly available cryptographic systems on the possibilities of intelligence gathering and legal interception. For example, Germany is seriously thinking about possible regulations on cryptography. Also, the topic is being discussed by the Senior Officials Group on Information Security (SOG-IS) in Europe and the Organization for Economic Cooperation and Development (OECD).

4.5 AUTHENTICATION

In general, *authentication* refers to the process of verifying the claimed identity of a principal. Authentication results in authenticity, meaning that the verifying principal (the *verifier*) can be sure the verified principal (the *claimant*) is the one he or she claims to be. It is common to divide the techniques that are used for authentication into three categories, depending on whether a technique is based on

- Something the claimant knows (proof by knowledge);

- Something the claimant possesses (proof by possession);

- Some biometric characteristics of the claimant (proof by property).

---

[1] The Coordinating Committee for Multilateral Export Controls (COCOM) was an international munitions control organization that also restricted the export of cryptography as a dual-use technology. Formally dissolved in March 1994, COCOM member countries included Australia, Belgium, Canada, Denmark, France, Germany, Greece, Italy, Japan, Luxemburg, The Netherlands, Norway, Portugal, Spain, Turkey, United Kingdom, and the United States. Cooperating members included Austria, Finland, Hungary, Ireland, New Zealand, Poland, Singapore, Slovakia, South Korea, Sweden, Switzerland, and Taiwan.

Examples for the first category are personal identification numbers (PINs), passwords, and transaction authentication numbers (TANs), whereas examples for the second category are keys, identification cards, and other physical devices or personal tokens. Historically, the first biometric characteristics that were used for authentication were fingerprints. Today, it is possible to use other characteristics such as facial images, retinal images, and voice patterns. However, the use of biometric characteristics in computer networks and distributed systems also requires some form of liveness testing that randomizes the biometric patterns that are matched. As this is difficult to achieve, most authentication mechanisms in use today are still based on proof by knowledge. Let's have a look at password-based and address-based authentication next, before we turn to more secure cryptographic authentication schemes.

4.5.1   Password-Based Authentication

In computer networks and distributed systems, protection of resources is usually achieved by direct login to each host accessed using passwords, with users selecting passwords and transmitting them in the clear and unprotected. Password-based authentication has several drawbacks, and we mention only two of them:

- First, users tend to select passwords that are easy to remember. Consequently, such passwords are not randomly distributed and easy to guess [22,23]. Password guessing is the process of correctly guessing the password of a legitimate user. Dan Klein analyzed the feasibility of password guessing attacks for approximately 15,000 user accounts back in 1990. As a result, he found that he could guess 2.7% of the passwords in the first 15 minutes and 21% within the first week [24]. It is assumed that these numbers haven't changed much since their original publication in 1990.

- Second, the transmission of a password (that may be well chosen or not) is exposed to passive eavesdropping and subsequent replay attacks.

Mainly because of the second drawback, password-based authentication is not suitable for use in computer networks and distributed systems. Passwords sent across a network are generally too easy to intercept and use to impersonate users. While this vulnerability has been long known, it was not until recently that it was demonstrated on a large scale with the discovery of planted password collecting routines at critical points within the Internet.[2]

---

[2]Compare CERT Advisory CA-94:01, "Ongoing network monitoring attacks," February 3, 1994.

4.5.2   Address-Based Authentication

One way to overcome the problems of password-based authentication is address-based authentication, as incorporated in the BSD UNIX r-tools (`rlogin`, `rsh`, and `rcp`). Address-based authentication does not rely on sending passwords around the network, but rather assumes that the identity of the source can be inferred based on the network address from which packets arrive. The basic idea is that each host stores information that specifies accounts on other hosts that should have access to its resources. Each host may have a file named `/etc/hosts.equiv` containing a list of trusted hostnames. Users with the same username on both the local and the trusted host may use the r-tools without having to supply a password. Individual users may set up a similar private equivalence list with the `.rhosts` file in their home directories. Each line in this file may contain a hostname and a username separated by a space. An entry in a user's remote `.rhosts` file permits the user who is logged into the system specified by hostname to log into the remote system without having to supply a password. Instead of logging into the host, the user can also remotely execute commands or copy files.

Note that the idea of trusted hosts is no general solution to the authentication problem in computer networks and distributed systems, and trusted hosts may even pose more serious security threats. The point is that host authentication mechanisms can always be defeated, and if an attacker is able to break into an account in a host that is trusted by other hosts, the user's accounts on these other hosts are usually compromised as well. The use of `.rhosts` files poses an additional security threat because the system administrator is, in general, unable to exclusively control access to the system via the r-tools. Users are likely to tailor their `.rhosts` files more for convenience than for security. Depending on the environment, address-based authentication may be more or less secure than sending passwords in the clear. In either case, it is more convenient, and it is therefore the authentication mechanism of choice in many networked environments.

4.5.3   Cryptographic Authentication

The basic idea of a cryptographic authentication is that a claimant A proves his or her identity to a verifier B by performing a cryptographic operation of a quantity that either both know or B supplies. The cryptographic operation performed by A is based on a cryptographic key that can either be a secret key from a secret key cryptosystem or a private key from a public key cryptosystem [25].

The simplest form of cryptographic authentication is the use of one-time passwords. The idea of using one-time passwords is to dynamically generate unpredictable passwords that are valid for only a single access to the security system. A second attempt to log on using the same one-time password generates an error and results in rejection of the login request. One-time password systems often are implemented using token cards, although some software-based implementations are available as well. Since one-time passwords can't be reused, their theft should not pose any security risk. Examples of token cards are SecurID from Security Dynamics, and SecureNet Key from Digital Pathways. SecurID tokens basically contain a DES chip and a clock. The clock is synchronized with the computer's clock and all a user should do to authenticate himself or herself is to read the one-time password on the display and type it in at the login prompt. In this case, the one-time password is usually a timestamp generated from the local clock encrypted with the DES key. Examples of software-based implementations are S/Key originally designed by Leslie Lamport and developed at Bell Communications Research (Bellcore) [26], as well as the One-Time Passwords in Everything (OPIE) developed at the U.S. Naval Research Laboratory (NRL). S/Key and OPIE both conform to the one-time password system specified in [27]. S/Key has been publicly available on the Internet for quite a long time,[3] whereas OPIE version 2.31 was not released until March 1997.[4]

In general, cryptographic authentication can be made more secure than either password-based or address-based authentication. In addition to that, new techniques based on zero-knowledge proofs may provide even more powerful authentication mechanisms [28,29]. These techniques demand rather intensive mathematical computations, but they present attractive features for authentication:

- First, they allow the claimer to prove that he or she knows the right identification secret without actually transferring any knowledge about that secret to the verifier.

- Second, some of the zero-knowledge schemes that have been proposed so far are such that verification of the authentication messages of any claimer all require the same public information, which avoids altogether the problem of key distribution exhibited by DES- or RSA-based authentication mechanisms.

Despite the apparent simplicity of the basic design principles for cryptographic authentication protocols, designing realistic protocols is notoriously difficult and several published protocols have exhibited substantial or subtle security problems. During the last decade, research efforts have focused on providing tools needed for

---

[3] ftp://thumper.bellcore.com/pub/nmh/skey
[4] ftp://ftp.nrl.navy.mil/pub/security/opie

developing authentication and key distribution protocols with some formal assurance of security. Most notably, formal tools for testing protocols were developed; for example, the BAN logic [30] and its successor, the GNY logic [31]. Instead of devising specific protocols, these methodologies provide a means for showing that appropriate beliefs are attained as a result of running an authentication protocol.

4.6 KEY DISTRIBUTION

Most of the security services that are enumerated in the OSI security architecture are based on cryptographic mechanisms, and the use of these mechanisms generally requires a corresponding key management infrastructure. According to the ISO, *key management* has to deal with "the generation, storage, distribution, deletion, archiving and application of keys in accordance with a security policy." Key management is carried out with protocols, and many of the important properties of key management protocols do not depend on the underlying cryptographic algorithms, but rather on the structure of the messages exchanged. Therefore, security leaks and vulnerabilities do not come from weak cryptographic algorithms, but rather from mistakes in higher levels of the protocol design.

The working group (WG) 802.10 of the Institute of Electrical and Electronic Engineers (IEEE) was formed in May of 1988 to address the security needs of local and metropolitan area networks. The WG is cosponsored by the IEEE Technical Committee on Computer Communications and by the IEEE Technical Committee on Security and Privacy. Within IEEE 802.10, work on cryptographic key management began in May of 1989. The key management model and protocol that is being standardized by IEEE 802.10 supports three classes of key distribution techniques, namely manual key distribution, center-based key distribution, and certificate-based key distribution [32].

4.6.1 Manual Key Distribution

Manual key distribution techniques use offline delivery methods to establish pairwise or multicast cryptographic keys. Manual key distribution techniques, in general, may be cumbersome and have scalability problems. Also, they do not provide any authentication other than that provided by the corresponding offline delivery method. Therefore, the strength of the procedures used for offline delivery of the cryptographic keys is extremely important.

In many cases, however, manual delivery of cryptographic keys is required at least once per user, and distribution of additional keying material can be performed using the manually distributed key as a *key encryption key* (KEK). The encrypted keying material can then be distributed using any convenient method. Manual key distribution is suitable in multicast environments, where a single group key must be delivered to potentially many participants. In fact, manual key distribution is often the most efficient way to deliver group keys, especially to larger groups. We will further address multicast key distribution in Section 9.3, when we talk about the possibilities to key the IP Security Protocol (IPSP) in a multicast environment.

4.6.2   Center-Based Key Distribution

Center-based key distribution techniques may be used to establish pairwise or multicast cryptographic keys between communicating peers via a trusted third party. This trusted third party can act as

- A *key distribution center* (KDC);

- A *key translation center* (KTC).

Center-based key distribution covers both KDCs and KTCs. The corresponding key distribution protocols depend upon the manual distribution of KEKs to provide confidentiality and integrity protection of for the distributed keys.

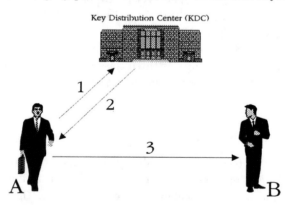

Figure 4.4   The pull model for center-based key distribution.

Most existing key distribution methods have been tailored to specific scenarios and applications. For example, any scheme relying on timestamps favors the local environment, where all users have access to a commonly trusted time server.

While requiring tightly synchronized clocks in the wide area is conceivable, it is certainly harder. More importantly, existing schemes make specific assumptions about network configuration and connectivity models. For instance, they may dictate a specific communication paradigm for contacting a trusted server or KDC. When a principal A needs a key to communicate with another principal B, Kerberos, for example, requires that A obtains the desired key from the KDC prior to communicating with B. This paradigm is sometimes referred to as the *pull model*. The pull model for center-based key distribution is illustrated in Figure 4.4.

By contrast, in the same situation, the U.S. standard for financial institution key management (ANSI X9.17) specifies that A must contact B first, and let B get the necessary key from the KDC. This paradigm is sometimes referred to as the *push model*. The push model for center-based key distribution is illustrated in Figure 4.5). In short, A pushes B to contact the KDC and request a session key accordingly.

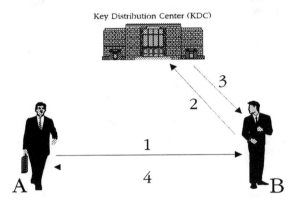

Figure 4.5   The push model for center-based key distribution.

It is important to note that neither the push model nor the pull model is better than the other, and that both models are justified in their respective environments. In a local area environment, for which Kerberos was originally designed, requiring clients to obtain the keys makes a lot of sense because it distributes the burden over many clients, thus alleviating the task of the few shared servers. In a wide area environment for which X9.17 was designed, however, the opposite approach is justified because there are typically many more clients than servers, and KDCs are typically located closer to servers than clients. Under such circumstances, the amount of system definition in terms of configuration, and the costs of the connections between clients and the KDCs required by the Kerberos approach may become prohibitive in a wide area environment.

It is even possible to combine the two approaches and to come up with a mixed model for center-based key distribution. The corresponding mixed model for center-based key distribution is illustrated in Figure 4.6.

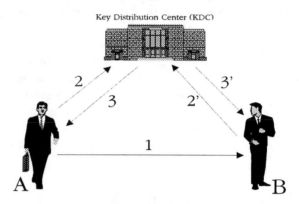

Figure 4.6   The mixed model for center-based key distribution.

4.6.3   Certificate-Based Key Distribution

Certificate-based key distribution techniques may be used to establish pairwise cryptographic keys. There are two classes of certificate-based key distribution techniques to be distinguished:

- A public key cryptosystem is used to encrypt a locally generated cryptographic key and to protect it while it is being transferred to a remote key management entity. This is called a *key transfer*.

- A cryptographic key is cooperatively generated at both the local and remote key management entity. This is called a *key exchange* or *key agreement*. The best example for a key agreement protocol is the Diffie-Hellman key exchange as discussed earlier in this chapter.

In general, certificate-based key distribution techniques may not be directly used to establish multicast keys. However, once pairwise cryptographic keys are established, they can be used to further protect the distribution of multicast keys.

4.7 NOTATION

In general, a *protocol* specifies the format and relative timing of information exchanged between communicating parties. A *cryptographic protocol* is a protocol that makes use of cryptographic techniques. The following notation is used in this book to describe cryptographic protocols:

- Capital letters, such as A, B, C, ..., are used to refer to principals, whereas the same letters put in italics are used to refer to the corresponding principal identifiers. Note that many publications on cryptography and cryptographic protocols use names, such as Alice and Bob, to refer to principals. This is a convenient way of making things unambiguous with relatively few words, since the pronoun "she" can be used for Alice, and "he" can be used for Bob. However, the advantages and disadvantages of this naming scheme are controversial, and we are not going to use it in the rest of this book either.

- K is used to refer to a secret key, which is basically a key of a secret key cryptosystem.

- The pair (k, k^{-1}) is used to refer to a public key pair, whereas k is used to refer to the public key and k^{-1} is used to refer to the corresponding private key.

  In either case, key subscripts may be used to indicate principals. In general, capital letter subscripts are used for long-term keys, and small letter subscripts are used for short-term keys. For example, K_A is used to refer to A's long-term secret key, whereas k_b is used to refer to B's short-term public key.

- The term $\{M\}K$ is used to refer to a message M that is encrypted with the secret key K. The same key K is used for decryption, so $\{\{M\}K\}K$ equals M. If K is used to compute and verify a message authentication code (MAC) for message M, then the term $\langle M \rangle K$ is used to refer to $\{h(M)\}K$, with h being a collision-resistant one-way hash function.

- Similarly, the term $\{M\}k$ is used to refer to a message M that is encrypted with the public key k. The message can only be decrypted with the corresponding private key k^{-1}. If a public key cryptosystem is used to digitally sign messages, the private key is used for signing and the corresponding public key is used for verifying signatures. Referring to the terminology of the OSI security architecture, the term $\{M\}k^{-1}$ is used to refer to a digital signature giving message recovery, and $\langle M \rangle k^{-1}$ is used to refer to a digital signature with appendix. Note that in the second case, $\langle M \rangle k^{-1}$ in fact abbreviates $M, \{h(M)\}k^{-1}$, with h being again a collision-resistant one-way hash function.

- In accordance with international standardization, $X \ll Y \gg$ is used to refer to a certificate that has been issued by X for Y's public key. Note that $X \ll Y \gg$, in principle, implies that X has certified the binding of Y's long-term public key k_Y with Y's identity.

- T is used to refer to a *timestamp*. Timestamp subscripts may be used to imply a temporal ordering.

- N is used to refer to a *nonce*. In short, a nonce is a quantity that any given user of a cryptographic protocol is supposed to use only once. Various forms of nonce are a timestamp, a sequence number, or a large and unpredictable random number. In our notation, we use small letters in nonce subscripts to indicate particular principals. Small letters are used mainly because of the short-term nature of nonces.

- Finally, M, N is used to refer to the concatenation of the two message strings M and N.

In the protocol descriptions that follow, the term

i: A $\longrightarrow$ B : M

is used to refer to step i, in which principal A is assumed to transmit a message M to principal B. Note that the notation of $\longrightarrow$ must be interpreted with care. The messages are sent in environments, where error, corruption, loss, and delay may occur. There is nothing in the environment to guarantee that messages are really made in numerical order by the principals indicated, received in numerical order or at all by the principals indicated, or received solely by the principals indicated.

REFERENCES

[1] B. Kaliski, "The MD2 Message-Digest Algorithm," Request for Comments 1319, April 1992.

[2] R.L. Rivest, "The MD4 Message-Digest Algorithm," Request for Comments 1320, April 1992.

[3] R.L. Rivest, and S. Dusse, "The MD5 Message-Digest Algorithm," Request for Comments 1321, April 1992.

[4] NIST, "Secure Hash Standard (SHS)," FIPS PUB 180-1, April 1995.

[5] H. Dobbertin, A. Bosselaers, and B. Preneel, "RIPEMD-160: A strengthened version of RIPEMD," *Proceedings of Fast Software Encryption Workshop*, 1996, pp. 71 – 82.

[6] P. van Oorschot, and M. Wiener, "Parallel Collision Search with Applications to Hash Functions and Discrete Logarithms," *Proceedings of ACM Conference on Computer and Communications Security*, November 1994.

[7] H. Dobbertin, "The Status of MD5 After a Recent Attack," *RSA Laboratories' CryptoBytes*, Vol. 2 (1996), No. 2.

[8] NIST (former NBS), "Data Encryption Standard," FIPS PUB 46, January 1977.

[9] X. Lai, *On the Design and Security of Block Ciphers*, Ph.D. Thesis ETH No. 9752, ETH Zürich, Switzerland, 1992.

[10] B. Schneier, "Description of a New Variable-Length Key, 64-Bit Block Cipher (Blowfish)," *Proceedings of Fast Software Encryption Workshop*, 1994, pp. 191 – 204.

[11] J.L. Massey, "SAFER K-64: A Byte-Oriented Block Ciphering Algorithm," *Proceedings of Fast Software Encryption Workshop*, 1994, pp. 1 – 17.

[12] W. Diffie, and M.E. Hellman, "New Directions in Cryptography," *IEEE Transactions on Information Theory*, IT-22(6), 1976, pp. 644 – 654.

[13] B. Pfitzmann, *Digital Signature Schemes*, Springer-Verlag, Berlin, Germany, 1996.

[14] R.L. Rivest, A. Shamir, and L. Adleman, "A Method for Obtaining Digital Signatures and Public-Key Cryptosystems," *Communications of the ACM*, 21(2), February 1978, pp. 120 – 126.

[15] T. ElGamal, *Cryptography and Logarithms Over Finite Fields*, Ph.D. Thesis, Stanford University, 1984.

[16] T. ElGamal, "A Public Key Cryptosystem and a Signature Scheme Based on Discrete Logarithm," *IEEE Transactions on Information Theory*, IT-31(4), 1985, pp. 469 – 472.

[17] NIST, *Digital Signature Standard (DSS)*, FIPS PUB 186, May 1994.

[18] ITU-T X.509, *The Directory — Authentication Framework*, November 1987.

[19] ISO/IEC 9594-8, *Information technology — Open Systems Interconnection — The Directory — Part 8: Authentication framework*, 1990.

[20] M. Blaze, W. Diffie, R.L. Rivest, B. Schneier, T. Shimomura, E. Thompson, and M. Wiener, "Minimal Key Lengths for Symmetric Ciphers to Provide Adequate Commercial Security," *Business Software Alliance*, January 1996.

[21] L.J. Hoffman, *Building in Big Brother: The Cryptographic Policy Debate*, Springer-Verlag, New York, NY, 1995.

[22] R. Morris, and K. Thompson, "Password Security: A Case History," *Communications of the ACM*, Vol. 22, 1979, pp. 594 – 597.

[23] D.C. Feldmeier, and P.R. Karn, "UNIX Password Security — Ten Years Later," *Proceedings of CRYPTO '89*, 1990, pp. 44 – 63.

[24] D.V. Klein, "Foiling the Cracker: A Survey of, and Improvements to, Password Security," *Proceedings of USENIX UNIX Security Symposium*, August 1990, pp. 5 – 14.

[25] N. Haller, and R. Atkinson, "On Internet Authentication," Request for Comments 1704, October 1994.

[26] N. Haller, "The S/KEY One-Time Password System," Request for Comments 1760, February 1995.

[27] N. Haller, and C. Metz, "A One-Time Password System," Request for Comments 1938, May 1996.

[28] A. Fiat, and A. Shamir, "How to Prove Yourself: Practical Solutions to Indetification and Signature Problems," *Proceedings of CRYPTO '86*, 1987, pp. 186 – 194.

[29] J.J. Quisquater, and L. Guillou, "How to Explain Zero-Knowledge Protocols to Your Children," *Proceedings of CRYPTO '89*, 1990, pp. 628 – 631.

[30] M. Burrows, M. Abadi, and R. Needham, "A Logic of Authentication," *ACM Operating Systems Review*, Vol. 23, 1989, pp. 1 – 13.

[31] L. Gong, R. Needham, and R. Yahalom, "GNY Logic Fill In," *Proceedings of the IEEE Symposium on Security and Privacy*, 1990, pp. 234 – 248.

[32] IEEE 802.10c/D10, Standard for Interoperable LAN/MAN Security: Clause 3 — Key Mangement Protocol, September 1995.

Part II

ACCESS CONTROL

Chapter 5

Overview

In the second part of this book we focus on the firewall technology that is mainly used to provide access control services for corporate intranets. We start with an advertising query and answer that Trusted Information Systems, Inc.[1] (TIS) put on its WWW home page early in 1997 to promote the Gauntlet Internet Firewall System:

What do the CIA, MGM/Universal Studios, and the Nation of Islam have in common? — Their Web sites were hacked and vandalized in 1996.

There are two conclusions drawn in the advertisement: First, one must protect a Web site, and second, one must use a Gauntlet Internet Firewall System to do so. While one can agree with the first conclusion, the second one is not very obvious and is mainly drawn by TIS marketing people.

The aim of this chapter is to introduce the firewall technology. In Section 5.1, we start with a brief overview of the rationale and the basic principles that underlie the technology, and in Section 5.2, we describe and further discuss the basic components of a firewall configuration.

---

[1]http://www.tis.com

5.1   INTRODUCTION

While Internet connectivity offers enormous benefits in terms of increased avail-ability and access to information, Internet connectivity is not always a good thing, especially for sites with low levels of security. As we have discussed in the first part of this book, the Internet suffers from glaring security problems that, if ignored, could have disastrous impacts for unprepared sites. Inherent problems with the TCP/IP protocols and services, the complexity of host and site configuration, vulnerabilities introduced in the software development process, and a wide variety of other factors all contribute to making unprepared sites open for intruder activities and other security-related threats. For example, host systems and access controls are usually complex to configure and test for correctness. As a result, they are sometimes acci-dentially misconfigured, and this may result in intruders gaining unauthorized and illegitimate access to system and information resources. It is a rather astonishing fact that some UNIX vendors still ship their systems with access controls config-ured for maximum (i.e., least secure access), which can result in unauthorized and illegitimate access if left as is. Furthermore, a number of security incidents have occurred that are due in part to vulnerabilities discovered by intruders. Since many UNIX systems have their network code derived from BSD UNIX that is publicly available in source code, intruders have been able to study the code for bugs and error conditions that may be exploited to gain unauthorized and illegitimate access. The bugs exist in part because of the complexity of the software and the inability to test it under all circumstances and in all the environments it must operate in. Sometimes the bugs can be discovered and corrected; other times, however, little can be done except to rewrite the entire software, which is usually the option of last resort.

Consequently, host security is hard to achieve and does not scale well in the sense that as the number of hosts increases, the ability to ensure that security is at a high level for each host usually decreases. Given the fact that secure management of just one single system can be a demanding task, managing many such systems could easily result in mistakes and omissions. A contributing factor is that the role of system administration is often undervalued and performed in a hassle. As a result of this, some systems will be less secure than others, and these systems will probably be the ones that ultimately break the security of either a site or an entire corporate intranet.

This book does not address host and site security. There is an RFC specifying a site security handbook published in July 1991 [1]. There is also an IETF Site

Security Handbook (SSH) WG being chartered in the User Services Area.[2] The IETF SSH WG is revising and periodically updating the site security handbook in corresponding Internet Drafts.[3] The latest draft was released for public scrutiny in March 1997.

In days of old, brick walls were built between buildings in apartment complexes so that if a fire broke out, it would not spread from one building to another. Quite naturally, these walls were called firewalls. Today, when a private network is connected to a public network its users are usually enabled to reach and communicate with the outside world. At the same time, however, the outside world can also reach and interact with the private network. In this dangerous situation, an intermediate system can be plugged between the private network and the public network to establish a controlled link, and to erect a security wall or perimeter. The aim of this intermediate system is to protect the private network from network-based attacks that may originate from the outside world, and to provide a single choke point where security and audit can be imposed. Note that all traffic in and out of the private network can be enforced to pass through this single, narrow checkpoint. Also note that this checkpoint provides a good place to collect information about system and network use and misuse. As a single point of access, the intermediate system can record what occurs between the private network and the outside world. Quite naturally, these intermediate systems are called *firewall systems*, or *firewalls* in short. In other literature, Internet firewalls are sometimes also referred to as *secure Internet gateways* or *security gateways*. We are not going to use these alternative terms in this book.

In essence, a firewall represents a blockade between a privately owned and protected network (that is assumed to be secure and trusted) and another network, typically a public network or an internet (that is assumed to be nonsecure and untrusted). The purpose of a firewall is to prevent unwanted and unauthorized communications into or out of the protected network.

In addition to the physical firewall analogy mentioned above, there are other analogies that may help to better understand and motivate for the use of firewalls:

- Passports are generally checked at the border of a country;

- Apartments are usually locked at the entrance and not necessarily at each door;

---

[2]Note that that there is also an IETF SSH WG being chartered in the Security Area. In this case, SSH abbreviates Secure Shell and refers to a transport layer security protocol. We further address the SSH transport layer security protocol in Chapter 10.

[3]`draft-ietf-ssh-handbook-*.txt`

- Similarly, offices don't usually have a door to the outside world;

- And yet, a bank still has a vault to store money and valuable goods.

Other analogies include the toll booth on a bridge, the ticket booth at a movie theatre, and the check-out line at the supermarket. These analogies and the first three analogies listed above illustrate the fact that it sometimes makes a lot of sense to aggregate security functions at a single point. Nevertheless, the last analogy listed above illustrates that additional security precautions may be required under certain circumstances. Note that a firewall is conceptually similar to locking the doors of a house or employing a doorperson. The objective is to ensure that only properly authenticated and authorized people are able to physically enter the house. Unfortunately, this protection is not foolproof and can be defeated with enough effort. The basic idea is to make the effort too big for an average burglar, so that he or she will eventually go away and find another, more vulnerable, target. However, just in case the burglar does not go away and manages to enter the house, we usually lock up our valuable goods in a safe. According to this analogy, the use of a firewall may not always be sufficient, especially in high-security environments we typically live in these days.

In their book on firewalls and Internet security [2], William Cheswick and Steven Bellovin define a firewall (system) as a collection of components placed between two networks that collectively have the following properties:

- All traffic from inside to outside, and vice versa, must pass through the firewall;

- Only authorized traffic, as defined by the local security policy, will be allowed to pass;

- The firewall itself is immune to penetration.

Note that these properties are design goals. A failure in one aspect does not necessarily mean that the collection is not a firewall, simply that it is not a good one. Consequently, there are different grades of security that a firewall can achieve. Also note that there must be a security policy for the firewall to enforce.

Another possibility to define a firewall has been developed by the Swiss Federal Office of Information Technology and Systems (BFI) for its network security policy (NSP). According to this NSP, a system is called a firewall if it is able:

- To enforce strong authentication for users who wish to establish (inbound or outbound[4]) connections;

- To associate data streams that are allowed to pass through the firewall with previously authenticated and authorized users.

Again, it is a policy decision if a data stream is allowed to pass through the firewall. So this definition also leads to the necessity of an explicit firewall policy. Later in this chapter, we will distinguish between packet filters and application gateways. It is interesting to note at this point that the second definition requires the use of application gateways. Since application gateways operate at the higher layers of the OSI-RM, they typically have access to more information than simple packet filters and can therefore be programmed to operate more intelligently and to be more secure as well. Some vendors, for marketing reasons perhaps, blur the distinction between a packet filter and a firewall to the extent that they call any packet-filtering device a firewall. For the sake of clarity, however, this book makes a clear distinction between packet filters (operating at the network and transport layers of the OSI-RM) and firewalls (operating at the higher layers of the OSI-RM). This distinction is emphasized by the second definition given above. Note that the definition can be applied not only to TCP/IP-based firewalls, but also to modem pools with serial line interfaces that provide support for strong user authentication as well.

From a more pragmatic point of view, a firewall refers to a collection of hardware, software, and policy that is placed between a private network, typically a corporate intranet, and an external network, typically the Internet. As such, the firewall implements parts of an NSP by enforcing all data traffic to be directed to or routed to the firewall, where it can be examined and evaluated accordingly. In essence, a firewall seeks to prevent unwanted and unauthorized communications into or out of a corporate intranet, and to allow an organization to enforce a policy on traffic

---

[4]In this book, the terms "inbound" and "outbound" are used to refer to connections or IP packets from the point of view of the protected network, which is typically the intranet. Consequently, an outbound connection is a connection initiated from a client on an internal machine to a server on an external machine. Note that while the connection as a whole is outbound, it includes both outbound IP packets (those from the internal client to the external server) and inbound IP packets (those from the external server to the internal client). Similarly, an inbound connection is a connection initiated from a client on an external machine to a server on an internal machine. Following this terminology, the inbound interface for an IP packet refers to the physical network interface on a screening router that the packet actually appeared on, while the outbound interface refers to the physical network interface the packet will go out on if it isn't denied by the application of a specific packet filter rule.

flowing between its intranet and the Internet. Typically, a firewall also requires its users to strongly authenticate themselves before any further action is deployed. The second definition given above has made this requirement mandatory for a firewall system to provide. In this case, strong authentication mechanisms are used to replace password-based and address-based authentication.

The general reasoning behind firewall usage is that without a firewall, a site is more exposed to inherently insecure host operating systems, TCP/IP protocols and services, as well as probes and attacks from the Internet. In a firewall-less environment, network security is totally a function of each host, and all hosts must, in a sense, cooperate to achieve a uniformly high level of security. The larger the network, the less manageable it usually is to maintain all hosts at the same level of security. As mistakes and lapses in security become more common, break-ins can occur not only as a result of complex attacks, but also because of simple errors in configuration files and inadequatly chosen passwords. Assuming that software is buggy, one can conclude that most host systems have security holes that can eventually be exploited by intruders. Firewalls are designed to run less software, and hence may potentially have fewer bugs, vulnerabilities, and security holes than conventional hosts. In addition, firewalls generally have advanced logging and monitoring facilities and can be professionally administered. With firewall usage, only few hosts are exposed to attacks from the Internet.

Later in this part of the book, we will discuss the advantages and disadvantages of the firewall technology as a whole. Probably one of the main disadvantages is due to the fact that a firewall can't protect sites and corporate intranets against insider attacks. For that matter, internal firewalls may be used to control access between different administration and security domains, or to protect sensitive parts of a corporate intranet. Internal firewalls are sometimes also called *intranet firewalls*. From a purely technical point of view, there is nothing that distinguishes an intranet firewall from an Internet firewall except for the policy it enforces. Consequently, we are not going to differentiate between intranet and Internet firewalls in this book.

There are many books available that entirely cover the firewall technology. As a matter of fact, most books that have addressed Internet and intranet security in the past are actually books on firewalls [2,3,4], or put the main emphasis on the firewall technology [5]. There are also some scientific papers and reports available that address specific topics related to firewalls [6,7]. The design of a former firewall configuration at AT&T is described in [2,8], and the design of the DEC SEAL Screening External Access Link (SEAL[5]) firewall configuration is addressed in [9].

---

[5]Meanwhile, DEC has renamed its firewall product and service line. Today, DEC offers a

Meanwhile, the U.S. National Institute of Standards and Technology (NIST) has also started activities related to the Internet and security-related problems. In particular, it has made publicly available a document that provides a basic overview of firewall components and the general reasoning behind firewall usage [10]. In Europe, the German Information Security Agency (GISA) has extended its IT Baseline Protection Manual with a section that covers the firewall technology in 1996 [11]. In addition to these specific documents, there are several FTP sites that can be used to download arbitrary material on firewalls. Examples are `ftp.greatcircle.com` and `ftp.tis.com` in their relative subdirectories `pub/firewalls`.

5.2 BASIC COMPONENTS

We have said that a firewall provides basic access control services for sites and corporate intranets. In accordance with a specific security policy, the firewall intercepts data traffic and permits only authorized and legitimate traffic to pass through. The access control services can be provided either at the network and transport layers using packet filters, or at a higher layer using application gateways. In this section we overview the basic components a firewall typically consists of: a firewall policy, packet filters, and application gateways.

5.2.1 Firewall Policy

There are two levels of policy that directly influence the design, installation, and use of a firewall system:

- The higher-level policy, the *service access policy*, defines the TCP/IP protocols and services that should be allowed or denied from the protected network, how theses services should be used, and how exceptions to this policy are handled.

- The lower-level policy, the *firewall design policy*, describes how the firewall actually goes about restricting access and filtering the TCP/IP protocols and services according to the service access policy.

---

firewall family consisting of three types of firewall systems to meet specific user requirements: (1) the high-end *Digital Firewall Service*, which addresses high-performance and high-availability demands coupled with custom security policy needs; (2) the midlevel, single-system *Digital Firewall for UNIX*, which meets current needs but is expandable to a multisystem firewall to accommodate increases in traffic volumes and security complexity; and (3) the entry-level *BorderWare* firewall from Border Network Technologies, Inc. In this family, the Digital Firewall Service actually refers to the former SEAL firewall.

Before we further address the two levels of policy, we want to note that a firewall policy should always be as flexible as possible. This need for flexibility is mainly due to the fact the Internet itself is in flux, and that an organization's needs may change over time as the Internet offers new services, methods, and possibilities for doing business. New TCP/IP protocols and services are emerging on the Internet, which offer more benefits to organizations using the Internet, but sometimes also result in new security concerns. Consequently, a firewall policy must be able to reflect and adequately address these concerns.

Service Access Policy

In short, a *network security policy* (NSP) is a document that describes an organization's network security concerns and specifies the way network security should be achieved in that organization's environment. Parts of the NSP must include a *service access policy* that defines the TCP/IP protocols and services that should be accessible for internal and external use. As such, the service access policy extends the overall organizational policy regarding the protection of informational resources.

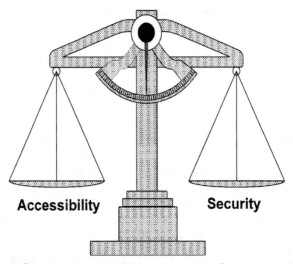

Accessibility   **Security**

Figure 5.1   Trade-off between the accessibility and security of intranet resources.

A firewall can implement a number of service access policies. Generally, a service access policy is focused more on keeping outsiders out than trying to police insiders. For example, a typical policy is to allow no inbound access to an intranet, but to allow full outbound access to the Internet. Another typical policy would be to allow some inbound access from the Internet, but perhaps only to selected systems, such as information servers or e-mail gateways. Also, firewalls sometimes implement service access policies that allow access from the Internet to selected internal systems, but this access would be granted only if necessary and only if it is combined with strong user authentication.

For a firewall to be successful, its service access policy must be realistic and reflect the level of security required for the intranet. For example, a site with top secret and classified data doesn't need a firewall at all. They shouldn't be hooked up to the Internet in the first place, or the systems with the really secret data should be isolated from the rest of the intranet. A realistic service access policy is one that provides a balance between protecting intranet resources from known risks, while still protecting users access to external resources, such as the Internet.

In general, there is a trade-off between the accessibility and security of intranet resources. This trade-off can be symbolized with a balance as illustrated in Figure 5.1. It is quite easy to provide either full accessibility or full security. In the first case, one simply connects a corporate intranet to the Internet without caring about security, whereas in the second case, one established two physically separated networks, one with Internet connectivity and one without. The challenge is to find an appropriate balance between the accessibility and security of intranet resources, and this balance must be reflected in the service access policy of the corresponding firewall configuration.

Firewall Design Policy

The service access policy must be refined in a *firewall design policy* that is unique to a firewall configuration. The firewall design policy specifies the rules used by the firewall to implement the service access policy.

Formulating a firewall design policy is a difficult task, since one cannot design it in a vacuum isolated from understanding issues such as firewall capabilities and limitations, as well as threats and vulnerabilities associated with the TCP/IP protocols and services. A key decision in the firewall design policy is the stance of the firewall design. The stance reflects the attitude of the firewall designers. It is determined by the cost of failure of the firewall and the designers' estimate of that likelihood. Obviously, it is also based on the designers' opinions of their own abilities. In general, a firewall may implement one of the following two stances:

- Permit any service unless it is expressly denied;

- Deny any service unless it is expressly permitted.

A firewall that implements the first stance allows all TCP/IP protocols and services by default, with the exception of those that the service access policy identifies as disallowed. In other words, anything that is not expressly prohibited is permitted by default. From a security point of view, this stance is less desirable, since it offers more avenues for circumventing and getting around the firewall. For example, users could access new services currently not denied by the policy or run denied services at nonstandard ports that are not expressly denied by the policy.

A firewall that implements the second stance denies all TCP/IP protocols and services by default, and passes only those that are identified as allowed. Obviously, this stance better fits the traditional access control model that is usually used in information security: anything that is not expressly permitted is prohibited by default. From a security point of view, this stance is preferable. Note, however, that it is usually also more difficult to implement and may impact users more in that certain TCP/IP protocols and services must be blocked or restricted heavily.

5.2.2   Packet Filters

In short, a *packet filter* is a multiported internetworking device that applies a set of rules to each incoming IP packet in order to decide whether it will be forwarded or discarded. IP packets are filtered based on information that is usually found in packet headers, such as

- Protocol numbers;

- Source and destination IP addresses;

- Source and destination port numbers;

- TCP connection flags;

- Some other options.

Figure 5.2   The placement of a packet filter between an intranet and the Internet.

In general, packet filters are stateless, meaning that each IP packet is examined isolated from what has happened in the past, forcing the filter to make a decision to permit or deny each packet based upon the packet filter rules.

Figure 5.2 illustrates the placement of a packet filter between an intranet and the Internet. In the chapters that follow, we are going to use the black rectangle as a symbol referring to a packet filter in firewall configurations. Packet filters are further addressed in Chapter 6. Routers that are able to screen and selectively filter IP packets are also called *screening routers*. Note that a screening router is always a packet filter, whereas the opposite is not always the case. A packet filter may not be able to route IP packets, so a packet filter is not necessarily a screening router. However, in the text that follows we are going to use the terms packet filter and screening router synonymously most of the time.

The firewall configuration shown in Figure 5.2 is sometimes also referred to as a *packet-filtering-only firewall*, or *packet filter gateway* in short. Perhaps one justification of the term gateway is that filtering based on port numbers and TCP connection flags done at the transport layer is not a pure function of a router that typically operates at the network layer of the OSI-RM. The packet-filtering-only firewall is perhaps the most common and easiest to employ for small, uncomplicated sites. However, it suffers from a number of disadvantages and is less desirable than the other firewall configurations that are discussed in Chapter 8. Basically, one installs a screening router as a gateway to the Internet and configures the packet filter rules in accordance with a specific firewall policy. More often than not, such a policy allows internal systems to fully access the Internet, while all or most access from the Internet is blocked.

5.2.3 Application Gateways

Usually, an *application gateway* or *gateway* refers to an internetworking device that interconnects one network to another for a specific application. Therefore, the gateway must understand and implement the corresponding application protocol. In the client/server model, an application gateway refers to an intermediate process running between the client that requests a particular service and the server that provides the service. In this model, the application gateway functions as a server from the client's point of view, and as a client from the server's point of view.

Again referring to the Internet model, an application gateway can either work at the application layer or at the transport layer [2]:

• If the gateway works at the application layer, it is usually called an *application-level gateway*, or *proxy server* in short.

- If the gateway works at the transport layer, it is usually called a *circuit-level gateway*.

Most gateways actually used in firewall configurations work at the application layer and represent application-level gateways or proxy servers. In either case, the application gateway runs on a firewall host and performs a specific function as a proxy on the user's behalf. If the application gateway is an application-level gateway, then the function is application-specific. Otherwise, the function is not application-specific and the application gateway is actually a circuit-level gateway.

Typically, when a client contacts an application gateway using one of the TCP/IP application protocols, such as Telnet or FTP, the gateway asks for some valid user identification and authentication information. In the easiest case, this information simply consists of a username and a corresponding password. However, if a firewall is accessible from the Internet, it is strongly recommended to use strong authentication mechanisms, such as those provided by one-time passwords or challenge-response systems. If the gateway accepts the user identification and authentication information, it asks for the name of the remote system to be accessed on the user's behalf. It is now up to the user to respond accordingly and to provide the name of a remote system. The application gateway, in turn, contacts the remote system and establishes a secondary TCP/IP connection to that system. Having established this secondary TCP/IP connection, the application gateway simply relays data between the two connections. Note that the entire process of contacting an application gateway before connecting to the remote system can be made fully transparent by using modified clients that establish the required connections on the user's behalf. Also note that in the case of an application-level gateway, the data can additionally be scanned for specific protocol commands or data contents. It is even possible to enforce specific restrictions on inbound or outbound data traffic. For example, the DEC SEAL firewall could be configured so that outbound FTP traffic was restricted to authorized users and to a limited bandwidth. The intent here is to prevent theft of valuable programs or data. While of limited utility against insiders who could easily copy the desired files on removable storage media, the technique is useful and effective against intruders who lack physical access.

Figure 5.3   The placement of an application gateway between an intranet and the Internet.

Figure 5.3 illustrates the placement of an application gateway between an intranet and the Internet. In the chapters that follow we are going to use the computer system as a symbol referring to an application gateway in firewall configurations (either a circuit-level gateway or an application-level gateway). Application gateways are further addressed in Chapter 7.

The Internet community often uses the term *bastion host* to refer to an exposed firewall system that hosts an application gateway. The term bastion comes from the heavily fortified projections on the exteriors of castles in medieval times. A bastion host should be configured to be particularly secure since it is exposed to direct attacks from the Internet. Typically, a bastion host is located in a secure environment by residing on a secure operating system. In this case, the secure operating system must protect the firewall code and files from outside attacks. More often than not, the firewall code is the only application that is permitted to execute on the bastion host. Absence of other applications reduces the possibility of unauthorized attempts to penetrate the firewall. In spite of the fact that most bastion hosts run a modified and downstripped version of the UNIX operating system, there is increasing demand for Windows NT-based firewalls. Also, there are some firewalls that come along with a special and highly secure operating system. One example of this kind is the Sidewinder firewall developed and marketed by the Secure Computing Corporation.

Depending on its basic components and configuration, several grades of firewall security can be obtained. For example, there is no security by allowing unrestricted access between a corporate intranet and the Internet. Next, packet filters can be added to obtain a certain level of traffic interception. As well, the firewall can include both packet filters and application gateways. A variety of application-level or circuit-level gateways can be added along with different strengths of the corresponding authentication schemes. We can also improve the overall security for the intranet by adding e-mail gateway and name services to the firewall. The firewall can also reside on a secure operating system, thereby improving the underlying security for the firewall code and files. A firewall can also provide support for Internet layer security protocols, such as the IP security protocol (IPSP) and Internet key management protocol (IKMP) that we are going to describe and further discuss in Chapter 9. This facility can be used to build secure tunnels between firewall-protected sites and to build virtual private networks (VPNs) accordingly. Finally, a company can also deny any access to and from the Internet, thereby ensuring isolation and complete security from the outside world. Although this is seemingly a theoretical option in the euphoric time for Internet access we live in these days, for certain highly secure environments it is still the only prudent approach to follow.

Packet filters, application gateways, and the combination of these two basic components in firewall configurations are described and further discussed in the remaining chapters of this part. However, it is only fair to mention at this point that some firewall vendors are also using *stateful inspection* as a replacement or enhancement for application gateways. The stateful inspection technology was originally developed by the firewall market leader, CheckPoint Software Technologies Ltd., for its FireWall-1 product.[6] CheckPoint has filed a patent application for the stateful inspection technology that is still pending.

Remember that packet filters are stateless, meaning that each IP packet is examined isolated from what has happened in the past, forcing the packet filter to make a decision to permit or deny each packet based upon the packet filter rules. Stateful inspection, in turn, handles packet filtering in a different way. It looks at the same headers as packet filters do, but can also peek into the payload data where the transport and application data usually appear. More importantly, stateful inspection maintains state information about past IP packets. It compares the first packet in a connection to the packet filter rules, and if the packet is permitted, state information is added to an internal database. One might think of this state information as representing an internal virtual circuit in the firewall on top of the transport layer association. This information permits subsequent packets in that association to pass quickly through the firewall. If the rules for a specific type of service require examining application data, then part of each packet must still be examined. As an example, FireWall-1 can react to seeing an FTP PORT command by creating a dynamic rule permitting a connection back from the FTP server to that particular port number on the client's side. Logging, or authentication as required by the rules, typically occurs at the application layer. Although the opportunity for better logging is present, stateful inspection firewalls typically only log the source and destination IP addresses and port numbers, similar to logging with a packet filter or screening router. Today, several router vendors, including Cisco and Bay Networks, are exploiting adding stateful inspection to their products.

In summary, the placement of the firewall components introduced in this chapter in the four layers of the Internet model is illustrated in Figure 5.4. Let's assume that the end system on the left side wants to communicate with its peer on the right side, and that an intermediate system acts as an internetworking device between them. If the intermediate system covers the network access and Internet layers, it typically works as a packet filter or screening routers. This situation is illustrated in

---

[6]According to an IDC market survey, CheckPoint's FireWall-1 led the worldwide firewall market with a 40% share in 1996.

(1). If the intermediate system additionally covers the transport layer, it typically works as a circuit-level gateway. This situation is illustrated in (2). Finally, if the intermediate system covers all layers and is able to control traffic accordingly, it typically works as an application-level gateway for that particular application. This situation is illustrated in (3). Obviously, the more layers an intermediate system is able to cover, the better security it is usually able to provide. Note, however, that stateful inspection does not match well to this model, since the rules specified for each application may indicate the level of traffic interception.

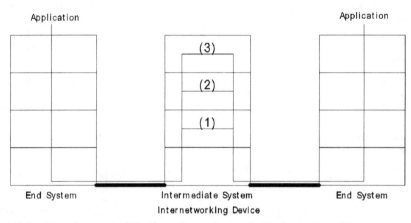

Figure 5.4   The placement of the firewall components in the Internet model.

Finally, we want to point out that there have been several cryptographic Internet access control schemes and protocols proposed in the past [12,13]. Although interesting from a theoretical point of view, these schemes are not addressed in this book and there are two reasons for that:

- First and foremost, the schemes make use of public key cryptography and do not work efficiently enough to be used and widely deployed at the Internet layer. We will see later in this book that cryptographic protection at the Internet layer is typically restricted to keyed one-way hash functions and secret key cryptography.

- Secondly, some of the basic properties of an Internet access control scheme can also be supported by Internet layer security protocols, such as IPSP and IKMP. Again, these protocols will be described and discussed in Chapter 9.

Consequently, we hardly see any activities going on with regard to the development of new Internet access control schemes or the integration of existing schemes in the TCP/IP protocol stack. This is reason enough for us to skip the topic.

REFERENCES

[1] P. Holbrook, and J. Reynolds, "Site Security Handbook," Request for Comments 1244, July 1991.

[2] W.R. Cheswick, and S.M. Bellovin, *Firewalls and Internet Security: Repelling the Wily Hacker*, Addison-Wesley, Reading, MA, 1994.

[3] K. Siyan, and C. Hare, *Internet Firewalls and Network Security*, New Riders Publishing, Indianapolis, IN, 1995.

[4] D.B. Chapman, and E.D. Zwicky, *Internet Security Firewalls*, O'Reilly & Associates, Sebastopol, CA, 1995.

[5] S. Garfinkel, and G. Spafford, *Practical UNIX and Internet Security*, 2nd Edition, O'Reilly & Associates, Sebastopol, CA, 1996.

[6] F. Avolio, and M. Ranum, "A Network Perimeter With Secure Internet Access," *Proceedings of the Internet Society Symposium on Network and Distributed System Security*, February 1994, pp. 109 – 119.

[7] W.R. Cheswick, and S.M. Bellovin, "Network Firewalls," *IEEE Communications Magazine*, September 1994, pp. 50 – 57.

[8] B. Cheswick, "The Design of a Secure Internet Gateway," *Proceedings of USENIX Summer Conference*, June 1990, pp. 233 – 237.

[9] M. Ranum, "A Network Firewall," *Proceedings of World Conference on System Administration and Security*, July 1992, pp. 153 – 163.

[10] J.P. Wack, and L.J. Carnahan, *Keeping Your Site Comfortably Secure: An Introduction to Internet Firewalls*, NIST, Draft Version, October 1994.

[11] German Information Security Agency (GISA), *IT Baseline Protection Manual*, 1996.

[12] D. Estrin, and G. Tsudik, "Secure Control of Transit Internetwork Traffic," *Computer Networks and ISDN Systems*, Vol. 22(5), 1991, pp. 363 – 382.

[13] H. Park, and R. Chow, "Internetwork Access Control Using Public Key Certificates," *Proceedings of IFIP SEC' 96*, May 1996, pp. 237 – 246.

Chapter 6

Packet Filters

In this chapter we focus on packet filters. In Section 6.1, we briefly introduce the technology; in Section 6.2, we address packet filter rules; and in Section 6.3, we conclude with a brief discussion of packet filters used in firewalls.

6.1 INTRODUCTION

A *router* is an internetworking device that usually runs a custom operating system to transfer packets between two or more physically separated network segments.[1] It operates at the network layer in the OSI-RM, or the Internet layer in the Internet model, respectively. As such, it routes IP packets by consulting tables that indicate the best path the packet should take to reach its final destination. More precisely, a router receives an IP packet on one network interface and forwards it on another network interface, possibly in the direction of the destination IP address. If the router knows on what interface to forward the packet, it does so. Otherwise, it is not able to route the packet. In this case, the router usually returns the packet using an ICMP destination unreachable message to its source IP address.

---

[1]In spite of the fact that most routers in use today are able to route multiple protocols, we mainly focus on IP routing in this book. This is because IP is by far the most dominant network layer protocol used in the Internet.

Because every IP packet contains a source and destination IP address, packets bound for a particular host or network segment can be selectively filtered by a packet filtering device. Also, transport layer protocols such as TCP or UDP add a source and destination port number to each message as part of the header information. These port numbers indicate which processes on each host will finally receive the message encapsulated within the IP packet. This information can also be used for packet filtering.

Many commercial router products provide the capability to screen IP packets and filter them in accordance with a set of packet filter rules that implement a specific service access policy. For example, Cisco routers use a fairly simple syntax to define packet filter rules. Each network interface on a Cisco router can be assigned an access group, which is basically an integer number that references the interface. Packet filtering commands for that interface are then expressed in access lists[2] that are associated with access groups. The router, in turn, matches each IP packet routed to a particular network interface against the access lists associated with the access group of that particular interface [1,2].

We said in the previous chapter that routers that provide packet filtering capabilities are called screening routers. In general, screening routers can provide an efficient mechanism to control the type of network traffic that can exist on a particular network segment. By controlling the type of network traffic that can exist on a network segment, they can also control the types of services that may exist. Services that may compromise the security of the network segment can therefore be effectively restricted.

Remember that a packet filter or screening router is a multiported internetworking device that applies a set of rules to each incoming IP packet to decide whether it will be forwarded or discarded. As such, the packet filter or screening router has several ports or network interfaces. Each port may connect the packet filter to a network segment, and the network segments are classified as either internal or external. Internal network segments belong to the intranet, and external network segments belong to the Internet. Consequently, it is up to the packet filter to intercept and control data traffic between internal and external network segments.

Upon receiving an IP packet, the packet filter parses the header of the packet and applies the corresponding packet filter rules in order to determine whether the packet should be forwarded towards its destination IP address or dropped and discarded. We saw in the previous chapter that IP packets are filtered based on

---

[2]More precisely, Cisco routers provide support for two types of access lists: standard access lists and extended access lists. We refer to the corresponding product documentation for more information on this topic.

information that is usually found in packet headers, such as

- Protocol numbers;

- Source and destination IP addresses;

- Source and destination port numbers;

- TCP connection flags;

- Some other options.

Note that routers do not normally look at port numbers when making routing decisions, but for filtering purposes, knowing the source and destination port number allows selective filtering based on the service being used. For example, a Telnet server usually uses port 23, and an SMTP server usually uses port 25. Selective filtering by port numbers also takes advantage of how ports are assigned. Although a Telnet server uses port 23 most of the time, a Telnet client port number is not fixed, but assigned dynamically. In general, the client port is assigned a number greater than 1023. Also note that although screening routers can filter on any of the TCP connection flags summarized in Table 2.4, the flags that are most frequently used for packet filtering are the SYN and ACK flags.

Some packet filtering implementations with only rudimentary capabilities don't actually parse the headers of IP packets, but instead require the administrator to specify byte ranges within the header to examine, and the patterns to look for in those ranges [3]. This is almost useless, since it requires the administrator to have a very detailed understanding of the structure of an IP packet. Also, it is totally unworkable for packets using IP option fields, which cause the location of the beginning of the transport layer protocol headers, such as TCP or UDP headers, to vary. This variation, in turn, makes it very difficult to find and examine the TCP or UDP port number fields.

In addition to the header information itemized above, some packet filtering implementations also allow the administrator to specify packet filter rules based on which network interface an IP packet actually came in on, and on which interface the packet is destined to go out on. Being able to specify filters on both inbound and outbound interfaces allows an administrator significant control over where the packet filter appears in the overall scheme and is very convenient for useful filtering on screening routers with more than two network interfaces. As described in Chapters 7 and 8, this ability has turned out to be very useful, and essential to counter sequence number and IP spoofing attacks. Unfortunately, not all screening routers can actually filter on both inbound and outbound interfaces, and many routers implement packet filtering only on the outbound interface for efficiency reasons. Note that for outgoing IP packets, the filter rules can be applied when the router consults its routing tables to determine the interface to send the packet out on. At this point, however, the router no longer knows on which interface the packet came in; it has lost some important information.

Not all screening routers are able to filter IP packets based on all header fields mentioned above. For example, some screening routers are not able to take into consideration the source port of an IP packet. This can make packet filter rules more complex and can even open up holes in the entire packet filtering scheme. There is, for example, such a problem if a site wishes to allow both inbound and outbound SMTP traffic. Remember that in the case of a client establishing an SMTP connection to a server, the client's source port number would be randomly chosen at or above 1024, and the destination port number would be 25, the port an SMTP server usually resides at. Consequently, the SMTP server would return IP packets with a source port number of 25 and a destination port number equal to the port number randomly chosen by the client. In this scenario, a packet filter must be configured to allow destination and source port numbers greater than 1023 to pass through in either direction. If the router is able to filter on the source port, it can block incoming SMTP traffic with a destination port greater than 1023 and a source port other than 25. Without this ability, however, the router can't take into consideration the source port and must therefore permit incoming SMTP traffic with a destination port greater than 1023 and an arbitrary source port number. Consequently, legitimate but malicious users could conceivably make use of this situation and run servers at ports greater than 1023 to circumvent the service access policy enforced by the packet filter. For example, a Telnet server that normally listens at port 23 could be told to listen at port 7777 instead. Users on the Internet could then use a normal Telnet client to connect to this internal server even if the packet filter blocks destination port 23.

Screening routers filter IP packets according to packet filter rules. More precisely, when an IP packet arrives at a network interface of a packet filter, the packet headers are parsed. As described above, most packet filters examine the fields in only the IP and the TCP or UDP headers. Each packet filter rule is applied to the packet in the order in which the packet filter rules are stored. If a rule blocks the transmission or reception of a packet, the packet is not allowed. If a rule allows the transmission or reception of a packet, the packet is allowed to proceed. If a packet does not satisfy any rule, it is either allowed or blocked depending of the stance of the firewall design. In general, it is good practice to block the IP packet in this case.

We have mentioned previously that packet filters are stateless, meaning that each IP packet must be examined isolated from what has happened in the past, forcing the filter to make a decision to permit or deny each packet based upon the packet filter rules. Routers are generally optimized to shuffle IP packets quickly. The packet filters of a screening router take time and can defeat the overall optimization efforts. In fact, packet filtering is a slow operation that may considerably reduce routing throughput. Logging of IP packets also occurs without regard to past history, and enabling logging results in another hit on performance. More often than not, packet filtering and logging are not enabled in routers primarily to achieve better performance. If enabled and used, packet filtering and logging are typically installed at the edge of an administrative domain.

6.2 PACKET FILTER RULES

We have seen in the previous chapter that the service access policy defines the TCP/IP protocols and services that are allowed or denied to pass through a firewall, and that the firewall design policy describes how the firewall actually goes about restricting access and filtering TCP/IP protocols and services. Consequently, packet filter rules must adequately reflect and implement the service access and firewall design policies. Note that packet filter rules are often defined at firewall installation time, although they may be modified, added, or deleted later as well.

In essence, a *packet filter rule* consists of two parts, namely an action field and a selection criteria:

- The *action field* of a packet filter rule specifies the action to be taken if an IP packet meets the selection criteria and is selected by that rule. Two types of action are usually permitted: BLOCK (or DENY) and PERMIT (or ALLOW). In short, BLOCK implies that the selected IP packet should be rejected and discarded, whereas PERMIT implies that the selected IP packet should be accepted and forwarded towards its destination IP address.

- The *selection criteria* of a packet filter rule uses information found in packet headers, and related to the network interfaces, the packets appear to decide whether a particular IP packet should be selected or not, and whether the appropriate action specified in the action field of the packet filter rule should be taken.

With regard to source and destination IP address, a selection criterion can work either with full IP addresses or address masks. Therefore, an address selection is usually accomplished by specifying two dotted-decimal IP addresses. In this case, the first IP address is the desired address and the second IP address is an address mask that selects the relevant bits in the address field. If a mask bit is 1, the corresponding bit in the address is ignored and any value is allowed. For example, suppose we want to select any packet with a source IP address that begins with 157.4.5. Therefore, we put 157.4.5.0 as the desired source IP address and 0.0.0.255 as the address mask for selecting the relevant bits. So, for this address mask, the first 3 bytes of the mask would select all of the 24 bits of the first 3 bytes of a packet's source IP address. Next, the selected 24 bits are compared against 157.4.5. If there is a match, the packet is selected. Obviously, an equal mechanism can be used for the destination IP address as well.

It is worth mentioning that most packet filtering implementations apply the rules in the sequence specified by the administrator until they find a rule that meets the selection criteria for a particular IP packet. When an IP packet arrives at a packet filter, it is tested against the first packet filter rule. If the rule applies to the packet, the specified action for that rule is carried out (the packet is forwarded or discarded). If the rule does not apply to the packet, the second rule is checked, and so on. Note that for each rule, if the IP packet satisfies the selection criteria, the action specified for that rule is carried out and the filter processing for that packet is completed. Suppose the IP packet is not selected by any of the rules, up to the last one. The last rule, however, specifies to discard all packets. So, the last rule takes effect, and the packet is discarded. Consequently, the default action for packet filtering in this case would be to discard the packet, unless otherwise specified by a previous packet filter rule. This is a strongly recommended policy that may help prevent unauthorized IP packets getting into the protected area of a corporate intranet. Unfortunately, there are also some packet filtering implementations that enforce a particular order of rule application based on the selection criteria in the rules, such as source and destination IP address, regardless of the order in which the rules are specified. Some implementations, for example, apply packet filter rules in the same order as routing table entries; that is, they apply rules referring to more specific addresses before rules with less specific addresses. In general, routers that apply packet filter rules in the order specified by the administrator, without reordering them, are easier to understand, configure, and manage, and are therefore also more likely to yield correct and complete rulesets.

Packet filtering can be used in a variety of ways to block IP traffic from or to specific sites and network segments. For example, a site may wish to block connections from certain IP addresses that it considers to be hostile or untrustworthy. Alternatively, a site might also wish to block connections from all IP addresses external to the site (with certain exceptions, such as SMTP connections for handling e-mail messages).

As an example of a packet filtering scenario, consider a service access policy that permits only certain connections to a network of address 123.4.*.*. Telnet connections will be allowed to only one host, 123.4.5.6, which may be a Telnet application gateway. Similarly, SMTP connections will be allowed to two hosts, 123.4.5.7 and 123.4.5.8, which may be e-mail application gateways. NNTP traffic is allowed only from the site's feed system, 129.6.48.254, and only to the site's NNTP server, 123.4.5.9, wheras NTP traffic is allowed to all hosts. All other services and corresponding IP traffic must be blocked by default. Packet filter rules that implement this policy are summarized in Table 6.1. Note that each type of packet filtering device usually has its own set of rules and syntax on how to program packet filter rules. Therefore, one must read the packet filtering device documentation and learn the peculiarities of the packet filter rules syntax for that particular device. In our example of packet filter rules we use an abstract syntax that is not usually found in commercial products.

Table 6.1

Example of Packet Filter Rules

No.	Type	Source Address	Dest. Address	Source Port	Dest. Port	Action
1	tcp	*	123.4.5.6	> 1023	23	Permit
2	tcp	*	123.4.5.7	> 1023	25	Permit
3	tcp	*	123.4.5.8	> 1023	25	Permit
4	tcp	129.6.48.254	123.4.5.9	> 1023	119	Permit
5	udp	*	123.4.*.*	> 1023	123	Permit
6	*	*	*	*	*	Deny

The first rule allows TCP traffic from any source IP address and port number greater than 1,023 on the Internet to the destination address of 123.4.5.6 and port number 23 on the intranet. This port number is associated with the Telnet server, and all Telnet clients should have unprivileged source ports of 1,024 or higher. The second and third rules work in a similar fashion, except that traffic to destination addresses 123.4.5.7 and 123.4.5.8, and port number 25 for SMTP, is permitted. The fourth rule permits IP packets to the site's NNTP server, but only from source IP address 129.6.48.254 to destination IP address 123.4.5.9 and port number 119. Note that 129.6.48.254 is the only NNTP server that news should be received from, thus access for NNTP is restricted to only that IP address. The fifth rule permits NTP traffic, which uses UDP as opposed to TCP, from any source to any destination address on the intranet. Finally, the sixth rule denies all other traffic and corresponding IP packets. If this rule weren't present in the ruleset, the router may or may not deny all subsequent packets.

In Chapter 2, we briefly mentioned the problem of IP fragmentation. Note that IP (at least IPv4) supports the notion that any router along a packet's delivery path may fragment that packet into smaller packets to accomodate the limitations of underlying transport media, to be reassembled into the original IP packet at the destination. For example, a fiber distributed data interface (FDDI) frame may be much larger than an Ethernet frame. So, a router between an FDDI ring and an Ethernet network may split an IP packet that fits in a single FDDI frame into multiple fragments that fit into the smaller Ethernet frames. The problem with this, from a packet filtering point of view, is that only the first of the IP fragments comprises the upper-layer protocol headers (TCP or UDP headers) from the original packet, which may be necessary to make a useful filtering decision concerning the fragment. Different packet filtering implementations take a variety of responses to this situation. Some implementations apply packet filter rules only to the first fragment of an IP packet that actually contains the upper-layer protocol header, and simply route the remaining fragments. The assumption is that if the first fragment of an IP packet is dropped by the packet filter, the rest of the fragments can't be reassembled into a full IP packet and will therefore cause no harm. Note, however, that it is dangerous to suppress only the first fragment of an outbound IP packet; one may still be leaking valuable data in the subsequent fragments that are routed on out of the intranet. To defeat this problem, it is possible to keep a cache of recently seen first fragments and the filtering decision that was reached, and to look up nonfirst fragments in this cache in order to apply the same decision. This approach is conceptually very closely related to stateful inspection, which we introduced in Chapter 5.

The question on how to filter TCP/IP application protocols and services depends on the chosen service access policy (i.e., which systems should have Internet access and the type of access to permit). Many books have been written in the past that focus entirely on that question. Again, we refer to the books that have been referenced in Chapter 5. In particular, we refer to the book of William Cheswick and Steven Bellovin. In Appendix B, they address packet filtering characteristics for the various TCP and UDP ports. Also, the book of Brent Chapman and Elizabeth Zwicky contains a thorough analysis of the various TCP/IP protocols and services.

In summary, there are many TCP-based application protocols and services that can be effectively addressed with packet filters and screening routers. Examples include FTP, Telnet, SMTP, DNS, Gopher, HTTP, and NNTP as summarized in

Table 6.2
TCP-Based Application Protocols and Services

Protocol	Full Name (if any)	Port(s)
FTP	File Transfer Protocol	21/20
Telnet		23
SMTP	Simple Mail Transfer Protocol	25
DNS	Domain Name System	53
Gopher		70
HTTP	Hypertext Transfer Protocol	80
NNTP	Network News Transfer Protocol	119

Table 6.2. With regard to FTP, it is worth mentioning that two TCP connections are actually used between a client and a server: a control connection (port 21 on the server's side) and a data transfer connection (port 20 on the server's side). It is up to the client to establish the control connection, whereas it is up to the server to establish backwards the data transfer connection. In general, it is difficult to correctly handle the second connection establishment with a packet filter, since it corresponds to a connection establishment initiated from the outside world. Under certain circumstances, however, a bypass is available if one has the FTP client software in source code. In this case, one can modify the client software to issue a PASV command to the server, directing it to do a passive open and thus permitting an outgoing call through the packet filter to establish the data connection. This approach is further addressed in [4].

With regard to DNS it is also worth mentioning that the service can be based on TCP or UDP, and is usually provided at port 53 (in either case). The UDP-based service is usually used for queries, while the TCP-based service is used for server-to-server zone transfers. One implementation characteristic of the Berkeley Internet Name Daemon (BIND) is that server-to-server proxy queries are made via UDP with both ends of a connection using port 53. Packet filter rules can take advantage of this characteristic, since DNS is sometimes the only UDP-based protocol that is allowed bidirectionally between internal machines and the outside world.

Not all systems require general access to all services. For example, restricting Telnet or FTP access from the Internet to only those systems that actually require it can improve the overall security at almost no cost to user convenience. Other protocols and services such as NNTP may seem to pose little threat, but restricting them to only those systems that actually require them may help to create a cleaner intranet environment and reduce the likelihood of exploitation from yet-to-be-discovered vulnerabilities and corresponding threats.

Unfortunately, the are also some TCP/IP protocols and services that can't be addressed effectively with packet filters and screening routers. Let's briefly overview some examples:

- Remember that ICMP is a control protocol layered on top of IP. Most packet filtering implementations can filter ICMP messages by type in the same way as they can filter TCP and UDP by port number. Most ICMP message types are informational and useful for network management and debugging purposes. They should almost certainly be permitted to pass through. Other ICMP message types, however, are instructions that may influence future routing decisions. These messages should probably not be permitted to pass through.

- The Trivial FTP (TFTP, port 69) is used for booting diskless workstations, terminal servers, and routers. It should never be allowed from outside a protected network, since it has no password security and, if badly configured, allows anybody to make copies of arbitrary files or even replace them. This poses a problem with regard to password files.

- RPC-based protocols and services offer a special challenge for packet filtering techniques, since they don't reliably appear on a specific port number. The only RPC-related service that is guaranteed to be at a certain port number is the portmapper service (port 111). This service maps an RPC service number to the particular UDP or TCP port number that the service is currently using on the machine being queried. Since RPC-based protocols and services might be on any port, the filtering implementation has no sure way of recognizing what is and what isn't RPC.

- The Berkeley r-tools are another tricky case because they generally use privileged ports for both the server (port 512 for rexec, 513 for rlogin, and 514 for rsh and rcp), and client (a random privileged port). A typical packet filter ruleset that allows outbound services by allowing outbound packets to specific privileged ports and inbound packets to nonprivileged ports won't allow any of these services, since their inbound packets will be coming to random privileged ports. If one allows inbound packets to random privileged ports, however, one has just opened up all services on privileged ports to attacks from the outside world. One possible solution to this problem is to allow only packets from established connections inbound, if the packet filter or screening router is able to consider the SYN and ACK flags.

- Most UNIX systems currently provide support for the X11 window system. Network access is an important feature of this system, and X11 servers are tempting targets for intruders. As a matter of fact, an intruder with access to an X11 server may be able to get screen dumps, and read or inject keystrokes. To make things worse, X11 authentication features are seldom used in the name of user convenience. Consequently, X11 and other window systems aren't secure enough to be used across the Internet and should be filtered out accordingly. The window systems vary in what ports they use. X11, for instance, typically uses TCP port 6,000 for the first display on a given machine, port 6,001 for the second display, and so on. To protect machines running X11 servers, one must filter ports 6,000 to 6,000+n, where n is the maximum number of X11 servers running on any single machine behind the packet filtering device. Contrary to X11, OpenWindows uses port 2,000.

TCP/IP protocols and services that are inherently vulnerable to abuse should generally be blocked by a screening router being part of a firewall configuration.

We have mentioned the sequence number and related IP spoofing attacks several times throughout the previous chapters of this book. Let's now have a brief look at the way a firewall and its packet filtering component can be configured to thwart them. Remember that these attacks usually exploit the weakness that the source address of an IP header must not be authentic (since it is not authenticated). A host can very easily change the source IP address of a packet to appear as if it is coming from another host, such as a trusted host. In this case, the packet may include a system command that would be executed without prior authentication of the corresponding user.

To prevent this kind of attack, the packet filter rules must be designed to discard any packet arriving at an inbound network interface that contains a source IP address of an internal machine. The reason is that a packet originating from the outside with the source IP address of an internal machine implies that the packet is somehow fraudulent. Consequently, the packet filter rules must specify to discard the packet. Suppose the network or firewall administrator has detected that a certain host on the Internet is sending fraudulent packets by spoofing the source IP address. The administrator can then add a new rule to discard packets arriving from any host with that particular source IP address. Similarly, if a given host is under attack, the new filter rule can discard IP packets destined for that particular host. The new rule should be added at the beginning of the existing ruleset, thereby avoiding any impact to other network traffic.

6.3   DISCUSSION

Today, a steadily increasing number of commercial router products provide support for packet filtering capabilities. In addition, there are tools and utilities available on the Internet that can be used for packet filtering purposes. For example, a version of the **screend** screening software is publicly and freely available for both the ULTRIX and DEC UNIX kernel [5].[3] The software was originally developed by Jeff Mogul at DEC and is now maintained by Paul Vixie. It incorporates a kernel modification that permits a user process to pass on each packet before it is forwarded. In either case, it is always a good idea to disable IP source routing on a packet filtering device. Whether IP source routing can be disabled at all, whether it is enabled or disabled by default, and how to disable it varies from product to product. For example, for a Cisco router, one can usually disable source routing by using the command **no ip source-route**.

There are also some PC-based packet filtering products available that are not able to route IP packets and therefore act as a bridge between the network segments they interconnect. Probably the two most widely deployed examples are the KarlBridge and the Drawbridge:

- The KarlBridge is actually a PC program written by Doug Karl at Ohio State University. It is an inexpensive two-port Ethernet-to-Ethernet bridge that provides packet filtering capabilities based on IP addresses and port numbers. Besides IP, the KarlBridge can also filter other network layer protocols, such as Novell Netware, DECnet, and AppleTalk. A shareware working demo of the KarlBridge is publicly and freely available on the Internet.[4] Although this is just a limited-function version of the commercially available KarlBridge and KarlBrouter products, it is still very functional and, for many situations, has just the right features to be useful. The commercial versions of the KarlBridge and KarlBrouter have additional features, such as data encryption and IP routing capabilities. KarlBridges and KarlBrouters are manufactured and sold in the United Kingdom by Sherwood Data Systems, Ltd., and other resellers exist worldwide. In the United States, the main commercial supplier of the KarlBridge is KarlNet, Inc.

- The Drawbridge packet filtering package comes along with the copyrighted but publicly and freely available Texas A&M University (TAMU) security tools [6].[5]

---

[3]ftp://gatekeeper.dec.com/pub/DEC/screend/screend.tar.Z
[4]ftp://ftp.cis.ohio-state.edu/pub/kbridge/
[5]ftp://net.tamu.edu/pub/security/TAMU/

There are currently two versions of the Drawbridge package: one with DES support for data encryption, and one without DES support. Because of U.S. export restrictions, only U.S. domestic sites can download the Drawbridge package with DES support.

Installation and configuration of the KarlBridge and Drawbridge are described in a book authored by Karanjit Siyan and Chris Hare that was referenced in Chapter 5, as well as corresponding product information and manuals.

Packet filters and screening routers are used and widely deployed on the Internet today, and there are at least three reasons for that:

- First and foremost, packet filtering is a low-cost technology. We have seen that packet filtering capabilities are already integrated into many commercial router products today.

- Secondly, the use of packet filtering is transparent to both application programs and users. There is no need to make an application program aware of packet filtering devices.

- Thirdly, vendors have promoted the technology, since it is not based on cryptography and is not export-controlled accordingly. This allows a worldwide distribution and promotion of products that make use of packet filtering technologies.

Due to these advantages, it is possible and very likely that we will see a further proliferation and sophistication of packet filtering techniques and corresponding implementations in the near future. Stateful inspection as discussed in the previous chapter is just one example of this more general trend.

But IP packet filtering is not a panacea for network security, particularly in the form in which it is currently implemented by many vendors. As a matter of fact, packet filters and screening routers suffer from a number of weaknesses and disadvantages [3]. The primary weakness relates to the complexity of correctly configuring and managing packet filter rules. There are two points here:

- First, correctly specifying packet filter rules is a difficult and error-prone process.

- Secondly, reordering packet filter rules makes correctly specifying rules even more difficult by turning a ruleset that works if evaluated in the order given into a ruleset that doesn't work. The difficulty is somehow related to the complexity of correctly setting up rules in knowledge-based expert systems.

In general, the way in which packet filter rules must be specified and the order in which they are applied are key determinants of how useful and powerful given packet filtering capabilities really are. Most implementations require the administrator to specify filters in ways that make the filters easy to parse and apply, but make them rather difficult for the administrator to comprehend and consider. Also, the configuration process requires intricate knowledge of TCP/IP networking and addressing. Note that most users still consider networking activities in terms of "connections," while packet filtering, by definition, is concerned only with IP packets that eventually make up a connection or virtual circuit on a higher layer. For example, an inbound connection must usually be translated into at least two packet filter rules, namely one for the inbound IP packets from the client to the server and one for the outbound packets from the server back to the client. To make things worse, the concept of a connection is applied even when considering a connectionless protocol, such as ICMP, UDP, or UDP-based application protocols. This mismatch between the abstractions commonly used and the mechanisms provided by many packet filtering implementations contributes to the difficulties of correctly and completely specifying packet filter rules.

As a result, network and firewall administrators may very well commit mistakes in setting up packet filter rules. Oftentimes, exceptions to rules must be made to allow certain types of access that normally would be blocked. Unfortunately, such exceptions make a packet filter ruleset so complex as to be unmanageable. For example, it is relatively simple and straightforward to specify a rule to block all inbound connections to a Telnet server that is running on port 23. If exceptions are made (i.e., if certain systems need to accept direct Telnet connections from the outside), then a rule for each system must be added in the ruleset. Sometimes the addition of certain rules may complicate the entire packet filtering scheme. This is due to the fact that the simple syntax used in most packet filtering implementations makes it easy for the screening router but difficult for the administrator. Brent Chapman compares the task of specifying packet filter rules with the task of programming in assembly language [3]. Instead of being able to use some high-level language abstractions, the administrator is still forced to produce a tabular representation of the packet filter rules. However, the desired behavior may or may not map on to a tabular representation. Fortunately, the industry direction is to make it more simple to specify packet filter rules and not require intricate knowledge of TCP/IP networking and addressing. In addition, utilities and tools are being developed to test and validate packet filter rules, perhaps including test suites and automatic test case generators. There are also tools available that can be used to derive packet filter rules directly from a given router network specification.

In summary, the advantages of packet filters and screening routers are simplicity and low cost, whereas the disadvantages are related to the difficulties in setting up packet filter rules correctly, as well as the lack of user authentication. It is very important to note that any packet filter has to decide whether to forward or discard packets based on information that must not be authentic. Since the authenticity of an IP source address is not protected, a given host can spoof another host by simply changing the source IP address of the packets it sends out. The sequence number attack described previously exploits this kind of vulnerability. A countermeasure to reduce or even eliminate this vulnerability is Internet layer security such as provided by IPSP. Using such a protocol, a screening router could be configured to drop and silently discard any IP packet that is not properly authenticated with a valid and legitimate authentication header (AH).

REFERENCES

[1] B. Corbridge, R. Henig, and C. Slater "Packet Filtering in an IP Router," *Proceedings of the USENIX Large Installation and System Administration Conference*, October 1992, pp. 227 – 232.

[2] S. Carl-Mitchell, and J.S. Quarterman, "Building Internet Firewalls," *UNIX World*, February 1992, pp. 93 – 101.

[3] D.B. Chapman, "Network (In)Security Through IP Packet Filtering," *Proceedings of USENIX UNIX Security Symposium III*, September 1992, pp. 63 – 76.

[4] S.M. Bellovin, "Firewall-friendly FTP," Request for Comments 1579, February 1994.

[5] J.C. Mogul, "Simple and Flexible Datagram Access Controls for UNIX-based Gateways," *Proceedings of USENIX Summer Conference*, 1989, pp. 203 – 221.

[6] D.R. Safford, D.K. Hess, and D.L. Schales, "The TAMU Security Package: An ongoing response to Internet intruders in an academic environment," *Proceedings of USENIX UNIX Security Symposium*, October 1993, pp. 91 – 118.

Chapter 7

Application Gateways

In this chapter we focus on application gateways. In Section 7.1, we introduce the technology and distinguish between application-level gateways or proxy servers, and circuit-level gateways, such as those provided by the SOCKS software package. In Sections 7.2 and 7.3, we further address proxy servers and SOCKS, and in Section 7.4, we discuss the relative merits of application gateways as compared to packet filters and screening routers.

7.1 INTRODUCTION

There are several possibilities to counter the weaknesses and disadvantages of packet filters and screening routers. In the previous chapters, we introduced and discussed stateful inspection as a possible enhancement for simple packet filtering. In this chapter, we further elaborate on application gateways as introduced in Chapter 5. Remember that an application gateway can either work at the application or transport layer, and that one distinguishes application-level gateways and circuit-level gateways accordingly.

As an example, consider the situation in which a firewall blocks all incoming Telnet and FTP connections using a screening router. The screening router allows

Telnet and FTP traffic only to a bastion host of the firewall configuration. The bastion host, in turn, houses an application gateway in terms of an application-level or circuit-level gateway. The situation is slightly different in either case:

- If the application gateway works at the application layer (actually representing an application-level gateway), Telnet and FTP proxy servers must be running on the bastion host.

- If the application gateway works at the transport layer (actually representing a circuit-level gateway), a SOCKS server must be running on the bastion host.

In either case, a user who wishes to connect inbound to an inside machine, would have to have his or her Telnet client connect to the application gateway running on the bastion host. The application gateway would then authenticate and authorize the user. In the positive case, it would set up a secondary TCP/IP connection to the inside machine and relay application data between the two TCP/IP connections forth and back. More precisely, the procedure would comprise the following steps:

- First, a Telnet client acting on the user's behalf requests a connection to the application gateway running on the bastion host. If a screening router is put in place, the connection must be authorized according to the packet filter rules.

- The application gateway, in turn, checks the source IP address of the client machine. The connection request is accepted or rejected according to some preconfigured access criteria.

- In addition to the source IP address check of the client machine, the user may also need to authenticate himself or herself.

- If the user is properly authenticated, he or she must provide the address or name of the inside machine he or she wants to get connected to.

- The application gateway now sets up a secondary TCP/IP connection to the destination machine. Again, this connection request may have to pass through a screening router. In this case, the packet filter rules of the screening router must be configured so that they let packets through that are originated by the application gateway.

- After having successfully established the secondary TCP/IP connection to the destination machine, the application gateway relays Telnet application data between the two TCP/IP connections forth and back. If the application gateway is an application-level gateway, it may also scan for specific Telnet commands and eventually filter them out. In either case, the application gateway can log the connection.

In order to properly authenticate the user, the application gateway must have some identification and authentication information. In principle, this information can either be locally stored or remotely archived and made available through a security server. Obviously, the second approach is preferable since it makes it possible to aggregate security management functions for several firewall systems and network access servers (NAS) at a single point. Typically, a standardized protocol is used to retrieve the information required to authenticate and authorize users from a security server. There are two competing proposals for such a protocol:

- Livingston Enterprises, Inc. has developed a protocol named Remote Authentication Dial-In User Service (RADIUS) [1]. In short, the RADIUS protocol can be used to carry authentication, authorization, and configuration information between a NAS that desires to authenticate its users and a shared authentication or security server. Livingston Enterprises, Inc. has also made publicly and freely available RADIUS security server software. A companion protocol that can be used to carry accounting information between a NAS and a shared authentication or security server server is specified in [2].

- Cisco has developed a similar protocol called Terminal Access Controller Access System (TACACS) [3], as well as an updated version of TACACS called TACACS+.

Both protocols are widely supported by commercial firewall systems and network access servers today.

There are also some other proposals to handle user authentication. For example, Ravi Ganesan has implemented an application gateway that uses Kerberos to authenticate connection requests [4]. We address the Kerberos system in Chapter 11, when we talk about authentication and key distribution systems. Once the application gateway has satisfied itself about the identity of the requesting user, it establishes a corresponding connection to the destined server. With this design, the Kerberos authentication server should be run by the firewall administrator, since the party that controls the server also controls the authentication, and hence the ability to pass connections through the gateway.

In practice, application gateways are used for TCP-based applications, such as Telnet, FTP, Gopher, HTTP, and SMTP. There are, however, some problems related to the handling of UDP-based applications. Note that UDP is a connectionless transport layer protocol, meaning that no connection is established before application data is transmitted. Consequently, there is no possibility for the application gateway to receive a connection request, to authenticate and authorize the requesting user, and to set up a secondary TCP/IP connection accordingly. Each UDP datagram must be treated individually. We will address the handling of UDP-based applications, especially with regard to multicast environments, later in this chapter. Let's now have a closer look at application-level and circuit-level gateways, as represented by proxy servers and SOCKS.

7.2   PROXY SERVERS

An application-level gateway that is running on a bastion host typically houses several proxy servers. Each proxy server acts as a proxy on the user's behalf. More precisely, if an intranet user wants to access a specific TCP/IP application server on the Internet, he must have his client establish a TCP/IP connection to the proxy server running for that particular application on the bastion host. The proxy server, in turn, must authenticate and authorize either the user requesting access or the client machine acting on the user's behalf. Several authentication and authorization schemes are possible at this point:

- The simplest scheme is notably to have the proxy server hold a list of client IP addresses that are allowed to connect to external application servers. This scheme is not very secure, since anybody can spoof authorized IP addresses to get Internet access. In many cases, the authorized IP addresses are well known in organizations and can be spoofed accordingly.

- A more secure scheme is to use strong authentication mechanisms between the user and the proxy server, and to handle authorization accordingly. In this case, it is no longer possible for a user to simply spoof the IP address of another user's authorized client machine to get Internet access.

In practice, the firewall policy should define the authentication and authorization schemes that must be used in either direction and for each service. Many policies use the simple scheme described above for outbound connections, and the more secure scheme for inbound connections. Typically, RADIUS, TACACS, or TACACS+ is used to verify the authentication information with a centralized security server.

After having successfully authenticated and authorized the client and user, the proxy server sets up a secondary TCP/IP connection to the requested application server on the Internet. From the user's point of view, a secondary authentication may now be required and actually take place, since the application server may want to authenticate and authorize the user as well. This secondary authentication step is beyond the scope of the firewall. If the user is successfully authenticated and authorized, the application server usually starts serving the request. From that moment on, the proxy server simply relays application data forth and back between the two TCP/IP connections. It may also implement some rules, saying that certain commands are not allowed for the application protocol for which it has been designed for. Also, for any IP packet flowing from the internal client to the external server, the proxy server usually replaces the source IP address with its own address. In this case, the internal IP addresses used on the intranet are entirely hidden and not exposed to the Internet.

Since proxy servers run at the application layer, separate servers are usually required for each application. Commercial firewalls typically come along with proxy servers for Telnet, FTP, SMTP, HTTP, and some other TCP/IP applications. On the client's side, the use of proxy servers usually requires some customization and modification of either user procedures or client software.

- The customization and modification of user procedures is an obvious approach to implement proxy server support. As a matter of fact, the preceding discussion of proxy servers is based entirely on this approach. An important benefit is that the customization of user procedures, in general, requires no impact to client software. Given the extensive presence of client software, this approach is attractive for implementing Internet access. The main disadvantage of this approach is that the user has to be trained for an extra step to logon to the proxy server. For organizations that have been using TCP/IP applications for a long time, the corresponding user training may be a time-consuming and expensive process.

- The other approach to implement proxy server support is to customize and modify the client software. The main advantage of this approach is that it may provide transparency to users in accessing the Internet. This transparency is attained by implementing additional software at the client and the firewall that intercepts and directs the application traffic. The main disadvantage, however, is that it obviously requires modifications to client software. This is not always possible, and is very seldom easy to accomplish. In the following section we will overview and discuss a circuit-level gateway called SOCKS. SOCKS is notably the most widely deployed example of firewall software that follows the approach of using customized client software.

Note that both approaches to implement proxy server support have severe disadvantages, since they require customization and modification of either user procedures or client software. It would be nice to have a firewall that maintains all the software modifications required for proxy support in the firewall. In this case, neither the user procedures nor the client software would have to be customized and modified accordingly. Fortunately, some firewall vendors have come up with solutions to this problem. They usually call their firewall systems transparent, since they provide transparency to their users. Note, however, that transparency is not necessarily provided in both directions. As a matter of fact, inbound transparency is seldom used, since users must usually authenticate themselves at a firewall system. If a firewall is used that provides outbound transparency, a user sends out a request to connect to an Internet server to the proxy server of the firewall system. The proxy server, in turn, intercepts the request, authenticates and possibly authorizes the user, and sets up the secondary TCP/IP connection on the user's behalf. Note that this approach still requires that all messages to and from the Internet be transmitted through the firewall. However, the existence of a firewall system can be hidden entirely from the users.

There are advantages and disadvantages related to the use of application-level gateways in general and proxy servers in particular. First and foremost, it is important to note that application-level gateways allow only those TCP/IP protocols and services for which a proxy server actually exists. In other words, if a firewall hosts proxy servers for Telnet and FTP, then only Telnet and FTP traffic is allowed into and out of the protected area of a corporate intranet, and all other services are blocked. In many cases, this degree of security is important, as it guarantees that only those services that are considered trustworthy are actually allowed through the firewall. It also prevents other untrusted services from being implemented behind the backs of the firewall administrator.

Another benefit of using application gateways is that application protocols can be screened and filtered. Some firewalls, for example, can screen FTP traffic and filter out the FTP PUT command, which is useful if one wants to guarantee that users cannot write to, say, an anonymous FTP server. Another example is a firewall that screens HTTP traffic to filter out Java applets and ActiveX controls in order to protect internal hosts from executable content and software-driven attacks. The possibilities of executable content and software-driven attacks are further elaborated in Chapter 8, when we discuss the limitations of the firewall technology.

We have already mentioned one of the main disadvantages of application gateways, namely that they are not good at handling UDP-based applications. Another disadvantage is related to proprietary application protocols. To code and set up a proxy server, one must know the underlying application protocol. This is not always the case, since proprietary application protocols are in widespread use. Examples include Lotus Notes, SQLnet, and SAP.

In addition to commercial firewall products, there are also software packages available today that can be used to build and customize a firewall system. For example, TIS has developed a firewall toolkit (FWTK) [5]. Since the TIS FWTK is written in the C programming language it should, with some effort at portability, run on most versions of the UNIX operating system. It is important to note that the TIS FWTK does not constitute a turnkey firewall solution, but rather provides the components from which an application-level gateway can be assembled and built. Components of the FWTK, while designed to work together, can also be used in isolation or can be combined with other firewall software components. The TIS FWTK provides proxy servers for most TCP-based applications in use today, such as Telnet, Rlogin, FTP, HTTP, Gopher, SMTP, NNTP, and X11. Also, the toolkit provides an authentication server that all proxy servers can utilize. The authentication server, in turn, supports many authentication mechanisms, ranging from simple passwords to one-time passwords and challenge-response mechanisms. For example, S/Key from Bellcore, SecureNet Key from Digital Pathways, and SecurID from Security Dynamics are all supported by the FWTK authentication server. Also, the toolkit supports several firewall configurations, including dual-homed firewalls, screened host firewalls, and screened subnet firewalls. We are going to address these configurations in Chapter 8.

The TIS FWTK software was officially released in October 1993. It is publicly and freely available,[1] but is copyrighted and must be licensed for commercial use. The toolkit has also been used at the Institute for Computer Science and Applied Mathematics (IAM) of the University of Berne to experiment with the firewall technology [6]. Much of the functionality of the commercial Gauntlet Internet Firewall System from TIS is built on top of the FWTK.

7.3 SOCKS

We have mentioned previously that *SOCKS* refers to a circuit-level gateway.[2] More precisely, SOCKS is a networking proxy mechanism that enables hosts on one side of a SOCKS server to gain full access to hosts on the other side of the SOCKS server without requiring direct IP reachability. It works by redirecting a connection request

---

[1] ftp://ftp.tis.com/pub/firewalls/toolkit/fwtk-v1.2.tar.Z
[2] http://www.socks.nec.com

from a host on one side to a host on the other side to a SOCKS server, which authenticates and authorizes the request, establishes a proxy connection to the destined host, and relays data traffic forth and back between the two TCP/IP connections. As a circuit-level gateway, SOCKS runs at the transport layer and therefore relays connections without looking into the corresponding application data. We have also mentioned previously that SOCKS follows a customized client approach, meaning that SOCKS requires customizations and modifications to client software, but no change is usually required to user procedures. More precisely, SOCKS requires modifications either to the client software or the TCP/IP stack to accommodate the interception at the firewall between the client on the intranet and the server on the Internet.

A client that has been modified to handle SOCKS interactions is commonly referred to as a socksified client. Following this terminology, the Netscape Navigator, Microsoft Internet Explorer, and NCSA Mosaic are socksified HTTP clients, as they accommodate interactions with a SOCKS server (at least in their latest releases). A socksified client issues SOCKS calls that are transparent to the users. Note that socksified TCP/IP stacks are also available, which may obviate the need for client software modifications. In either case, the SOCKS server resides at the firewall and interacts with the socksified clients or TCP/IP stacks. There are no further changes required for the servers that reside on the Internet.

Table 7.1
Socket Calls and SOCKS Counterparts

SOCKS Call	Socket Call
Rconnect	connect
Rbind	bind
Rlisten	listen
Rselect	select
Rgetsockname	getsockname
Raccept	accept

SOCKS and the SOCKS protocol for communications between a socksified client and a SOCKS server were originally developed by David and Michelle Koblas in 1992 [7]. Today, the software is now maintained by Ying-Da Lee. There are also several SOCKS software packages publicly and freely available on the Internet.[3] They typically consist of two components: a SOCKS server or daemon called socksd,

---

[3]ftp://ftp.nec.com/pub/socks or ftp://ftp.cup.hp.com/dist/socks/socks.tar.gz

and a SOCKS library that can be used to replace regular Socket calls in the client software. More precisely, one must recompile and link the client software with a few preprocessor directives to intercept and replace the regular Socket calls with their SOCKS counterparts as summarized in Table 7.1.

The design goal of SOCKS was to provide a general framework for TCP/IP applications to securely use the services of a firewall. Complying with these design goals, SOCKS is independent of any supported TCP/IP application protocol. When a socksified client requires access to an Internet server, it must first open a TCP/IP connection to the appropriate port on the SOCKS server residing at the firewall system. The SOCKS server is conventionally located on TCP port 1,080. If the TCP/IP connection is established, the client sends a connection relay request to the SOCKS server. This request includes the following information:

- Desired destination address;

- Desired destination port;

- Authentication information.

The SOCKS server evaluates the information in the connection relay request. During this evaluation, it may perform various functions, such as authentication, authorization, message security-level negotiation, and so on. The SOCKS server either accepts the request and establishes a corresponding connection to the Internet application server or rejects the request. The evaluation depends on the configuration data of the SOCKS server. In either case, the SOCKS server sends a reply back to the client. Among other things, the reply includes information indicating whether the request was successful. Once the requested connection is established, the SOCKS server simply relays data between the client and server.

There are currently two versions of SOCKS available: SOCKS version 4 and SOCKS version 5. SOCKS V4 has been widely used in firewalls. However, as SOCKS evolves from version 4 to version 5, the application scope of SOCKS has also been extended. Firewall is just one, a traditional one, of the SOCKS V5 applications. Today, work on SOCKS V5 is mainly driven by NEC Corporation.[4] Also, the SOCKS V5 protocol is being standardized by the IETF AFT WG and specified in [8]. Compared to SOCKS V4, SOCKS V5 has added several new functions:

- SOCKS V5 supports a handshake between the client and the SOCKS server for authentication method negotiation. The first message is sent by the client to the

---

[4]Note that SOCKS5 and SOCKS5Toolkit are registered trademarks of NEC Corporation.

SOCKS server. It declares the authentication methods the client is currently able to support. The second message is sent from the SOCKS server back to the client. It selects a particular authentication method according to the SOCKS server's security policy. If none of the methods declared by the client meets the security requirements of the SOCKS server, communications will be dropped.

- After the authentication method has been negotiated, the client and SOCKS server start the authentication process using the chosen method. Two authentication methods are specified in corresponding RFCs: password-based authentication [9] and Kerberos V5 GSS-API authentication [10]. Again, we will address Kerberos and the Generic Security Service Application Programming Interface (GSS-API) in Chapter 11. The approach for use of GSS-API in SOCKS V5 is to authenticate the client and server by sucessfully establishing a security context. This context can then be used to protect messages that are subsequently exchanged. Prior to use of GSS-API primitives, the client and server should be locally authenticated and have established default GSS-API credentials.

- Depending on the underlying authentication methods implemented via GSS-API, a client can negotiate with the SOCKS server about the security of subsequent messages. In the case of Kerberos V5, either integrity and/or confidentiality services can be provided for the rest of messages, including the client's proxy request, the SOCKS server's replies, and all application data.

- One of the connection requests in SOCKS V5 is for a UDP association that results in a virtual proxy circuit for traversing UDP-based application data. Consequently, the SOCKS V5 library can be used to socksify both TCP- and UDP-based applications, while the SOCKS V4 library can only be used to socksify TCP-based applications.

Due to their fundamental differences, the SOCKS V5 protocol specification does not require any provision for supporting the SOCKS V4 protocol. However, it is a simple matter of implementation to enable SOCKS V5 servers to communicate with V5 and V4 clients and servers. For example, the NEC Corporation has made publicly available a SOCKS V5 reference implementation for both UNIX and Windows NT that supports the SOCKS V4 protocol as well. Also, the implementation supports the two authentication methods mentioned above, and has a built-in address resolution proxy that enables clients to be fully operational without having DNS support. A client can pass the name, instead of the resolved IP address, to the SOCKS server and the server will resolve the address on the client's behalf.

7.4 DISCUSSION

In summary, the advantages of application gateways are user authentication, application protocol control, logging, and accounting. We discussed user authentication and application protocol control in this chapter. With regard to the other points it is important to note that an application gateway always acts as an intermediate process that can handle logging and accounting in a simple and fairly straightforward way. The disadvantages of application gateways are related to the fact that for full benefit, a proxy server must be built specifically for each application protocol. This fact may severely limit the deployment of new applications. A clear advantage of SOCKS is its generality, meaning that a SOCKS server can act as a proxy server for any TCP/IP application. This generality, however, also has negative impacts on security. For example, a SOCKS server is not able to scan application data for specific commands or executable content. Due to the increased availability of transparent firewalls and socksified client software, users can nowadays generally access Internet servers without requiring any awareness of intervening firewalls. As such, there is no user training required when a firewall is installed to control access to intranet resources.

The security of an application gateway relies heavily on the underlying authentication scheme, and a weak authentication scheme can easily defeat the purpose of the entire firewall. A typical TCP/IP application, such as Telnet or FTP, uses a password-based authentication scheme that is inherently weak. Unless otherwise protected, the passwords are transmitted in the clear. It has to be distinguished whether the client contacts the application gateway from the intranet or from the Internet. If the client contacts the application gateway from the intranet, the authentication information also travels through the intranet, which is assumed to be comparatively secure. But if the client contacts the application gateway from the Internet, the authentication information also travels through the Internet. In this case, a strong authentication scheme is strongly recommended. This is especially true for administrator access.

In Chapter 2, we introduced and discussed the TCP SYN flooding attack. In this attack, a number of SYN messages are sent to a server in order to flood its buffer area. It is important to note that conventional packet filters or screening routers are not able to defend against TCP SYN flooding attacks, since they lack the necessary capability to perform stateful inspection. However, many companies are working together to devise improvements to existing TCP/IP implementations and to improve kernel resistance against this type of attack. When these improvements become available, it is strongly recommended to install them on all systems as soon as possible. In the meantime, however, there are some ad-hoc solutions offered by firewall vendors. For example, CheckPoint Software Technologies, Ltd. offers *SYNDefender* for its FireWall-1 product line. SYNDefender provides two different solutions for the problem of defending against TCP SYN flooding attacks:

- SYNDefender Relay

- SYNDefender Gateway

The *SYNDefender Relay* counters TCP SYN flooding attacks by making sure that a three-way connection establishment handshake with an external host is completed before an initial SYN message is actually sent to an internal host. Therefore, the SYNDefender Relay that resides on the firewall and receives a SYN message from an external host returns a SYN-ACK message to that host. The external host must then finish the connection establishment with an ACK message, before the SYNDefender Relay sets up a secondary TCP/IP connection to the internal host on the external host's behalf. From then on, the SYNDefender Relay simply relays data between the two TCP/IP connections forth and back. The corresponding message flows are illustrated on the top of Figure 7.1. Note that one of the key capabilities the SYNDefender Relay employs is the ability to translate the sequence numbers, which are now different for each half of the connection.

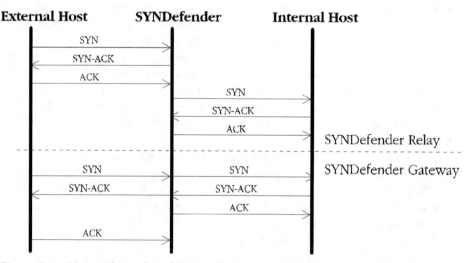

Figure 7.1   Message flows of the SYNDefender Relay and the SYNDefender Gateway.

In order for the resetting of SYN connection attempts to be effective against the TCP SYN flooding attack, the reset timer must be small enough to keep the server's backlog queue from filling up, while at the same time being big enough to allow users coming over slow links to connect. The *SYNDefender Gateway* solution surmounts this problem by making sure that an ACK message is sent in immediate response to the server's SYN-ACK message. When the server receives the ACK message, the connection is moved out of the backlog queue and becomes an open connection. Again, the SYNDefender Gateway resides on the firewall. Whenever it receives a SYN message from an external host, it simply forwards the message to the internal host. The internal host, in turn, sends back a SYN-ACK message that the SYNDefender Gateway forwards to the external host. Additionally, the SYNDefender Gateway returns an ACK message to the internal host in order to establish the connection. If a proper ACK message from the external host is received within a certain timeframe, the destined connection is established and the SYNDefender Gateway simply relays data forth and back. If, however, the SYNDefender Gateway does not receive a proper ACK message from the external host, it closes the connection by sending an RST message to the internal host. The message flows of the SYNDefender Gateway are illustrated at the bottom of Figure 7.1.

The main advantage of the SYNDefender Relay is that the internal host will not receive any invalid connection establishment attempts. If the host has limited memory or often reaches an overloaded state, then the SYNDefender Relay's filtering of invalid connection establishment attempts might be advantageous in the event of an attack. Users making connections to the host may, however, experience a slightly longer connection setup time, which is not the case with the SYNDefender Gateway solution.

We have mentioned that there are some problems related to the handling of proprietary application protocols, as well as UDP traffic. There is little that can be done about proprietary application protocols, except for a collaboration with the corresponding vendors. With regard to UDP traffic, however, an interesting question is related to the handling of multicast traffic. Note that multicast traffic, as deployed on the Multicast Backbone (MBone), is based on UDP as a transport layer protocol [11]. The MBone holds great potential for many organizations because it supports low-cost audio and video conferencing and carries live broadcast of an increasing number of public interest events. MBone conferences are transmitted via unauthenticated multicast traffic, which unfortunately convey significant security vulnerabilities to any system that receives them. For this reason, most application gateways block MBone traffic sent from the Internet and prevent it from reaching internal hosts. It is not until recently that firewall vendors have begun to address the

UDP and multicast challenge. For example, TIS has extended its set of proxy servers for the FWTK version 2.0 with a set of facilities that can be used to participate in MBone conferencing [12]. The basic idea is to have proxy servers running on the firewall that forward inbound multicast traffic using unicast addressing on the corporate intranet. Obviously, this approach is appropriate for individual users participating in MBone conferencing. However, this approach is not very efficient and may run into scalability problems if too many users on the corporate intranet want to participate. In this case, the efficiency advantages of multicast routing are entirely lost.

Now that the basic components of a firewall configuration have been introduced and examined, we can combine packet filters and application gateways to provide some higher levels of security and flexibility than if either were used alone. In the chapter that follows we are going to provide some examples of firewall configurations to give a more concrete and comprehensive understanding of the firewall technology as a whole.

REFERENCES

[1] C. Rigney, A. Rubens, W. Simpson, and S. Willens, "Remote Authentication Dial-In User Service (RADIUS)," Request for Comments 2058, January 1997.

[2] C. Rigney, "RADIUS Accounting," Request for Comments 2059, January 1997.

[3] C. Finseth, "An Access Control Protocol, Sometimes Called TACACS," Request for Comments 1492, July 1993.

[4] R. Ganesan, "BAfirewall: A Modern Design," *Proceedings of Internet Society Symposium on Network and Distributed System Security*, February 1994.

[5] F. Avolio, and M. Ranum, "A Network Perimeter with Secure External Access," *Proceedings of Internet Society Symposium on Network and Distributed System Security*, February 1994.

[6] P. Zumbrunn, "Firewalls im Rahmen einer ganzheitlichen Sicherheitspolitik," M.Sc. Thesis, University of Berne, Switzerland, September 1995.

[7] D. Koblas, and M.R. Koblas, "SOCKS," *Proceedings of USENIX UNIX Security III Symposium*, September 1992, pp. 77 – 82.

[8] M. Leech, M. Ganis, Y. Lee, R. Kuris, D. Koblas, and L. Jones, "SOCKS Protocol Version 5," Request for Comments 1928, March 1996.

[9] M. Leech, "Username/Password Authentication for SOCKS V5," Request for Comments 1929, March 1996.

[10] P. McMahon, "GSS-API Authentication Method for SOCKS Version 5," Request for Comments 1961, June 1996.

[11] V. Kumar, "MBone: Interactive Multimedia on the Internet," New Riders Publishing, Indianapolis, IN, 1996.

[12] K. Djahandri, and D.F. Sterne, "An MBone Proxy for a Firewall Toolkit," *Proceedings of IEEE Symposium on Security and Privacy*, May 1997.

Chapter 8

Firewall Configurations

Packet filters and application gateways are usually combined in firewall configurations. In this chapter we are going to overview and discuss three firewall configurations that are used and widely deployed on the Internet today. In particular, we address dual-homed firewalls in Section 8.1, screened host firewalls in Section 8.2, and screened subnet firewalls in Section 8.3. In Section 8.4, we focus on firewall certification, and in Section 8.5 we conclude with a brief discussion of the firewall technology as a whole.

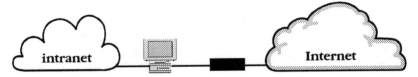

Figure 8.1   A dual-homed firewall configuration.

8.1 DUAL-HOMED FIREWALLS

In TCP/IP terminology, the term *multihomed host* is generally used to refer to a host with multiple network interfaces. Usually, each network interface is connected to a separate network segment and the multihomed host can either route or forward IP packets between those network segments. If, however, IP routing and IP forwarding are disabled on the multihomed host, it provides isolation between the network segments and may be used in a firewall configuration accordingly. To disable IP routing is usually a relatively simple and straightforward task. It basically means to turn off any program that might be advertising the host as a router. To disable IP forwarding is considerably more difficult, and may require modifying the operating system kernel. Fortunately, these days a number of UNIX vendors provide supported parameters for turning off IP forwarding.

A *dual-homed host* is a very special example of a multihomed host, namely one that has two network interfaces. Again, IP routing and IP forwarding are disabled to provide isolation between the two network segments the dual-homed host interconnects.

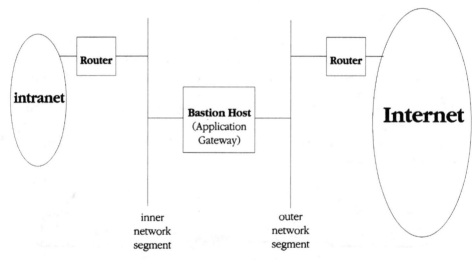

Figure 8.2   The entire architecture of a dual-homed firewall configuration.

A *dual-homed firewall* configuration is built around and makes use of a dual-homed host. Figure 8.1 illustrates the basic layout of a dual-homed firewall configuration. In its simplest form, the configuration comprises a bastion host with two network interfaces and with the IP forwarding and routing capabilities disabled so that IP packets can no longer be routed between the two network segments. The application gateways are running on the bastion host. In addition to that, a screening router is typically placed between the bastion host and the Internet.

In this configuration, the bastion host's external network interface is connected to an outer network segment that hosts the screening router. This router, in turn, is connected to the Internet. Its aim is to ensure that any IP packet arriving from the Internet is correctly addressed to the bastion host. If a packet arrives with another destination IP address, it must be dropped and discarded. Note that the outer network segment between the bastion host and the external screening router can also host specialized systems, such as information or network access servers. Also note that some firewall configurations have a second screening router placed between the bastion host and the intranet. In this case, the bastion host's internal network interface is connected to an inner network segment that hosts another screening router. This router, in turn, is conneted to the intranet. Figure 8.2 illustrates the entire architecture of such a dual-homed firewall configuration with two screening routers. In this configuration the bastion host interconnects two network segments that, in turn, are connected to the intranet or Internet, respectively. An important consideration is that the security of the bastion host must be very high, since the use of any vulnerable services or techniques on the host could lead to break-ins. If the bastion host is compromised, an intruder could potentially subvert the entire firewall by simply (re)enabling the IP forwarding and routing capabilities.

Note that the bastion host of a dual-homed firewall can also be replicated for efficiency reasons. The resulting configuration is sometimes also referred to as a *parallel dual-homed firewall configuration*. It may consist of several bastion hosts that are all connected to both the inner and outer network segments. In this case, the various proxy and SOCKS servers may run on different hosts. In the discussions that follow, we are going to use the term dual-homed firewall to possibly include parallel dual-homed firewall configurations as well.

Unlike the packet-filtering-only firewall introduced and briefly discussed in Chapter 5, the dual-homed firewall is a complete block to IP packets flowing between an intranet and the Internet. Intranet access can only be provided by proxy or SOCKS servers that are running on the bastion host. Nevertheless, there are some elder dual-homed firewall configurations that do not use proxy or SOCKS servers at all, but require users to have accounts on the bastion host. These configurations, however, are not recommended for any but the smallest sites, since maintaining multiple user accounts on a firewall system can lead to administration mistakes, which in turn can lead to attacks and successful intruder break-ins.

In summary, the dual-homed firewall is a simple but very secure configuration. Since no services pass except those for which proxy or SOCKS servers actually exist, a dual-homed firewall inherently implements the second stance of a firewall design, which is to deny any service unless it is expressly permitted. While the use of dual-homed firewalls is interesting from a security point of view, there are some practical problems related to the fact that until today no proxy servers existed for proprietary TCP/IP application protocols, such as Lotus Notes, SQLnet, and SAP. In this case, the dual-homed firewall configuration turns out to be rather inflexible, and this inflexibility could turn out to be disadvantageous for some sites.

8.2   SCREENED HOST FIREWALLS

Whereas a dual-homed firewall configuration provides services from a host that is attached to multiple networks and that has routing turned off, a *screened host firewall* configuration provides services from a host that is attached to only the internal network. Figure 8.3 illustrates the screened host firewall configuration. Similar to the dual-homed firewall, the screened host firewall combines an application gateway with a screening router that filters IP packets originated from or destined to the Internet. But unlike the dual-homed firewall configuration, the application gateway in the screened host firewall configuration has just one network interface and does not need a separate network segment between the application gateway and the screening router. This is advantageous primarily with regard to the number of IP addresses that a site requires for its firewall configuration.

Figure 8.3   A screened host firewall configuration.

In the screened host firewall configuration, the screening router that connects the intranet to the Internet must be configured so that it sends all IP traffic originated from the Internet to the application gateway that is running on the bastion host. Before it forwards IP traffic to the bastion host, however, the screening router must apply its packet filter rules. Only traffic that passes the rules is diverted to the bastion host; all other traffic is rejected. Consequently, the routing tables of the screening router must be configured so that inbound traffic is always forwarded to the bastion host. The same tables must be heavily protected from intrusion and unauthorized access or change. If a routing table entry is changed so that the traffic is no longer forwarded to the bastion host but sent directly to an internal machine, the bastion host is bypassed and the entire firewall is effectively circumvented.

The screened host firewall configuration permits the firewall to be made more flexible, but perhaps also less secure, by permitting the screening router to pass certain trusted services around the application gateway and directly to internal machines. The trusted services might be those for which proxy servers don't exist, but might be trusted in the sense that the risk of using the services has been considered and found acceptable. For example, less risky services, such as those provided by the network time protocol (NTP), could be permitted to pass through the screening router directly to an internal time server. Also, if internal machines required access to the domain name system (DNS), DNS traffic could be permitted to bypass the application gateway as well.

In summary, the screened host firewall is based on a more flexible configuration than the dual-homed firewall. However, this flexibility is achieved with some cost to security. It is technically impossible to pass traffic through a dual-homed firewall unless there is a corresponding proxy or SOCKS server available on the firewall, whereas this is possible in the case of a screened host firewall. Screened host firewalls are appropriate for sites that need more flexibility and less security than that provided by dual-homed firewalls.

8.3   SCREENED SUBNET FIREWALLS

The *screened subnet firewall* configuration adds an extra layer of security to the screened host firewall configuration by adding a network segment that further isolates the protected network from the Internet.

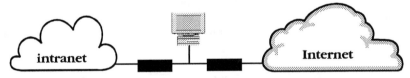

Figure 8.4   A screened subnet firewall configuration.

Figure 8.4 illustrates the screened subnet firewall configuration. It consists of two screening routers that are used to create an inner, screened subnet. This subnet is sometimes also referred to as a sandbox or demilitarized zone (DMZ). The DMZ may host an application gateway that is running on a bastion host, as well as some additional servers that require carefully-controlled Internet access. Note that the two screening routers provide redundancy in that an attacker would have to subvert both routers in order to reach internal machines. Also note that the bastion host and the additional servers on the DMZ could be set up such that they would be the only systems seen from the Internet; no other system name needs to be known or used in a DNS database that is made accessible to the outside world.

Figure 8.5 illustrates the entire architecture of a screened subnet firewall configuration. Again, there are two network segments: an outer and an inner network segment. Both segments are interconnected with a screening router. The bastion host is located on the outer network segment. Again, it can be replicated for efficiency reasons to get a *parallel screened subnet firewall.*

A screened subnet firewall, like the screened host firewall, can be made more flexible by permitting certain services to pass around the application gateway. As an alternative to passing services directly between the intranet and Internet, one could also locate the systems that need these services directly on the screened subnet. We have already mentioned that the DMZ may house servers that require carefully controlled Internet access in addition to the bastion host. For example, a site that needs to but does not permit X11 or NFS traffic between the Internet and some systems, could still locate these systems on the screened subnet. The systems could maintain access to internal systems by connecting to the application gateway and reconfiguring the routers to the inner network segment or the intranet, respectively. This is not a perfect solution, but an option for sites that require a high degree of security.

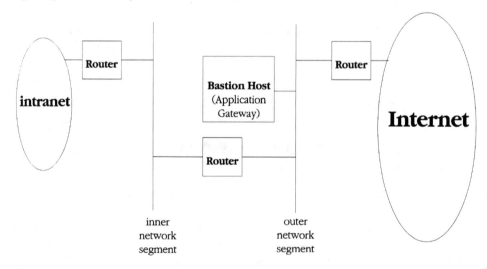

Figure 8.5   The entire architecture of a screened subnet firewall configuration.

In summary, the screened host and screened subnet firewalls are more flexible but less secure than the dual-homed firewall. The dual-homed firewall is more secure because its service access policy can't be weakened (because the dual-homed firewall cannot pass services for which there is no proxy or SOCKS server available). However, where throughput and flexibility are important or required, the screened host and screened subnet firewalls may be preferable choices. Compared to the screened host firewall, the screened subnet firewall has the advantage of better security and the disadvantage of requiring a separate network segment to serve as DMZ.

Table 8.1
NCSA Certified Firewall Products (March 1997)

Vendor	*Firewall Product*
3Com	NETBuilder Router v9.1
Abhiweb	AFS 2000 v2.02
ANS Communications	ANS Interlock
Ascend	Pipeline Router Ver.4.6C
Atlantic Systems Group	TurnStyle Firewall system V2.1
Border Network Technologies, Inc.	BorderWare 4.0
CheckPoint Software Technologies, Inc.	CheckPoint Firewall-1 (UNIX or NT)
Cisco Ssystems	PIX Firewall
Cyberguard Corporation	CyberGuard FirewallV2.2.3
DEC	AltaVista (UNIX or NT)
Global Internet	Centri Firewall V3.1
Global Technologies Associates	GFX Internet FirewallSystem V2.5
IBM	Secure Network Gateway
Livermore Software Laboratories, International	Protus V2
Milkyway Networks, Inc.	Black Hole
NEC Technologies	PrivateNet 2.0
NetGuard	Guardian 2.0
Network-1	Firewall/Plus 1.1-4 (UNIX or NT)
ON Technology Corporation	ON Guard
OpenROUTE Networks, Inc.	GT Secure (60 or 70)
Radguard Ltd.	PyroWall Ver.1.1
Raptor Systems, Inc.	Eagle 4.0 (Solaris or NT))
Seattle Software Labs, Inc.	Watchguard Security Management
Secure Computing Corporation	Sidewinder 3.0
Sun Microsystems	SunScreen SPF-100 1.0
Technologic Inc.	Interceptor
TIS	Gauntlet Internet Firewall System

8.4   FIREWALL CERTIFICATION

The idea of having security properties of IT systems evaluated and certified by some trusted party is not new and has led to the development of various criteria catalogues, such as the Trusted Computer System Evaluation Criteria (TCSEC), also known as Orange Book in the United States, the Information Technology Security Evaluation Criteria (ITSEC) in Europe, and the Common Criteria (CC) for both of them. In theory, the same or slightly modified and enhanced versions of these catalogues could be used to evaluate and certify firewall systems as well. In practice, however, there are only a few firewalls that have been evaluated and certified so far.

Meanwhile, some companies and organizations have independently started to evaluate and certify the security properties of commercial firewall products. For example, the National Computer Security Association (NCSA[1]) has become active in the field. The association hosts an annual conference on firewalls and Internet security technology and publicly released a NCSA Firewall Policy Guide in November 1995. The NCSA also hosts a Firewall Product Developer's Consortium (FWPD) that has defined NCSA FWPD Criteria for firewall certification. In short, the NCSA FWPD Criteria version 2.0 defines functionality and security requirements for firewall products:

- The functionality requirements specify TCP/IP protocols and services that must be provided to internal clients and external users. In particular, the protocols include Telnet, FTP, HTTP (with and without SSL support), SMTP, and DNS. In addition to that, the functionality requirements also address firewall management.

- Upon demonstration of its functionality, a firewall product is also subjected to a couple of tests to demonstrate protection against a standardized and evolving suite of attacks. These tests are performed with several tools, including a port scanning tool, the ISS Security Scanner, and some tools developed by NCSA.

There are several firewall products that have met the NCSA FWPD Criteria and that are authorized to use the NCSA Certified logo in their marketing and other literature accordingly. The products are itemized in Table 8.1. Note that the table was compiled in March 1997, and that additional firewall products probably have been certified since then.

---

[1]http://www.ncsa.com

8.5 DISCUSSION

Firewall systems are a fact of life on the Internet today. If properly implemented and deployed, they can provide effective access control services for corporate intranets. Consequently, more and more network managers are setting up firewalls as their first line of defense against outside attacks. Nevertheless, the firewall technology has remained an emotional topic within the Internet community. Let's briefly summarize their main concerns:

- Firewall advocates consider firewalls as important additional safeguards, because they aggregate security functions in a single point, simplifying installation, configuration, and management. Many companies use firewalls as corporate ambassadors to the Internet, and use them to store public information about corporate products and services, files to download, bug fixes, and so forth. From a U.S. manufacturer's and vendor's point of view, the firewall technology is interesting mainly because it doesn't use cryptographic techniques and can therefore be freely exported. In addition to that, the technology's use is restricted neither to the TCP/IP protocols nor to the Internet, and very similar techniques can be used in any packet switched data network, such as X.25 or ATM networks.

- Firewall detractors are usually concerned about the difficulty of using firewalls, requiring multiple logins and other out-of-band mechanisms, as well as their interference with the usability and vitality of the Internet as a whole. They claim that firewalls foster a false sense of security, leading to lax security within the firewall perimeter.

At minimum, firewall advocates and detractors both agree that firewalls are a powerful tool for network security, but that they aren't by any means a panacea or a magic bullet for all network and Internet-related security problems. Consequently, they should not be regarded as a substitute for careful security management within a corporate intranet. Also, a firewall is useful only if it handles all traffic to and from the Internet. This is not always the case, since many sites permit dial-in access to modems that are located at various points throughout the site. This is a potential backdoor and could negate all the protection provided by the firewall. A much better method for handling modems is to concentrate them into a modem pool. In essence, a modem pool consists of several modems connected to a terminal server. A dial-in user connects to the terminal server and then connects from there to other internal hosts. Some terminal servers provide security features that can restrict connections to specific hosts, or require users to strongly authenticate themselves. Obviously, RADIUS, TACACS, and TACACS+ can again be used to secure communications between the terminal server and a centralized security server. Sometimes, authorized users also wish to have a dial-out capability. These users, however, need to recognize the vulnerabilities they may be creating if they are careless with modem access. A dial-out capability may easily become a dial-in capability if proper precautions are not taken. In general, dial-in and dial-out capabilities should be considered in the design of a firewall and incorporated into it. Forcing outside users to go through the strong authentication of the firewall should be reflected in the firewall policy. In addition to unauthorized modems, there are at least two types of security problems that firewalls can't address:

- Firewalls generally do not provide protection against insider attacks. A firewall simply intercepts data traffic between an intranet and the Internet. As such, an insider may still steal critical information or damage intranet resources without any awareness at the firewall. This threat can be addressed by implementing appropriate authentication, authorization, and access control mechanisms inside the firewall. Additionally, intranet firewalls can be used to reduce the risk of successful insider attacks.

- Also, firewalls do not provide protection against data-driven attacks, such as those employed by users downloading virus-infected software from Internet archives or transferring such programs in MIME-type attachments of e-mail messages. Since these programs can be encoded, compressed, and encrypted in any number of ways, a firewall can't scan such programs to search for virus signatures with any degree of accuracy. The same is also true for macro viruses that are hidden in data files. The virus problem still exists and must be handled with both policy and some dedicated antiviral software controls.

With regard to computer viruses, it is important to note that the use and wide proliferation of executable content, as provided for example by Java applets and ActiveX controls, has dramatically intensified the problems related to malicious code [1,2]. The problems are obvious: If a user downloads a Java applet or ActiveX control on a client that is configured to accept executable content, the Java applet or ActiveX control is automatically executed without asking the user for permission. As such, the Java applet or ActiveX control can compromise the security of the system.[2] The situation is quite dangerous, since the user imports a specific

---

[2]Access the WWW home page of DigiCrime, Inc. at URL http://www.digicrime.com to experience that executable content can in fact damage your system.

task to perform on his or her system without knowing exactly what the task is all about. This situation is somehow comparable to a reverse RPC. For this dangerous paradigm, Java has also been attributed to be an "automatic malicious software distribution system" [3]. With its lack of a virtual machine concept, ActiveX is going to pose even more security problems than Java. For example, the German Chaos Computer Club demonstrated the danger of using ActiveX when they wrote and put on the Web an ActiveX control that was actually a Trojan horse. In the background, the ActiveX control prepares a money transfer order for the Microsoft Quicken software and puts it in the corresponding payment queue. So, when the user has Quicken transfer its money orders the next time, the faked money transfer order generated by the Trojan horse is transferred as well. If the amount of transferred money is not too big, chances are that the user does not realize the manipulation.

It is also worthwhile mentioning that firewalls offer strong protection, but that tunnels can always be used to circumvent and bypass them. In essence, tunneling refers to the technique of encapsulating a data unit from one protocol in another, and using the facilities of the second protocol to traverse parts of the network. At the destination point, the encapsulation is stripped off, and the original data unit is reinjected into the local network. There are many uses for tunneling, and in some cases, a protocol may also be encapsulated within itself. For example, IP tunneling is used in both the evolving Multicast Backbone (MBone) as well as the IPv6 Backbone (6Bone).

- With regard to the MBone, IP multicast packets are tunneled using IP unicast packets. More precisely, IP packets with multicast destination addresses are encapsulated in IP packets with unicast destination addresses and tunneled through the existing Internet accordingly. Only destinations that are able to handle multicast traffic decapsulate the packets and eventually reinject them into their local networks.

- Similarly, IPv6 migration suggests the use of IP tunneling for transmitting IPv6 packets in the existing IPv4-based Internet. In this case, IPv6 packets are tunneled using IPv4 packets. More precisely, IPv6 packets are encapsulated in IPv4 packets and tunneled through the existing Internet. Only destinations that are able to handle IPv6 packets decapsulate the IPv6 packets and eventually reinject them into their local networks. Later on, when IPv6 becomes more widely deployed, it is possible and very likely that IPv4 traffic will be tunneled through an IPv6-based Internet.

Unfortunately, IP tunneling can also be misused to circumvent and bypass firewalls. Let's assume that a firewall permits at least one type of traffic to pass through bidirectionally. In this case, an insider and an outsider who dislike the firewall and wish to bypass it can build a tunnel between an inside host and an outside host. What they essentially do is encapsulte arbitrary IP packets in legitimate IP packets or some higher-layer messages that are authorized to pass through the firewall. As such, the legitimate IP packets or some higher-layer messages are transmitted to the destination host, where they are decapsulated to retrieve the original IP packets. Consequently, the two accomplices have established a tunnel that allows the free flow of IP packets through the firewall. From a security point of view, an unauthorized tunnel is far worse than a simple outbound connection, since inbound connections are usually permitted through the tunnel as well. Unauthorized tunnels are, in the final analysis, a management problem, not a technical one. If insiders don't generally accept the need for information security, firewall systems and other access control mechanisms will always be futile. The establishment of unauthorized tunnels is actually an insider problem, since it requires the cooperation of a legitimate user.

Last but not least, one should also notice that tunnels through firewalls have their good sides, too. When properly configured and employed, they can be used to bypass the limitations of a particular firewall configuration. For example, a tunnel could be used to interconnect two physically separated sites. Firewalls at each location would provide protection from the outside, while a tunnel provides connectivity. If the tunnel is entirely encrypted, then the risks of such a configuration are low and the benefits are high.

To some people, the notion of a firewall is questionable. They argue that in most situations, the network is not the resource at risk; rather, the endpoints of the network are threatened. Given that the target of the attackers is the hosts on the network, should they not be suitably configured and armored to resist all possible attacks? The answer is that they should be, but probably cannot be. There will be bugs, either in the network programs or in the administration of the systems. Consequently, firewalls have been constructed and are used for pragmatic reasons by organizations interested in a higher level of security than may be possible without them. According to Steven Bellovin, firewalls are not a solution to network security problems, but rather a network response to a host security problem [4]. More precisely, they are a response to the dismal state of software engineering. Taken as a whole, the industry has missed the opportunity to produce software that is correct, secure, and easy to administer.

Today, firewall technology is the most widely deployed security technique on the Internet. Many companies and organizations regularly perform market surveys and publish corresponding results. For example, the Computer Security Institute (CSI) performed a market survey in 1996 and summarized the results in a Firewall Product Matrix [5]. Similarly, the *Data Communications Magazine* reported from an exhaustive test of about 20 commercially available firewall products[3] [6]. The firewall products were tested for security and management, as well as performance. What was found is that firewalls aren't yet at the commodity stage where one product is as good as another. Tabbed for Tester's Choice awards were the following firewall products:

- Firewall-1 from CheckPoint Software Technologies, Inc.;

- CyberGuard Firewall from Cyberguard Corporation;

- Watchguard Security Management System from Seattle Software Labs, Inc.;

- SunScreen EFS from Sun Microsystems, Inc.

In addition to that, honorable mention went to a beta version of the Altavista Firewall 97 version 3.0 from Altavista Internet Software, Inc. The investigation also revealed a trend for Windows NT-based firewall systems. Today, in addition to UNIX, some firewall products also run on Windows NT, Novell Netware, and OS/2. In addition to that, vendors are quick to cite ease of use as an additional selling point.

Firewall systems provide basic access control services for corporate intranets. But firewalls are not going to solve all security problems. A pair of historical analogies can help us better understand the role of firewall technology for the current Internet [7]:

- Our Stone Age predecessors lived in caves, each inhabited by a family whose members knew each other quite well. They could use this knowledge to identify and authenticate one another. Someone wanting to enter the cave would have to be introduced by a family member trusted by the others. Human history has shown that this security model is too simple to work on a large scale. As families grew in size and started to interact with one another, it was no longer possible for all family members to know all other members of the community, or even to reliably remember all persons who had ever been introduced to them.

---

[3]http://www.data.com/lab_tests/firewalls97_web.html

- In the Middle Ages, our predecessors lived in castles and villages surrounded by town walls. The inhabitants were acquainted with each other, but this web of knowledge was not trusted. Instead, identification and authentication, as well as authorization and access control, were centralized at a front gate. Anyone who wanted to enter the castle or village had to pass the front gate and was thoroughly checked there. Those who managed to pass the gate were implicitly trusted by all inhabitants. But human history has shown that this security model doesn't work either. For one thing, town walls don't protect against malicious insider attacks; for another, the use of town walls and front gates doesn't scale easily. Many remnants of medieval town walls bear witness to this lack of scalability.

Using the above analogies, the Internet has just entered the Middle Ages. The simple security model of the Stone Age still works for single hosts and local area networks. But it no longer works for wide area networks in general and the Internet in particular. As a first (and let's hope intermediate) step, firewalls have been erected at the Internet gateways. Because they are capable of selectively dropping IP datagrams, firewalls also restrict the connectivity of the Internet as a whole. The Internet's firewalls are thus comparable to the town walls and front gates of the Middle Ages. Screening routers correspond to general-purpose gates, while application gateways correspond to more specialized gates.

We don't see town walls anymore. Instead, countries issue passports to their citizens to use worldwide for identification and authentication. The Internet may need a similar means of security. Trusted third parties (TTPs) could issue locally or globally accepted certificates for Internet principals, and these certificates could be used to provide security services such as authentication, data confidentiality and integrity, access control, and non-repudiation services. In the following parts of this book, we are going to further elaborate on these approaches to Internet and intranet security.

REFERENCES

[1] G. McGraw, and E.W. Felton, *Java Security: Hostile Applets, Holes and Antidotes*, John Wiley & Sons, New York, NY, 1996.

[2] A.D. Rubin, D. Geer, and M.J. Ranum, *Web Security Sourcebook*, John Wiley & Sons, New York, NY, 1997.

[3] R.R. Schell, "The Internet Rules but the Emperor Has No Clothes," *Proceedings of 12th Computer Security Applications Conference*, December 1996, pp. xiii – xix.

[4] S.M. Bellovin, "An Introduction to Firewalls," Presentation held at the IEEE Computer Society Symposium on Internet Security, San Francisco, CA, November 12, 1994.

[5] Computer Security Institute, *Computer Security Issues & Trends: CSI's 1996 Firewall Product Matrix*, Spring 1996.

[6] D. Newman, H. Holzbaur, and K. Bishop, "Firewalls: Don't Get Burned," *Data Communications Magazine*, March 1997, pp. 37 – 53.

[7] R. Oppliger, "Internet Kiosk: Internet security enters the Middle Ages," *IEEE Computer*, Vol. 28, October 1995, pp. 100 – 101.

Part III

COMMUNICATION SECURITY

Chapter 9

Internet Layer Security Protocols

In this chapter, we focus on the security protocols that have been proposed for the Internet layer. In particular, we have a look at previous work in Section 9.1, the IETF IPsec WG in Section 9.2, the IP security protocol (IPSP) in Section 9.3, and some proposals for a standardized Internet key management protocol (IKMP) in Section 9.4. We finally conclude with a brief discussion of Internet layer security in Section 9.5.

9.1 PREVIOUS WORK

The idea of having a standardized network or Internet layer security protocol is not new, and several protocols had been proposed before the IETF IPsec WG even started to meet:

- The *Security Protocol 3* (SP3) is a network layer security protocol developed and proposed by the U.S. National Security Agency (NSA) and the National Institute of Science and Technology (NIST) as part of the secure data network system (SDNS) suite of security protocols [1]. SP3 uses cryptographic techniques to provide security services for the connectionless version of the OSI network layer protocol. Messages generated by the transport layer are processed by SP3 before they are passed to lower network sublayers.

- The *Network Layer Security Protocol* (NLSP) was developed by the International Organization for Standardization (ISO) to secure the connectionless network protocol (CLNP) [2]. It is an incompatible descendent of SP3.

- The *Integrated NLSP* (I-NLSP) was developed and proposed by K. Robert Glenn from NIST to provide security services for both IPv4 and CLNP. Again, the security function of I-NLSP is roughly similar to that of SP3, although some details differ. In particular, I-NLSP provides additional functionality, such as security label processing. I-NLSP was specified in an Internet draft that expired a long time ago.

- A protocol named *swIPe* is yet another experimental Internet layer security protocol developed and prototyped by John Ioannidis and Matt Blaze [3]. The prototype implementation is publicly and freely available on the Internet.[1]

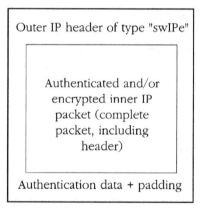

Figure 9.1   IP encapsulation as applied, for example, by the swIPe protocol.

The network and Internet layer security protocols listed above are more alike than they are different. In fact, they all use encapsulation as their enabling technique. What this basically means is that authenticated and/or encrypted network layer packets are contained within other packets. More precisely, outgoing plaintext packets are authenticated and/or encrypted and enclosed in outer network layer headers that are used to route the packets through the (inter)network. At the peer systems, the incoming packets are decapsulated, meaning that the outer network

---

[1]ftp://ftp.csua.berkeley.edu/pub/cypherpunks/swIPe/swipe.tar.Z

layer headers are stripped off and the inner packets are authenticated and/or decrypted, and forwarded to the intended destinations. Note that IP encapsulation requires no changes to the existing Internet routing infrastructure. Since authenticated and/or encrypted IP packets have an unencrypted, normal-looking outer IP header, they can be routed and processed as usual.

Figure 9.1 illustrates the idea of IP encapsulation as applied by the swIPe protocol. An authenticated and/or encrypted inner IP packet is encapsulated in an outer IP packet. This outer packet carries an IP header of protocol type swIPe.[2] In addition to the new IP header, authentication and padding data may be appended at the end of the packet as well.

9.2   IETF IPsec WG

When IPv6 was designed a couple of years ago, there was some heavy pressure to incorporate strong security functions. The primary objective was to make sure that the next generation of IP would have sufficiently strong cryptographic security mechanisms available for users who desire security. According to the design goals, the security mechanisms should be algorithm-independent so that the cryptographic algorithms can be altered without affecting the other parts of the implementation. The security mechanisms should also be useful in enforcing a wide variety of security policies, and yet they should be designed in a way that avoids adverse impacts on Internet users who do not employ security functions for the protection of their data traffic at all. The result of this effort was the specification of a comprehensive security architecture for IPv6 that comprises both authentication and encryption mechanisms.

In late 1992, the IETF chartered an IPsec WG to standardize both an IP Security Protocol (IPSP) and an Internet Key Management Protocol (IKMP). Soon it was realized that the same security architecture that had been designed for IPv6 could be adapted for IPv4 as well. Consequently, the security architecture today is common to IPv4 and IPv6. The main difference is that the security mechanisms specified in the architecture have to be retrofitted into IPv4 implementations, whereas they must be present in all IPv6 implementations right from the beginning.

The work of the IETF IPsec WG regarding IPSP and IKMP is overviewed in the following sections. We will see that IPSP and IKMP are coupled only via security associations (SAs) that are referenced by security parameters indexes (SPIs). In short, IKMP is used to set up SAs and initialize SPIs, whereas IPSP is used to

---

[2]The IANA has assigned protocol number 53 for swIPe.

employ these SAs and SPIs to cryptographically transform IP packets.

9.3   IP SECURITY PROTOCOL

We have already mentioned that the IPv6 security architecture comprises both data authentication and encryption mechanisms, and that the two mechanisms together constitute the IPSP. The two security mechanisms of IPSP can be characterized as follows:

- The *authentication header* (AH) is to provide data origin authentication and connectionless data integrity services. As such, it allows the recipient of an IP packet to verify that the originator is authentic and that the packet has not been altered during transmission.

- The *encapsulating security payload* (ESP) is to provide connectionless data confidentiality services. As such, it ensures that only the legitimate recipients of an IP packet are actually able to read it.

Both mechanisms are based on the concept of a *security association* (SA) and may be used together or separately. It should be noted at this point, however, that full protection against traffic analysis is not provided by any of the two security mechanisms. In Chapter 3, we saw that traffic padding and onion routing can be used to protect from traffic analysis. Another possibility is to use data link layer encryption in addition to some higher layer security protocol. Nevertheless, it is worth noting that only a few Internet users seem to be really concerned about traffic analysis.

For quite a long time, IPSP was specified in a set of related Internet drafts. It was not until August 1995 that the IESG approved IPSP as a Proposed Standard for the Internet. As such, the IPSP has entered the Internet standards process. The Internet drafts were rewritten and officially released in a set of related RFCs [4 – 8]. Note, however, that these RFCs don't describe an overall security architecture for the Internet; they just address Internet layer security. Also note that some of the RFCs have already been revised. For example, RFC 1825 that overviews the security architecture was updated in November 1996 in a corresponding Internet draft.[3] In the remaining part of this section, we overview the notion of an SA and further address the AH and ESP mechanisms.

---

[3]`draft-ietf-ipsec-arch-sec-01.txt`

9.3.1 Security Associations

The concept of an SA is fundamental to both the AH and ESP mechanisms. In short, an SA refers to an agreement between two or more parties on the security services that they want to use and how they are going to provide them. This agreement culminates in a common set of security-related parameters. This set typically consists of the following parameters, although some additional parameters may be supported as well:

- Authentication algorithm, mode, and keys for the AH mechanism.

- Encryption algorithm, mode, and keys for the ESP mechanism.

- The size and presence or absence of the encryption algorithm synchronization or initialization vector (IV). This information relates to the encryption algorithm and is required for the ESP mechanism only.

- The lifetime of the keys and the SA as a whole.

- The source address of the SA. In the event that more than one host actually shares the same SA, this may also be a network or subnet address.

- The sensitivity level of the secured data, such as CONFIDENTIAL, SECRET, or UNCLASSIFIED. This parameter is required only if the hosts claim to provide support for multilevel security (MLS).

When an IP packet is received, it can only be authenticated and/or decrypted if the receiver can link it with the context of an appropriate SA. Hence, the IP packet must convey a reference that points to the SA on the receiver's side. In IPsec terminology, this reference is called a *security parameters index* (SPI[4]). Each SA is uniquely identified by an SPI value and a destination address. The SPI is a 32-bit value that is normally negotiated during a key management protocol execution. A value of 0 implies that no SA currently exists, whereas the SPI values of 1 through 255 are reserved for future use.

Depending on the granularity of the keys that are used for authentication and/or encryption, three keying approaches are being distinguished to set up SAs (compare Figure 9.2):

---

[4]In earlier documents of the IETF IPsec WG, the SPI was sometimes also called a security association identifier (SAID). This term, however, should no longer be used, and should be replaced by SPI nowadays.

- The first approach, called *host-oriented keying*, has all users on one host share the same session key for use on traffic destined for all users on another host.

- The second approach, called *user-oriented keying*, lets each user on one host have one or more unique session keys for the traffic destined for another host; such session keys are not shared with other users.

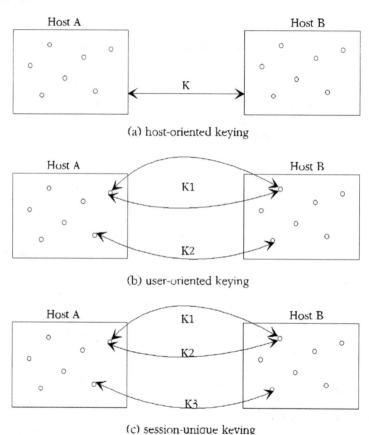

(a) host-oriented keying

(b) user-oriented keying

(c) session-unique keying

Figure 9.2   Three keying approaches for IPSP.

- The third approach, called *session-unique keying*, has a single session key being assigned to a given IP address, upper-layer protocol, and port number triple. For example, a user's FTP session may use a different key than the same user's Telnet session. In systems claiming support for MLS, a user typically has at least one key per sensitivity level in use.

The three keying approaches for IPSP are illustrated in Figure 9.2. In the case of (a) host-oriented keying, a single session key is shared between host A and host B. This key is used to secure all communications between the two hosts. In the case of (b) user-oriented keying, each user pair has one particular session key in common. Hence, if a user on host A communicates with another user on host B, they typically use a unique session key for all communications that may take place between them. This is slightly different in the case of (c) session-unique keying, where the two users may share one particular session key for each session that may take place between them. In this case, it may happen that two Telnet sessions between the same accounts are secured with different keys.

From a security point of view, it is obvious that user-oriented and session-unique keying are superior to host-oriented keying. This is due to the fact that in many cases, a single computer system will have at least two suspicious users that do not mutually trust each other. When host-oriented keying is used and mutually suspicious users exist, it is sometimes possible for a user to determine the host-oriented key via well-known methods, such as a chosen plaintext attack. Once this user has improperly obtained the key in use, he or she can read another user's encrypted traffic or even forge traffic from this user. When user-oriented or session-unique keying is used, certain kinds of attack from one user onto another user's data traffic are simply not possible.

It is also important to note that the use and handling of SAs and SPI values is different in situations where IP packets are sent to a unique receiver or a group of receivers:

- When packets are sent to a unique receiver (e.g., through a unicast IP address), the SPI is usually chosen by the receiver. It typically is the index into a local table of security contexts maintained by the receiver. The SPI to use is, in fact, a parameter of this particular SA and must be remembered to identify the SA accordingly.

- When packets are sent to a group of receivers (e.g., through a multicast IP address), the SPI must be common to all members of the group. Each member should be able to correlate the combination of group address and SPI with the key, algorithm, and other parameters used to secure group communications.

In general, SA and SPI management in a multicast environment is much more difficult than in a unicast environment. This is due to the fact that in a multicast environment all members of a host group must have the same key(s) to secure the data traffic accordingly. For example, we will see that the Photuris key management protocol and some related protocols, such as SKEME and OAKLEY, are not very useful in multicast environments since the Diffie-Hellman key exchange they use and depend on is not easily extendable to more than two parties. Similarly, we will see that the SKIP protocol addresses multicast only once a group interchange key (GIK) has been securely distributed to the legitimate members of the group.

As of this writing, multicast key distribution is an active area of research in the published literature. In spite of the fact that there is some work going on to develop conference key distribution systems (CKDS) for multicast environments, most of these schemes are not yet very efficient and do not scale well. Today, the distribution of group keys still relies on the existence of a key distribution center (KDC) that provides the legitimate members of a group with the key(s) they need to participate in secure communications [9]. In this case, however, it is perfectly reasonable to use one of the key management protocols mentioned above and further addressed in Section 9.4 to set up SAs between the group's KDC and each group member. There are some other approaches to handling key distribution in a multicast environment. For example, one approach is to reuse a multicast routing infrastructure to distribute multicast SAs, SPIs, and corresponding session keys [10,11]. Another approach is to delegate the task of controlling a group to the members of the group. This approach has led to a group key management protocol (GKMP[5]), mainly developed by SPARTA, Inc. A somewhat related approach is to introduce participants registration, and to couple this registration with an initial key distribution [12,13].

9.3.2   Authentication Header

The IPSP authentication header (AH) mechanism is to provide data origin authentication and connectionless data integrity services for IP packets. Depending on which cryptographic algorithm is actually in use and how keying is performed, it may provide non-repudiation of origin services as well. More recently, the AH mechanism has also been extended to optionally support replay protection. This option may be selected when an SA is established. As the AH mechanism does not provide data confidentiality services, implementations thereof may be widely deployed, even in countries where controls on encryption would preclude deployment of technology that potentially offered data confidentiality services.

---

[5]The GKMP is specified in the Internet drafts `draft-harney-gkmp-arch-*.txt` (protocol architecture) and `draft-harney-gkmp-spec-*.txt` (protocol specification).

The IPSP AH mechanism provides security by adding authentication data to IP packets. The authentication data is computed by using a cryptographic authentication algorithm and a corresponding key. The sender computes the authentication data prior to sending the IP packet, and the receiver verifies the data upon reception. One problem, however, is due to the fact that some fields of the IP packet header may change in transit. In the IPv6 header, for example, the Hop Count field value is decremented at each hop. If the routing header is used, the IPv6 destination and the next address are swapped at every relay of the source route, while the Address Index field value is decremented accordingly. In addition to that, some hop-by-hop options may also be updated in transit, as indicated by the change en route bit (C) of the option type. In the IPv4 header, the TTL field value may change in transit as well. Consequently, all changing fields must be omitted when computing and verifying the authentication data of the AH. What this usually means is that the sender must prepare a temporary version of the IP packet before computing the authentication data. This temporary version must be independent of any modification in transit. For example, the sender must perform the following steps to prepare authentication data computation for an IPv6 packet:

- The Hop Count field must be set to zero.

- If the routing header is used, the IP Destination field must be set to the final destination, the routing header content must be set to the value that it should have upon arrival, and the address index must be set accordingly.

- Options whose C bit is set must not be taken into account when computing the authentication data. Their content is temporarily replaced by a set of zero bytes.

Afterwards, the authentication data must be computed using a cryptographic algorithm. Note that conventional checksum algorithms, such as the 16-bit checksum used in IP or the 16- or 32-bit polynomial checksums typically used in serial links and Ethernet networks, should not be used here. Anybody who has sufficient knowledge of mathematics will understand that these algorithms are far too weak. Mainly due to their linearity, it is fairly simple to tweak some bits in a message so that the checksum remains the same. These checksum algorithms have been designed to protect messages against random errors caused by noisy channels, and not against determined offenders. Nonlinear cryptographic algorithms are required for message authentication instead.

The cryptographic authentication algorithm that was originally proposed for AH computation and verification is keyed MD5. The use of a keyed one-way hash function, such as MD5, to compute and verify message authentication codes (MACs) was originally proposed by Li Gong [14] and Gene Tsudik [15]. There were also some preliminary thoughts about using keyed one-way hash functions to secure messages in SNMP version 2. Prior to the use of keyed one-way hash functions, the usual way to compute and verify a MAC was

- To use a secret key cryptosystem such as DES;

- To encrypt the message in CBC mode;

- To take the last ciphertext block as MAC.

The idea of using a keyed one-way hash function for message authentication is to concatenate the message with a secret authentication key and to use the one-way hash function to compute a corresponding MAC from the concatenated message. Note that the one-way hash function should be collision-resistant, a feature usually attributed to MD5, SHA-1, RIPEM, and RIPEM-160. Also note that various methods can serve as concatenation functions, and that the secret prefix, secret suffix, and envelope methods were originally proposed in [15]. Keyed MD5 as proposed for IPSP operates by combining the message with a secret authentication key and then computing an MD5 hash value from the result. Referring to Tsudik's envelope method, the key is both prepended and appended to the message in order to prevent certain types of attacks. The exact sequence of operation is as follows:

- A temporary version of the message is prepared as described above.

- As MD5 operates on blocks of 16 bytes, the message is padded with null bytes to the next 16-byte boundary. Additionally, the authentication key is also padded with null bytes to the 16-byte boundary.

- The authentication data is computed as an MD5 hash value of a message obtained by concatenating the authentication key, the message, and again the authentication key.

The result of this general procedure is a hash value of a certain length. For example, using MD5 and RIPEM the result is a 128-bit hash value, whereas using SHA-1 and RIPEM-160 the result is a 160-bit hash value.

In general, the authentication algorithm is negotiated as part of the SA establishment. Keyed MD5 is specified as the default algorithm in RFC 1828 to make sure that all IPSP implementations can at least use one common algorithm [7]. One can reasonably expect that other algorithms will be used in the future, algorithms that will be faster to compute or harder to break than keyed MD5. For example, RFC 1852 specifies the use of keyed SHA-1 instead of keyed MD5 [16]. Note, however, that the RFC that specifies keyed SHA-1 is experimental and not submitted to the Internet standards track.

Remember our discussion in Section 4.1, where we have elaborated on the feasibility of building a machine to find collisions in MD5. It thus makes a lot of sense today to use SHA-1 instead of MD5. In addition, recent results in cryptographic research have shown that the use of a keyed one-way hash function in envelope mode is also vulnerable to specific attacks. It is therefore recommended to use alternative MAC constructions to compute and verify keyed one-way hash values. One-way hash functions were not originally designed to be used for message authentication. In particular, they are not keyed primitives, and it is not clear how they can be keyed in a secure way. Thus, one ought to be careful in using one-way hash functions for message authentication. A well-justified MAC construction is one under which the security of the resulting MAC can be related as closely as possible to the (assumed) security properties of the underlying one-way hash function. This rationale has led to some alternative MAC constructions that were independently proposed by Bart Preneel and Paul van Oorschot (MDx-MAC construction) [17], as well as by Mihir Bellare, Ran Canetti, and Hugo Krawczyk (NMAC and HMAC constructions) [18].

The HMAC construction is of utmost interest today. It can be used with any iterative one-way hash function h in combination with a shared message authentication key K. Remember that a one-way hash function is iterative if data is hashed by iterating a basic compression function on blocks of data. In this context, B denotes the byte length of such blocks ($B = 64$ for all the above-mentioned examples of iterative one-way hash functions), and L denotes the byte length of the resulting hash values ($L = 16$ for MD5 and RIPEM; $L = 20$ for SHA-1 and RIPEM-160). The authentication key K can be of any length up to B. Applications that use keys longer than B bytes will first hash the key using h and then use the resultant L byte string as the actual key for the HMAC construction. In any case, the minimal recommended key length for K is L bytes. In addition to that, two fixed and different 64-byte strings *ipad* and *opad* are defined as follows:

$$ipad = \text{the byte 0x36 repeated } B \text{ times}$$
$$opad = \text{the byte 0x5C repeated } B \text{ times}$$

The terms *ipad* and *opad* are mnemonics for inner and outer padding data. The HMAC construction takes as input the message M and the authentication key K, and produces as output the following expression (remember that a comma refers to concatenation):

$$HMAC_K(M) = h(K \oplus opad, h(K \oplus ipad, M))$$

Note that the HMAC construction uses the one-way hash function h as black box. Consequently, no modifications to the code for h are required to implement the HMAC construction. This makes it easy to use library code for h, and also makes it easy to replace a particular hash function with another, should the need to do so arise. The different realizations of HMAC are further referred to as HMAC-MD5, HMAC-SHA, and HMAC-RIPEMD.

A well-known practice with message authentication is to truncate the output of the MAC and output only part of the bits. As a matter of fact, Preneel and van Oorschot have shown some analytical advantages of truncating the output of hash-based MAC functions [17]. However, the results in this area are not absolute as for the overall security advantages of truncation and should be considered with care. In general, there are both advantages and disadvantages: advantages are that less information on the hash result is available to a potential attacker, whereas disadvantages are that the attacker must predict less bits. Applications of the HMAC construction can choose to truncate the result by outputting the t leftmost bits of the HMAC construction for some parameter t. Furthermore, the authors of [18] recommend that the output length t be not less than half the length of the hash value and not less than 80 bits. In general, the expression HMAC-h-t refers to a realization of the HMAC construction that uses hash function h with t bits of output. For example, HMAC-SHA1-96 denotes HMAC computed using SHA-1 with the output truncated to 96 bits. If the parameter t is not specified, it is assumed that all bits of the hash value are output.

The HMAC construction was recently chosen as the mandatory authentication transform for the IPSP AH mechanism. For this purpose, the HMAC construction has been described in a corresponding RFC [19]. Other Internet security protocols, such as the Secure Sockets Layer (SSL) protocol or the Secure Hypertext Transfer Protocol (S-HTTP), are being redefined to adapt and make use of the HMAC construction as well. We focus on these security protocols later in this part of the book.

The use of a keyed one-way hash function is attractive due to its simplicity and efficiency. However, it is also possible to use public key cryptography for AH computation and verification. In this case, the sender would digitally sign a message and the receiver would verify the digital signature accordingly. However, the use of public key cryptography not only requires more computation power on the sender's and receiver's sides, but also larger authentication data fields. A typical size of a digital signature is 1,024 bits, which is eight times as long as a keyed MD5 value. The main argument for using public key cryptography is notably the ability to provide non-repudiation of origin services. Note that if keyed one-way hash functions or secret key cryptography are used for AH computation and verification, it is always possible for the sender to repudiate having produced and appended specific authentication data. As the receiver holds the same authentication key, he or she won't be able to prove (for example, in court) that the sender has produced the authentication data. In situations where non-repudiation of origin services are required, the use of public key cryptography may seem to be mandatory. It is not clear at this point whether the Internet layer would be the right layer to provide this kind of functionality. An alternative approach would be to have specific applications provide non-repudiation services.

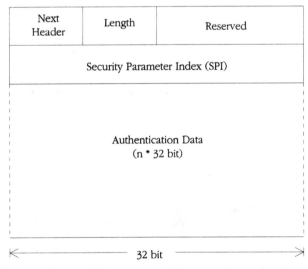

Figure 9.3 The IPSP authentication header format.

The format of the IPSP authentication header is simple and straightforward. It is illustrated in Figure 9.3. The AH starts with a 64-bit header that comprises the following fields:

- The 8-bit *Next Header* field refers to the type of the next payload header after the AH. The value of this field is chosen from the set of IP protocol numbers assigned by the IANA.

- The 8-bit *Length* field specifies the length of the authentication data in 32-bit words.

- The 16-bit *Reserved* field is reserved for future use. In the meantime, it must be set to zero.

- The 32-bit *SPI* field identifies the SA for the IP packet on the receiver' side.

This fixed 64-bit header is followed by the actual authentication data, encoded as a variable number n of 32-bit words. Typical values for n are 4 in the case of MD4, MD5, and RIPEM (128 bit), and 5 in the case of SHA-1 and RIPEM-160 (160 bit). Remember our discussion on using public key cryptography to digitally sign IP packets. In this case, the authentication data field could be 1,024 bits long, and the resulting value for n would then be 32.

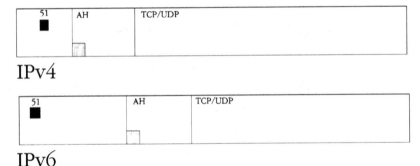

Figure 9.4   The placement of the AH in IPv4 and IPv6.

The IANA has assigned protocol number 51 for the IPSP AH. So, the header immediately preceding the AH should include the number 51 in the corresponding Header field. Figure 9.4 illustrates the placement of the AH in IPv4 and IPv6:

- In IPv4, the Protocol field of the IP header (black rectangle) must include the number 51 and the corresponding AH must be inserted between the IP header and the protocol data unit that is carried within the IP packet. Similarly, the Next Header field of the AH (grey rectangle) must include the number of the protocol that is transported by IP, such as 1 for ICMP, 6 for TCP, or 17 for UDP.

- In IPv6, the situation is simpler, since the AH is one of the generic extension headers. In this case, the extension header immediately preceding the AH must include the number 51 in the Next Header field (black rectangle), and the Next Header field of the AH (grey rectangle) must include either the number of the next extension header or the number of the protocol that is transported by the IP. For example, an authenticated TCP segment may contain an IPv6 header, an AH, and the TCP payload. But several variations are possible, for example when a routing header is inserted before the AH or when end-to-end options are inserted between the AH and the TCP payload.

It is important to note that the presence or absence of an AH does not change the behavior of the IP, nor in fact of any other network or transport layer protocol that is transported by the IP. The presence of an AH simply provides explicit insurance for the authenticity of the corresponding IP packet. TCP/IP protocol implementations may be instructed to reject IP packets that are not properly authenticated, and this might be a realistic policy in the near future. The use of the AH mechanism should .be sufficient to prevent most of the IP address spoofing and session hijacking attacks observed on the Internet today.

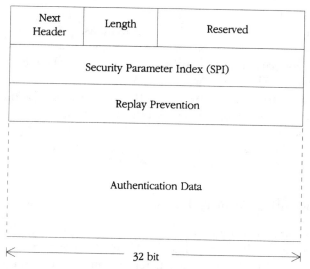

Figure 9.5   The revised IPSP authentication header format.

More recently, a revised format of the IPSP authentication header has been proposed as illustrated in Figure 9.5. Compared to the current AH format, there are two major differences:

- First, an optional 32-bit *Replay Prevention* field is inserted between the SPI and the Authentication Data field to provide protection against replay attacks and to guarantee that each IP packet exchanged between two parties is unique. It is up to the SA to specify whether replay prevention is used. If replay prevention is not used, the authentication data field may immediately follow the SPI.

- Second, the proposal to truncate keyed one-way hash values to 96 bits has been adopted for the AH HMAC construction. The value of 96 bits is commonly agreed to for both HMAC-MD5 and HMAC-SHA.

There is an RFC specifying HMAC-MD5 IP authentication with replay prevention [20] and a related Internet draft[6] specifying the same for SHA-1 instead of MD5.

In summary, the use of the IPSP AH mechanism has both advantages and disadvantages. On the positive side, the AH mechanism provides stronger security than now exists on the Internet. Also, the AH mechanism should not affect the exportability or significantly increase the implementation costs of corresponding products. On the negative side, however, the AH mechanism increases IP processing costs and communications latency in participating systems. The increased latency is primarily due to the calculation of the authentication data by the sender and the calculation and comparison of the authentication data by the receiver for each IP packet containing an AH.

Finally, we want to point out that the AH mechanism may be implemented by a security gateway on behalf of the hosts on the intranet protected by this gateway. However, this mode of operation is not encouraged. Whenever possible, the AH mechanism should be used from the sender to the final destination of an IP packet, so that full end-to-end protection may be provided.

9.3.3   Encapsulating Security Payload

In the previous subsection, we have overviewed and discussed the IPSP AH mechanism. In particular, we have seen that the AH mechanism does not transform the payload data of an IP packet, and that it remains in the clear; subject, for example, to eavesdropping. Consequently, another security mechanism must be deployed if data confidentiality services are required. In IPSP terminology, this security mechanism is called the encapsulating security payload (ESP). In short, the ESP mechanism provides data confidentiality services by encrypting and encapsulating

---

[6]`draft-ietf-ipsec-ah-hmac-sha-*.txt`

either the payload of an IP packet (transport mode) or the entire IP packet (tunnel mode). We will discuss the two modes for both IPv4 and IPv6 later in this section.

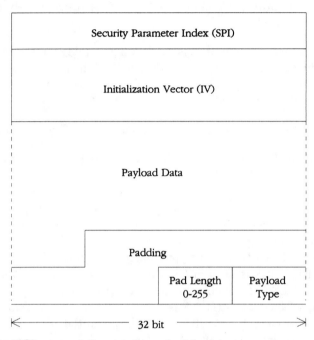

Figure 9.6   The IPSP encapsulating security payload format.

The format of the IPSP encapsulating security payload is illustrated in Figure 9.6. It includes the following fields:

- The 32-bit *SPI* field refers to the security parameters index on the receiver' side.

- The *Initialization Vector* (IV) field is composed of a variable number of 32-bit words, where the precise number is defined as a parameter of the SA. The content of the IV is normally the result of a random number generator. Its randomness is propagated to the remaining words of the message by a block cipher used either in cipher block chaining (CBC) mode or in one of the feedback modes that turn it into a stream cipher. When the size of the IV is 32 bits, a 64-bit IV is usually formed from the 32 bits concatenated with the bitwise complement of the 32-bit value.

- The variable-length *Payload Data* field includes the data that is encrypted with the algorithm specified in the current SA. Depending on whether the ESP mechanism is used in transport or tunnel mode, the payload data refers either to the encrypted upper-layer payload of an IP packet, or to an entirely encrypted and encapsulated IP packet.

- The variable-length *Padding* field is filled with preferably random bits. The length of the Padding field is chosen to make the length of the Payload Data and Padding fields equal to 6 modulo 8. For example, if the payload data length is 41, 5 bytes of padding are typically added.

- The 8-bit *Pad Length* field indicates the total length of the Padding field.

- Finally, the 8-bit *Payload Type* field includes the protocol number for the payload data.

The ESP has been designed so that only the SPI and the IV, if present, remain in the clear. Other fields, such as the Padding, Pad Length, and Payload Type fields, are encrypted together with the payload data. The precise format of the ESP depends on the particular encryption algorithm in use. The default algorithm suggested in RFC 1829 is DES in CBC mode [8]. But similar to keyed MD5 for authentication, DES-CBC is only a default algorithm for encryption. Other algorithms can be selected when the SA is being established. For example, RFC 1851 specifies the experimental use of Triple-DES [21], and the use of RC5 and CAST is specified in related Internet drafts. Note, however, that export, import, and use of specific encryption algorithms may be regulated in some countries.

The IANA has assigned protocol number 50 for IPSP ESP. So, the header immediately preceding the ESP should always include the number 50 in the Protocol or Next Header field. More precisely, the Protocol field of an IPv4 header should include the number 50 and the corresponding ESP must be placed as payload of the IP packet. Similarly, the Payload Type field of the ESP must include the protocol number of the encapsulated upper-layer protocol. In IPv6, the ESP header is always the last extension header. So, the Protocol field of the extension header immediately preceding the ESP should include the number 50. Let's now have a brief look at the ESP in transport and tunnel mode.

Transport Mode

We have already mentioned that the ESP mechanism in transport mode is used to encrypt and encapsulate the upper-layer protocol data that are carried as payload of an IP packet, such as ICMP, UDP, or TCP data. In this case, the bandwidth is approximately preserved, since there are no additional encrypted IP headers or options.

In ESP transport mode, the sending host first selects the upper-layer protocol data from the IP packet to be sent and encapsulates them in an ESP according to the format described above. Next, the sending host obtains the SA using the user identification and destination IP address and applies the cryptographic transformation defined by the SA to encrypt the payload data, padding, pad length, payload type, and possibly IV fields. The resulting ESP is then included as payload of the IP packet to be sent. Obviously, the IP header's protocol field is set to 50, and the ESP payload type field is set to the upper-layer protocol that is now encapsulated in the ESP. On the other side, the receiving host processes the IP header and plaintext part of the ESP to obtain the SPI value. This value is then used as an index into a local SPI table to find the negotiated SA parameters and cryptographic keys. The negotiated form of the IV also determines the size of the IV field. These bytes are removed, and an appropriate 64-bit IV value is constructed. Finally, the encrypted part of the ESP is decrypted using the encryption algorithm and key specified in the SA, as well as the IV just recovered.

Tunnel Mode

We have seen that ESP in transport mode is used to encrypt and encapsulate the upper-layer protocol data of IP packets. ESP tunnel mode uses a different technique. In this mode, entire network layer protocol data units, such as IP packets or IPX packets for Novell NetWare, can be encrypted and encapsulated in new IP packets. Tunnel-mode ESP is primarily used by security gateways for packets that are not originating on that gateway but must be securely transmitted on the Internet. Note, however, that tunnel-mode ESP can also be used to provide some form of partial traffic flow confidentiality service. As a matter of fact, tunnel-mode ESP can be used to create a secure tunnel between two security gateways so that anybody eavesdropping on the communications between the two gateways would not be able to learn what hosts are actually sending and receiving data behind the gateways. Consequently, IP tunnels and virtual private networks (VPNs) make heavy use of tunnel-mode ESP. We will come to these issues later in this chapter.

In ESP tunnel mode, the sending host obtains the SA using the user identification and destination IP address and applies the corresponding cryptographic transformation to encrypt the entire IP packet. The encrypted IP packet is then encapsulated in an ESP, and the resulting ESP is included as payload in a new IP packet. Obviously, the protocol field (in IPv4) or next header field (in IPv6) of the new IP header is set to 50, whereas the payload type field of the ESP is set to 4 (for IPv4) or 6 (for IPv6). As such, the new IP packet is routed through the Internet. On the other side, the receiving host processes the unencrypted IP header and plaintext part of the ESP to obtain the SPI value. This value is then used as an index into a local SPI table to find the negotiated SA parameters and cryptographic keys. The negotiated form of the IV also determines the size of the IV field. These bytes are removed, and an appropriate 64-bit IV value is constructed. The encrypted part of the ESP is decrypted using the encryption algorithm and key specified in the SA, as well as the IV just recovered. Finally, the receiving host is able to extract the IP packet that has been tunneled in ESP for transmission through the Internet.

Similar to the IPSP AH mechanism, the use of the IPSP ESP mechanism has both advantages and disadvantages. On the positive side, the ESP mechanism provides stronger security than now exists on the Internet. Also, it should not affect or significantly increase the implementation costs of corresponding products. On the negative side, however, hosts that implement the ESP mechanism experience some performance impact. First, there is the additional processing required for handling the ESP protocol at the sending and receiving hosts. Second, the sending host and the receiving host also expend some processor time to perform actual encryption and decryption. This additional processing is often directly proportional to the size of the packets and can increase the total time and the latency to transfer a packet. The actual performance impact depends on the specific processor and the ESP implementation in use. In certain cases, it may be preferable to incorporate appropriate additional hardware that encrypts and decrypts data traffic more easily. Also, the use of the ESP mechanism directly affects the exportability of corresponding products in some countries.

Note that the AH and ESP mechanisms have been designed independently and can be applied separately or together to an IP packet. For example, if data confidentiality is not required, the AH mechanism can be used alone. Only if data confidentiality is also required should the ESP mechanism be used as well. IP packets using both the AH and ESP mechanisms are not prohibited. It is, however, recommended in this case to use a security transform that includes cryptographic checksum in the encrypted data. There is an Internet draft[7] specifying a combined DES-CBC, HMAC and replay prevention security transform, as well as a related Internet draft[8] that specifies the use of Triple-DES instead of DES. The corresponding

---

[7]`draft-ietf-ipsec-esp-des-md5-*.txt`
[8]`draft-ietf-ipsec-esp-3des-md5-*.txt`

header formats are illustrated in Figure 9.7. In addition to the usual ESP header fields, there is a 32-bit *Replay Prevention Field* and a variable-length *HMAC Digest* field. So far, HMAC truncation has not been specified for this security transform. It is, however, assumed that this will happen fairly soon.

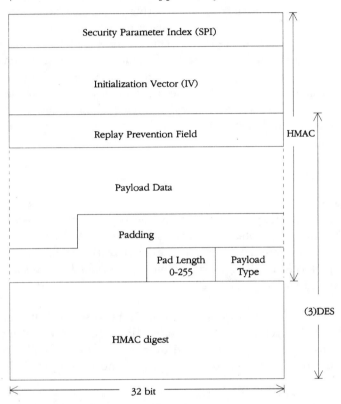

Figure 9.7   The DES-CBC, HMAC and replay prevention security transform header format.

9.4   INTERNET KEY MANAGEMENT PROTOCOL

The establishment of an SA requires shared keys that are known only to the legitimate members of the SA. For a few parties, these keys can be manually configured or distributed through out-of-band mechanisms, such as secure electronic mail or private phone calls. However, efficient key management protocols are required for a large number of parties with frequent additions or removals. As a matter of fact, the use and deployment of IPSP will require a standardized and efficient key management protocol, and the IETF IPsec WG is working towards a corresponding *Internet key management protocol* (IKMP).

Since the submission of the IPSP to the Internet standards track, the IETF IPsec WG has been struggling with several competing key management protocol proposals. In September 1996, a decision was made to put a key management protocol forward and proceed towards an IKMP. This protocol is basically a combination of two key management protocols. In spite of the fact that the situation is somehow cleared up today, it is still interesting and useful to overview and discuss the various key management protocols that have been proposed in the recent past. Without going into the details of the corresponding technical specifications, we are going to examine the protocols next. Prototype implementations exist and are readily available for all protocols.

9.4.1   MKMP

Prior to the standardization of IPSP and IKMP, Pau-Chen Cheng, Juan Garay, Amir Herzberg, and Hugo Krawczyk from the IBM Thomas J. Watson Research Center in Yorktown Heights, New York, had designed and prototyped a security architecture for the Internet layer. At the heart of this architecture is an *IP secure tunnel protocol* (IPST) and a corresponding *modular key management protocol* (MKMP) layered on top of UDP [22]:

- IPST follows the spirit of discussions in the IETF IPsec WG. It is an encapsulation protocol that defines the format of an IP packet that encapsulates another IP packet to be securely transmitted over the Internet. Similar to IPSP, the encapsulated IP packets may be authenticated and/or encrypted.

- MKMP refers to a (set of) protocol(s) that has been designed for the management of cryptographic keys as required for SAs in IPST. The protocol provides mechanisms for the derivation and periodic refreshing of session keys as required for the multiple cryptographic functions used with a single SA.

IPST and MKMP have been prototyped on AIX 3.2.5 and are being shipped with IBM's NetSP Secure Network Gateway firewall products. The IPST and MKMP functionality has been placed inside the kernel IP module and not in a network device driver such as for the swIPe prototype implementation mentioned previously. In addition to that, IBM has submitted several Internet Drafts describing the MKMP approach to the IETF IPsec WG for possible inclusion as part of the evolving IKMP. These Internet Drafts expired a long time ago and IBM is no longer promoting the MKMP approach. However, we will see later in this chapter that some design principles from the MKMP approach have been adapted by other key management protocols.

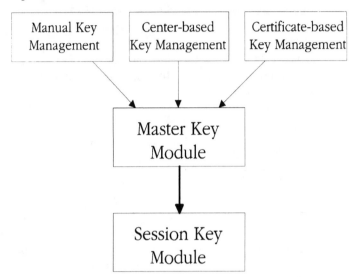

Figure 9.8   The two modules of the MKMP approach.

Figure 9.8 illustrates the MKMP approach. It assumes that a typical key management scheme consists of two modules:

- A master key module in which a master key may be exchanged or agreed upon between the communicating parties;

- A session key module in which a master key may be used for the derivation, agreement, and/or refreshing of session keys to be applied in the cryptographic transforms.

The split into two modules is not mandatory, and in fact, MKMP is unique in making this separation explicit. Assuming that master keys may be derived using any of the established methods — such as manual, center-based, or certificate-based key distribution — the MKMP provides a solution for the session key module only.

An important design goal of MKMP was simplicity and efficiency, namely to keep both the number of messages exchanged between entities and the computational overhead to a minimum. Another goal was to guarantee a basic security principle for session keys, namely that even if an eavesdropper were able to derive a session key, future session keys and the master key are not compromised.

Let's assume that the two principals, A and B, already share a master key K from the master key module and a nonce, N_b, from a previous MKMP execution. Keeping a shared nonce is not essential and can even be replaced by using timestamps or by adding an extra message flow to the protocol. Note, however, that the nonce also serves the purpose of alleviating the effect of a denial of service attack. In any case, the nonces do not require confidentiality and can be transmitted in the clear. A and B can now use the following handshake protocol to agree on a new session key SK:

$$1 : A \longrightarrow B : N_a, \langle N_a, N_b \rangle K$$
$$2 : B \longrightarrow A : N_b', \langle N_b', N_a \rangle K$$

In step 1, A provides B with both a nonce N_a and a MAC for the concatenation of N_a and N_b, computed with the master key K. B verifies the authenticity of the MAC and returns in the positive case another nonce N_b' and a MAC for the concatenation of N_b' and N_a, again computed with K in step 2. Finally A and B both use f_K, a pseudorandom function keyed with K, to come up with a session key $SK = f_K(N_b', N_a)$. Note that the session key is never transmitted between A and B. This avoids the need to authenticate and/or encrypt the key. Also note that usually one requires more than one session key for a particular SA. For example, one needs different keys for authentication and encryption, and in some cases the keys are even used unidirectionally. To derive more than one key is straightforward: instead of a single application of $f_K(.)$, one applies $f_K(tid,.)$ for each required key, where tid is a unique transformation identifier that identifies the algorithm for which the key is to be used, the key length, the direction, and some other parameters.

Obviously, the MKMP is of limited practical value since it does not provide a solution for the distribution of master keys. It is therefore assumed that IBM will adopt IPSP and IKMP as soon as standardization is complete. With regard to MKMP, more detailed design information, as well as source and binary code, can be obtained from the authors of [22].

9.4.2   SKIP

Most key distribution and management schemes and protocols are session-oriented, meaning that they establish and maintain an SA that lasts a certain amount of time. In contrast, many network and Internet layer protocols, such as IP and CLNP, are connectionless in nature and provide a connectionless datagram delivery service accordingly. In order to use a session-oriented key distribution scheme with IP, one has to create and implement a pseudosession layer underneath IP for the establishment and updating of IP traffic authentication and encryption keys. While this is possible, it may be far less cumbersome to use a scheme that does not entail the overhead of such a pseudosession layer. This rationale has led to the development of the *simple key-management for Internet protocols* (SKIP) [23]. SKIP has been designed to secure connectionless datagram delivery services, such as those provided by IP. The distinguishing feature of SKIP is that it requires no prior communication in order to establish and change IP traffic authentication and encryption keys. Instead of using session-oriented keys, SKIP uses packet-oriented keys that are communicated inline with the IP packets. The development and implementation of SKIP is mainly driven by Ashar Aziz, from the Internet Commerce Group of Sun Microsystems, Inc. The base SKIP protocol and its subprotocols are specified in a set of related Internet drafts.[9]

SKIP utilizes the fact that if each principal has a certified Diffie-Hellman public key, then each pair of principals implicitly shares a mutually authenticated key that is computable based solely on knowledge of the other principal's certified Diffie-Hellman public key. SKIP therefore requires an automated distribution and retrieval of Diffie-Hellman public key certificates, such as those provided by the certificate discovery protocol (CDP).

Let's assume that all principals share a large prime p and a generator g. Let's also assume that principal A has a private Diffie-Hellman key x_A and a corresponding public key $y_A = g^{x_A} (\bmod\ p)$, and that principal B has another private key x_B and a corresponding public key $y_B = g^{x_B} (\bmod\ p)$. Both public keys are distributed in the form of public key certificates. According to the Diffie-Hellman key exchange, A and B then share the secret key $K'_{AB} = g^{x_A x_B} (\bmod\ p)$. This key is implicit and does not need to be communicated explicitly to either principal. Each principal can compute the shared secret based on knowledge of the other principal's identity and public key certificate. This mutually authenticated long-term secret key K'_{AB} can then be used to derive a master or key encrypting key (KEK) K_{AB} to provide IP packet based authentication and encryption. K_{AB} can be derived, for example, by taking the low-order key size bits of K'_{AB}. However, that there are at least two reasons for updating the master key periodically:

- First, it minimizes the exposure of any given KEK, making cryptanalysis more

---

[9]`draft-ietf-ipsec-skip-*.txt`

difficult.

- Second, updating the master key prevents the reuse of compromised packet keys.

The master key is updated by sending in the packet a counter n that only increments and is never decremented. K_{AB} then becomes a function of this counter n as follows: $K_{ABn} = h(K'_{AB}, n)$. Again, h refers to a one-way hash or pseudo-random function, such as e.g. MD5, SHA-1, or RIPEM. A simple and stateless way of implementing n is to let n be equal to the number of time units since the more recent of A or B's certificate. In the absence of a clock, n can be constructed simply by using a counter.

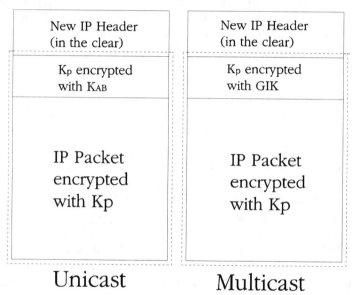

New IP Header (in the clear)	New IP Header (in the clear)
Kp encrypted with KAB	Kp encrypted with GIK
IP Packet encrypted with Kp	IP Packet encrypted with Kp
Unicast	Multicast

Figure 9.9   The use of SKIP to encrypt unicast and multicast packets.

In order to encrypt an individual IP packet, A randomly generates a packet key K_p and envelopes the packet with this key and the master key or KEK that he implicitly shares with the intended receiver B. More precisely, A encrypts both the packet with K_p and K_p with K_{AB}, and encapsulates both ciphertexts in a new IP packet. Note that since K_{AB} can be cached for efficiency, it allows packet keys to be modified very rapidly without incurring the computational overhead of public key operations. The packet keys can be changed as frequently as desired in line with a key management policy. If necessary, packet keys can be changed on a per-packet basis. Furthermore, since the keys are communicated in the packets themselves, there is no need to incur the overhead and complexity of a pseudo session layer underneath IP. When B receives the encrypted packet, he looks up A's certificate. Using the corresponding long-term public key and his own long-term private key, B can compute K'_{AB} and hence K_{AB}. Using K_{AB}, B can finally decrypt both K_p and the entire IP packet.

Figure 9.9 illustrates the use of SKIP to encrypt unicast and multicast packets. Previously in this chapter, we have seen that the traditional approach for key distribution in a multicast environment is to set up and run a KDC that distributes the traffic key(s) to the legitimate and authorized members of a group. This one shared key is then used by the group members to encrypt and decrypt data traffic. There are at least two problems related to this approach:

- The first problem is related to the fact that key change can't be done efficiently and does not scale well to large groups. Key change policies need to be a function of the amount of data encrypted with a given key, and not just a function of time alone. This means that for high-speed data transmission links the keys must be updated far more frequently than for slower links, for the same key change policy. For a large number of members in a multicast group, however, it may become increasingly difficult or prohibitive for a multicast KDC to be rapidly supplying updated keys to all group members.

- The second problem with using the same key by all members of a multicast group is that it precludes the use of certain stream ciphers. This is because using the same key will result in the same key stream being used to encrypt different plaintexts. Since key stream reuse is catastrophic to the security of some stream ciphers, it should be avoided generally. Nevertheless, it is important to allow stream ciphers to be used in conjunction with IP multicast. A common use of IP multicast is conferencing, especially videoconferencing. Since video is a demanding application in terms of speed and throughput, it is important to allow the use of ciphers that can be efficiently implemented in software. Some of the most widely used and efficient ciphers are stream ciphers such as RC4. Due to key stream reuse issues, it is not possible to use a stream cipher like RC4 for IP multicast if all members of the multicast group use the same traffic key.

A simple modification of the basic SKIP protocol solves both problems. Instead of distributing a traffic key to the group members, a group owner may distribute a group interchange key (GIK) to them. This GIK is in turn used as a KEK, similar to the way K_{AB} is used for unicast traffic. In order to send encrypted data to a multicast group, a member first has to request the GIK from the group owner. The group owner's identity has to be known to the requesting principal accordingly. This request is made using the unicast SKIP protocol. Once the group owner determines that the requesting principal is on the group's access control list (ACL), it will provide the GIK to him or her. The requesting principal then encrypts the multicast traffic using one (or more) randomly generated packet key(s). The packet keys are in turn encrypted using the GIK, and sent inline with the corresponding IP packets. Note that changing the multicast traffic encryption key is simple. Each source can do this by randomly generating a new traffic key and communicating it inline with the multicast IP packets (encrypted using the GIK). Multicast traffic encryption keys can be updated rapidly, even every packet if so desired, with no further communications overhead. Also note that since each source of encrypted traffic generates random traffic keys, all sources of encrypted traffic naturally use different keys. This allows any kind of stream cipher to be used for multicast traffic encryption as well.

So far, the description of SKIP has been provided using the number theoretic constructions of the classic Diffie-Hellman key exchange, namely exponentiation over a prime field. However, SKIP can also be generalized to make use of any public key agreement algorithm. In short, a public key agreement algorithm is a cryptographic construction that allows one to compute a shared secret using another party's public value and one's own private value. Examples of cryptographic constructions that also provide the public key agreement property include constructions that employ elliptic curves over finite fields.

SKIP does also support an ephemeral Diffie-Hellman key exchange to provide perfect forward secrecy (PFS) for situations that require PFS. The concept of PFS is aimed at guaranteeing that future communication is cryptographically protected, even in the event of compromise of current cryptographic keys. A key management protocol provides PFS if the disclosure or compromise of long-term keying material does not compromise the secrecy of the exchanged transient keys from previous communications and the data encrypted with them, provided that the keys are properly deleted from the system. PFS is provided by the independent generation of each key such that subsequent keys are not dependent on any previous key. Practically speaking, there is currently no other solution to provide PFS except for the Diffie-Hellman key exchange. SKIP PFS is a simple handshake protocol that uses an ephemeral Diffie-Hellman key exchange to provide PFS. The extension may also support principal anonymity if required. Let's assume that A and B already share an implicit master key K_{AB}. In addition to their long-term Diffie-Hellman public key pairs (x_A, g^{x_A}) and (x_B, g^{x_B}), A and B also possess short-term Diffie-

Hellman public key pairs (x_a, g^{x_a}) and (x_b, g^{x_b}). The short-term public key pairs are used for the ephemeral Diffie-Hellman key exchange that is authenticated with the master key. Consequently, the SKIP PFS protocol (without principal anonymity) can be formalized as follows:

$$1 : A \longrightarrow B : \langle g^{x_a}, g, p, \ll A \gg, EMKID_{BA} \rangle K_{AB}$$
$$2 : B \longrightarrow A : \langle g^{x_b}, g, p, \ll B \gg, EMKID_{AB} \rangle K_{AB}$$

In step 1, A provides B with his short-term public key g^{x_a} for the ephemeral Diffie-Hellman key exchange, g, p, a cerificate $\ll A \gg$ for his long-term Diffie-Hellman public key, as well as an ephemeral master key identifier $EMKID_{BA}$ for messages sent from B to A. The entire message is authenticated with the master key K_{AB}. In step 2, B returns his short-term public key g^{x_b}, g, p, a cerificate $\ll B \gg$ for his long-term Diffie-Hellman public key, as well as an ephemeral master key identifier $EMKID_{AB}$ for messages sent from A to B. Again, the entire message is authenticated with the master key K_{AB}. A and B can now use the newly shared secret $g^{x_a x_b} (\mathrm{mod}\ p)$ to compute an ephemeral master key EK_{ABn}. The formula to compute EK_{ABn} is as follows:

$$EK_{ABn} = h(K_{AB}, g^{x_a x_b}, n, 01), h(K_{AB}, g^{x_a x_b}, n, 00)$$

In this formula, K_{AB} refers to the master key shared berween A and B, $g^{x_a x_b}$ to the newly shared secret, n to the counter from the SKIP header, and 00 and 01 to 1 byte values containing the values 0 and 1, respectively. Again, h refers to a collision-resistant one-way hash function, and the comma refers to the concatenation. Consequently, EK_{ABn} is computed by concatenating two one-way hash values.

In addition to that, the protocol can also be modified to additionally support principal anonymity. The corresponding SKIP PFS protocol (with principal anonymity) can be formalized as follows:

$$1 : A \longrightarrow B : \langle g^{x_a}, g, p, \{\ll A \gg\} g^{x_a x_B}, EMKID_{BA} \rangle K_{AB}$$
$$2 : B \longrightarrow A : \langle g^{x_b}, g, p, \{\ll B \gg\} g^{x_a x_B}, EMKID_{AB} \rangle K_{AB}$$

In this protocol, the two certificates $\ll A \gg$ and $\ll B \gg$ are additionally encrypted with $g^{x_a x_B} (\mathrm{mod}\ p)$. Consequently, the identifiers encoded in the certificates are no longer visible from a party that is not involved in the key exchange.

It is important to note that any ephemeral Diffie-Hellman key exchange also introduces greater bilateral state and overhead than is present in the base SKIP protocol. Consequently, when using SKIP PFS, certain features of the base SKIP protocol that rely on its statelessness become unavailable. In general, there is an interesting trade-off between the stetelessness of a key management protocol and its ability to provide PFS [24].

More recently, Sun Microsystems, Inc. received two patents[10] for the SKIP technology and has dedicated its rights to the public domain. As a matter of fact, Sun Microsystems, Inc. has licensed all persons and companies to practice the SKIP procedures claimed in the patents without licensing fees.

Sun Microsystem's implementation of SKIP currently consists of a key manager daemon, a bulk data crypt engine, and a streams module:

- The SKIP key manager daemon maintains a database of certificate information about peer entities. It is responsible for calculating and caching the Diffie-Hellman long-term secret key and derived master key for each entity. The key manager also works with the SKIP kernel to generate pseudorandom packet keys.

- In conjunction with the user space key manager, the SKIP bulk data crypt engine offers bulk data encryption and decryption services to kernel clients. Within the SKIP engine are a number of generic cryptographic modules that implement algorithms such as DES-CBC, RC2-CBC, and RC4. These kernel modules are used by the SKIP bulk data crypt engine to perform packet encryption.

- The SKIP streams module is inserted between the TCP/IP protocol stack and the network interface. Using an access control list based on the peer's IP address, packets are either passed in the clear, dropped, or sent to the bulk data crypt engine for encryption or decryption. The access control lists can be maintained by some user-level management tools.

All communications between the SKIP kernel and the key manager take place using a pseudodevice driver. Solaris SKIP operates transparently and requires no modification either to existing applications or operating system software. During the system boot process, the SKIP streams module is inserted between the IP layer and the network interface. In this way, the SKIP module intercepts all packets entering and leaving the IP layer. SKIP counts the number of bytes encrypted

---

[10]U.S. patents 5,588,060 "Method and apparatus for a key-management scheme for internet protocols" and 5,548,646 "System for signatureless transmission and reception of data packets between computer networks."

using a given key and will request a new key once a configurable limit (512 KB by default) is exceeded.

Sun Microsystems is shipping SKIP for Solaris and has has source and binaries for SKIP Release 1.0 available for FreeBSD and SunOS. In addition to that, Sun Microsystems is participating in RSA's S/WAN initiative for interoperability testing (see Section 9.5). According to the SKIP WWW home page,[11] SKIP interoperability tests are currently occurring between commercial SKIP implementations from CheckPoint, Toshiba, Gemini, VPnet, Elvis+, and Sun Microsystems. Even without source code availability, installed systems can be upgraded to make use of SKIP. As a matter of fact, several implementations currently exist that can be integrated into a binary UNIX kernel for Solaris 2.4, SunOS 4.1.3, NetBSD, Nextstep, IRIX, and SCO UNIX. In addition to that, at least one Windows NT version is in work. Note, however, that most of these implementations are originating in the United States and are subject to export controls. Consequently, they may not be available outside the United States and Canada.

For noncommercial use, there are at least three SKIP versions available: Sun Microsystems' reference implementation that can be downloaded from the SKIP WWW home page, one version from Elvis+ in Russia, and another internationally available source code release called ENskip from the ETH Zürich in Switzerland [25].[12] More recently, Sun Microsystems has announced that is would import and sell through its distribution channels the software from Elvis+ under the name PC SunScreen SKIP E+ for Windows 3.11, Windows 95, and Windows NT. Corresponding evaluation copies are freely available on the Internet.[13] Obviously, it is the plan of Sun Microsystems to import cryptographic software instead of exporting it, and to circumvent current the U.S. export controls accordingly. At the time of this writing, it is not clear how the U.S. administration is going to react on this plan.

9.4.3 Photuris

Almost simultaneously with SKIP, Phil Karn from Qualcomm proposed another experimental key management protocol named *Photuris*. For once, the protocol name is not an acronym, but rather a tribute to some unknown engineers. "Photuris" is the Greek name used by zoologists to designate the firefly, and "firefly" in turn is the name of the classified key exchange protocol designed by the NSA

---

[11]http://skip.incog.com
[12]http://www.tik.ee.ethz.ch/ skip
[13]http://www.elvis-plus.com

for the STU-III secure telephone. A rumor tells that the design of Photuris is very closely related to that of the NSA's Firefly protocol. The Photuris protocol is also similar to the *station-to-station* (STS) protocol originally proposed by Whitfield Diffie, Paul van Oorschot, and Michael Wiener [26]. The Photuris key management protocol is specified in a pair of Internet Drafts coauthored by Bill Simpson.[14] Some of the techniques used in the Photuris protocol are covered by U.S. Patent 5,148,479, granted to IBM. In August 1995, IBM granted the conditional free use of the patented technologies in conjunction with Photuris or such derivates to the IETF [27].

When designing the Photuris protocol, Karn tried to keep the advantages of the Diffie-Hellman key exchange while addressing its major drawbacks, which are its vulnerability to the man-in-the-middle attack and its use of computationally intensive operations, such as modular exponentiation:

- In order to thwart the man-in-the-middle attack, Photuris combines the Diffie-Hellman key exchange with a subsequent authentication of the public values used for the key exchange.

- With regard to the use of computationally intensive operations, Photuris proposes the use of a set of predefined primes, mainly to avoid the long computation required to discover large primes as well as to enable some precomputation.

Also note that there is a potential Achilles heel in the design of any key management protocol that makes use of public key cryptography. As it requires computationally intensive operations, a protocol that makes use of public key cryptography is generally vulnerable to resource-clogging attacks. A complete defense against resource-clogging attacks seems to be impossible, so Karn designed a mechanism to make them at least more difficult. This mechanism has been named cookie exchange and is discussed further below. In short, the aim of a cookie exchange is to either thwart resource-clogging attacks or, at a minimum, oblige an attacker to disclose his or her IP address. As such, the cookie exchange must precede the Diffie-Hellman key exchange. However, the cookie exchange does not protect against a passive attacker who is able to copy a valid cookie, or an active attacker who can modify or substitute cookies. These attacks are mitigated somewhat with time-variant cookies and not further addressed in the Photuris design.

A Photuris key management protocol execution consists of the following three exchange phases:

---

[14]`draft-ietf-ipsec-photuris-*.txt` and `draft-simpson-photuris-schemes-*.txt`

- A *cookie exchange* phase that is used to thwart resource clogging attacks launched with bogus source IP addresses.

- A *value exchange* phase that is used to establish a shared secret between the two parties involved. A Diffie-Hellman key exchange is typically performed in this phase.

- An *identification exchange* phase that is used to identify the parties to each other, and to verify the authenticity and integrity of the values exchanged in the previous phases. This exchange is encrypted for privacy reasons with a key that is derived from the shared secret.

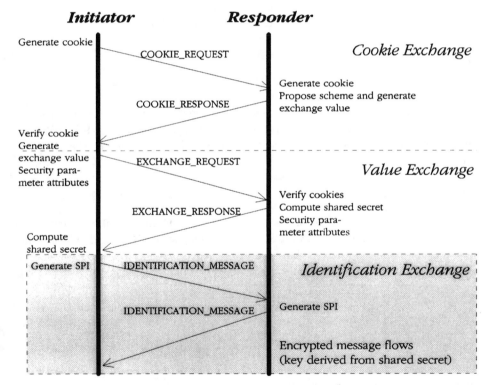

Figure 9.10   The Photuris key management protocol message flows.

Additional messages can be exchanged to periodically change the session keys, as well as to establish new or revised security parameters. These exchanges are also encrypted for privacy reasons in the same fashion as the identification exchange mentioned above.

Photuris is layered on top of UDP and IP. On each station, a Photuris server may await requests on UDP port 468. This port number has been officially assigned by the IANA for the Photuris protocol. The Photuris terminology refers to the client requesting an SA as an *initiator* and the server serving the request as a *responder*. In the protocol description that follows the letter "I" is used to refer to the initiator and the letter "R" is used to refer to the responder. The exchange phases mentioned above lead to the following six message flows:

1 : I	$\longrightarrow$	R :	COOKIE_REQUEST
2 : R	$\longrightarrow$	I :	COOKIE_RESPONSE
3 : I	$\longrightarrow$	R :	EXCHANGE_REQUEST
4 : R	$\longrightarrow$	I :	EXCHANGE_RESPONSE
5 : I	$\longrightarrow$	R :	IDENTIFICATION_MESSAGE
6 : R	$\longrightarrow$	I :	IDENTIFICATION_MESSAGE

The message flows and the major actions on the initiator's and responder's side of the Photuris key management protocol are overviewed in Figure 9.10. We are going to further address and discuss the three exchange phases of the Photuris protocol next.

Cookie Exchange

In step 1, I initializes some local state and sends a COOKIE_REQUEST message to R. The message includes a 128-bit initiator cookie, which is a randomized value that identifies the Photuris exchange and is used to later reject invalid response messages from R. A cookie may also be referred to as an anticlogging token (ACT).

On receipt of the COOKIE_REQUEST message, R determines if there are sufficient resources to begin another Photuris protocol exchange. When too many SAs and SPI values are already in use, or some other resource limit is reached, the execution stops and an ERROR_MESSAGE is sent back. Otherwise, R generates a responder cookie and returns a COOKIE_RESPONSE message to I in step 2. The message includes both cookies and a list of one or more key exchange schemes supported in increasing order of preference. According to the mathematical theory, each key exchange scheme refers to a group in which the discrete logarithm problem is intractable and where the Diffie-Hellman key exchange may take place. The protocol specification supplies a couple of numbers that have been assigned by the IANA. Most of these schemes are optional, whereas implementation of scheme number 2 is required for all Photuris implementations. This scheme specifies the use of a multiplicative group based on a 1,024-bit prime and the generator 2.

R creates no additional state at this point in time. Note that the exact technique by which a Photuris party generates a cookie is implementation dependent. A recommended technique is to calculate a cryptographic hash value over the IP source and destination addresses, the UDP source and destination port numbers, and a randomly generated value that is kept secret. Thus, an incoming cookie can be verified at any time by regenerating it locally from values contained in the incoming UDP datagram and the secret value.

The initiator and responder may use secret values to generate cookies in different ways:

- The initiator's secret value should change for each new Photuris exchange, and is thereafter internally cached on a per-responder basis. This provides improved synchronization and protection against replay attacks. An alternative is to cache the cookie instead of the secret value. Incoming cookies can then be compared directly without the computational cost of regeneration.

- The responder's secret value may remain the same for different initiators. The cookie is not cached per initiator to avoid saving state during the initial cookie exchange. Once the EXCHANGE_REQUEST message is received, both initiator and responder cookies are cached to identify the exchange.

I is supposed to associate a retransmission timer with each Photuris exchange. If a COOKIE_RESPONSE message does not arrive in due time, the cookie exchange will be retried. It should, however, be retried with a different initiator cookie, because the responder may very well keep copies of recently received COOKIE_REQUEST messages and refuse to serve them more than once, in an attempt to thwart replay attacks. Saturated receivers may also elect to ignore incoming cookie requests, for example, if too many SAs are active at the same time.

Value Exchange

On receipt of a legitimate COOKIE_RESPONSE message, I verifies the cookie, chooses an appropriate key exchange scheme and exchange value, and sends a corresponding EXCHANGE_REQUEST message to R in step 3. The message includes the cookies and a list of security parameter attributes supported by I, in increasing order of preference. I also starts a retransmission timer. If no valid EXCHANGE_RESPONSE message is obtained within a predetermined time limit, the same EXCHANGE_REQUEST message is retransmitted. Having the key exchange scheme chosen by I allows the greatest protocol flexibility, and follows the requirement that no state should be kept by R until the shared secret is calculated. Unfortunately, this also allows the weakest scheme to be chosen by I. This is no worse than the alternative, namely to have R choose from weak schemes offered by I.

On receipt of the EXCHANGE_REQUEST message, R validates the responder cookie and the key exchange scheme chosen by I. Whenever an invalid cookie or scheme is detected, R discards the message and returns an ERROR_MESSAGE to I. When a valid EXCHANGE_REQUEST message is received, R chooses an appropriate exchange value for the indicated key exchange scheme, and returns a corresponding EXCHANGE_RESPONSE message to I in step 4. Similar to the EXCHANGE_REQUEST message, the EXCHANGE_RESPONSE message also includes the cookies and a list of security parameter attributes supported by R, in increasing order of preference. R keeps a copy of the incoming EXCHANGE_REQUEST and the corresponding EXCHANGE_RESPONSE message. If a duplicate EXCHANGE_REQUEST message is received, R merely resends its previous EXCHANGE_RESPONSE message and takes no further action. At this point in time, R begins calculation of the shared secret. This may take a substantial amount of time.

Identification Exchange

So far, neither the cookie exchange nor the value exchange provides any identification or authentication for I and R, except for the fact that both can send and receive messages from their current IP addresses. The identification exchange is used to authenticate the public values of the Diffie-Hellman key exchange, and to thwart the man-in-the-middle attack accordingly.

On receipt of a valid EXCHANGE_RESPONSE message, I begins its parallel computation of the shared secret. After having successfully computed the secret, I sends an IDENTIFICATION_MESSAGE to R in step 5. The message includes the cookies, a SPI to be used for incoming communications, a lifetime that specifies the number of seconds remaining before the indicated SPI expires, an identity choice that is selected from the list of attributes offered by R, corresponding identification and verification fields, as well as some related fields that are of minor importance and therefore omitted here. The verification field typically comprises a digital signature that is computed for the previous messages. I also starts a retransmission timer. If no IDENTIFICATION_MESSAGE is returned by R within the time limit, I simply retransmits the IDENTIFICATION_MESSAGE.

When R completes its computation of the shared secret, and upon receipt of a valid IDENTIFICATION_MESSAGE from I, R returns an IDENTIFICATION_MESSAGE to I in step 6. The message includes the same fields as the IDENTIFICA-TION_MESSAGE sent from I to R. Similar to the value exchange phase, R keeps a copy of the incoming IDENTIFICATION_MESSAGE and its own IDENTIFICA-TION_MESSAGE. If a duplicate IDENTIFICATION_MESSAGE is received, R merely resends its previous message, and takes no further action.

Calculation of the shared secret by I and R is executed in parallel to minimize delay. The key exchange scheme, exchange values, and resulting shared secret may be cached for short-term storage for the exchange lifetime. When repetitive Photuris exchanges occur between the same parties, and the exchange values are discovered to be unchanged, the cached shared secret can be used to rapidly generate new session keys.

With regard to traffic anonymity, it is important to note that although each IP packet carries its source and destination address in the clear, the origin and final destination can be hidden by forwarding the packet through an encrypted tunnel. Also, if the source IP address has been dynamically allocated, it provides no useful information to a potential eavesdropper. This leaves us with the identifying information that the parties send to each other during the identification exchange. One would often like to deny this information to an eavesdropper, especially when this would reveal the current location of a user. Fortunately, the identification exchange can be protected by encrypting it with a key derived from the shared secret just established. This keeps a passive eavesdropper from learning the identities of the parties, either directly from the certificates or by checking signatures against a database of known public keys. This scheme is not foolproof. By posing as the responder, an active attacker can trick the initiator into revealing his or her identity. However, this attack is considerably more difficult than passive eavesdropping. For these reasons, the IDENTIFICATION_MESSAGES are encrypted using the privacy method indicated by the corresponding scheme. The keys that are used for this encryption are calculated by applying a hash function over the concatenated shared secret, initiator cookie, responder cookie, SPI owner (receiver) exchange value, SPI user (sender) exchange value, and, again, the shared secret. Since the order of the exchange value fields is different in each direction, the resulting session key are usually different in each direction. Each SA may have one or more session keys. These keys are generated based on the attributes of the SA. The derivation method is essentially the same as the method used to derive the key for the privacy method just mentioned above.

At any time after completion of the identification exchange, either party can send a CHANGE_MESSAGE. The message has effect in only one direction, namely from the SPI owner to the SPI user. It is required to be encrypted for privacy in the same fashion as the IDENTIFICATION_MESSAGE.

There is a small amount of state associated with a Photuris key exchange. This includes the cookies, exchange values, and the computed shared secret. It is characteristic, however, that the responder does not maintain any state during the initial cookie exchange. This prevents memory resource exhaustion and simple flooding attacks. Later exchange phases require saving of state to perform the key establishment calculations and authentication. Nevertheless, all retained exchange state is subject to periodic expiration. According to the Photuris specification, a typical value for this lifetime is 10 minutes. The lifetime values, however, are implementation dependent and not disclosed in any of the Photuris messages. When an exchange value expires or is replaced by a newer value, all related exchange state must be purged. The periodic expiration and purge of exchange state reduces the risk of key compromise, and is an important consideration in attaining PFS.

9.4.4   SKEME

The Photuris protocol is a sound and secure key distribution protocol that combines the most general and scalable cryptographic technique, namely public key cryptography, with the best secrecy-protecting key exchange scheme, namely the Diffie-Hellman key exchange. The main drawback is that the Photuris protocol enforces a single execution path, and that this singularity may not meet all requirements of the Internet community. The most demanding aspects of any key distribution and management protocol is the variety and heterogeneity of the possible scenarios, as well as the different security and trust models it should be able to support. Public key cryptography is nice to have if it is available. However, it is still common today to use manual key distribution and configuration, KDCs, as well as preshared keys that may be used to derive session keys. Similarly, the Diffie-Hellman key exchange is nice to have if it is available. The main advantage of the Diffie-Hellman key exchange is its ability to provide PFS. However, there are situations in which PFS is meaningless. The best example for this is the IPSP AH mechanism. In these situations it may be more efficient and appropriate not to do a Diffie-Hellman key exchange, but to use another key exchange or distribution mechanism instead. To cut a long story short, one can argue that a single security and trust model may be insufficient to address the needs of key distribution and management in all possible scenarios for the Internet.

Hugo Krawczyk, from the IBM T.J. Watson Research Center, has taken the underlying principles of STS and Photuris one step further and widened their scope accordingly. Early in 1996, he came up with a generalization of the protocols known as *Photuris Plus* or *SKEME* [28]. SKEME provides various modes for key exchange. Similar to the STS and Photuris protocols, the basic mode of SKEME provides key exchange based on public keys and a Diffie-Hellman key exchange. However, SKEME is not restricted to the combination of public key cryptography and the Diffie-Hellman key exchange. It addresses additional needs, such as a key exchange based on a previously shared session key. This supports many important and realistic scenarios, which include manual key installation and other forms of preshared master keys. Furthermore, it accomodates key exchange in the Kerberos model, where the parties share a key via a commonly trusted KDC. By using this key to authenticate a Diffie-Hellman key exchange, rather than using it directly as a session key, SKEME achieves a significant security improvement by reducing the trust required in the KDC. SKEME also provides for more efficient key exchange mechanisms for the cases in which the PFS property of the Diffie-Hellman key exchange can be relaxed, thus saving the computational cost associated with that mechanism. Such cases include applications where authenticity of information, rather than confidentiality, is at stake, or where the level of secrecy required is relatively low. Finally, a very important goal of SKEME is to provide a mode to perform fast and frequent key refreshing. This has the effect of shortening the lives of cryptographic keys, thus limiting the damage and potential of key exposure.

The various modes of SKEME are folded into a single protocol, with a small set of messages, a well defined set of options, and a compact representation. There are four basic phases in the SKEME protocol: COOKIES, SHARE, EXCH, and AUTH:

- The COOKIES phase is intended to thwart denial of service attacks. It is adopted from the Photuris key management protocol.

- The SHARE phase is intended to establish a session key K_{ab} based only on the parties having the public keys of each other. In this phase, A and B exchange half-keys encrypted under each other's public key and then combine the half-keys via a one-way hash function to produce K_{ab}. The SHARE phase can be formalized as follows:

$$1 : A \longrightarrow B : \{K_a\}k_B$$
$$2 : B \longrightarrow A : \{K_b\}k_A$$

In step 1, A randomly selects a half-key K_a, encrypts it with B's public key, which is k_B, and sends the result $\{K_a\}k_B$ to B. Similarly, in step 2, B randomly selects a half-key K_b, encrypts it with A's public key, which is k_A, and sends $\{K_b\}k_A$ to B. Finally, A and B use a previously agreed upon one-way hash function h to compute $K_{ab} = h(K_a, K_b)$. Note that this phase by itself does not authenticate the parties involved or the resulting K_{ab}. Also note that when anonymity of the parties is required, then the messages also include the senders' identities in encrypted form. In this case, the SHARE phase can be formalized as follows:

$$1 : A \quad \longrightarrow \quad B : \{id_A, K_a\}k_B$$
$$2 : B \quad \longrightarrow \quad A : \{id_B, K_b\}k_A$$

- In the SKEME modes that provide support for a Diffie-Hellman key exchange, the EXCH phase is used to perform the key exchange. Let's assume that A has picked a random number x_a that serves as Diffie-Hellman exponent, and that B has picked another number x_b. A and B can then use the following handshake protocol to perform a Diffie-Hellman key exchange and end up with a shared secret $g^{x_a x_b} (\text{mod } p)$ that may serve as shared secret:

$$1 : A \quad \longrightarrow \quad B : g^{x_a}(\text{mod } p)$$
$$2 : B \quad \longrightarrow \quad A : g^{x_b}(\text{mod } p)$$

Note that A and B can compute $g^{x_a}(\text{mod } p)$ and $g^{x_b}(\text{mod } p)$ offline by each party prior to the execution of the handshake. In the SKEME modes that don't provide support for a Diffie-Hellman key exchange, the EXCH phase is used to exchange freshly and randomly generated nonces.

- The authenticity of the parties involved in the execution of the protocol is accomplished in the AUTH phase, which uses the shared secret K_{ab} from the SHARE phase to authenticate either the Diffie-Hellman exponents or the nonces from the EXCH phase. If a Diffie-Hellman key exchange has been performed in the EXCH phase, the AUTH phase can be summarized as follows:

$$1 : A \quad \longrightarrow \quad B : \langle g^{x_b}, g^{x_a}, id_A, id_B \rangle K_{ab}$$
$$2 : B \quad \longrightarrow \quad A : \langle g^{x_a}, g^{x_b}, id_B, id_A \rangle K_{ab}$$

Otherwise, the Diffie-Hellman exponents are replaced by the corresponding nonces. In step 1, A provides B with a MAC that he computes with K_{ab} from the concatenation of both Diffie-Hellman exponents, g^{x_b} and g^{x_a}, as well as both identifiers, id_A and id_B. Similarly, B provides A with a MAC that he computes with K_{ab} from the concatenation of both Diffie-Hellman exponents and both identifiers in reverse order.

In the actual SKEME protocol design, the messages of the last three phases are combined to provide a more compact and communication efficient protocol scheme. This combined SKEME protocol includes three steps that can be summarized as follows:

$$
\begin{aligned}
1 : A &\longrightarrow B : [\{id_A, K_a\}k_B,]\ value_A \\
2 : B &\longrightarrow A : [\{K_b\}k_A,]\ value_B, \langle value_A, value_B, id_B, id_A \rangle K_{ab} \\
3 : A &\longrightarrow B : \langle value_B, value_A, id_A, id_B \rangle K_{ab}
\end{aligned}
$$

In step 1, A sends $value_A$ to B. If A and B both provide support for public key cryptography, then A additionally provides $\{id_A, K_a\}k_B$. In step 2, B returns $value_B$ and $\langle value_A, value_B, id_B, id_A \rangle K_{ab}$ to A. Again, if A and B provide support for public key cryptography, then B additionally provides $\{K_b\}k_A$. Anyway, in step 3, A sends $\langle value_B, value_A, id_A, id_B \rangle K_{ab}$ to B. The various modes of SKEME are summarized is Table 9.1 and discussed next. Let's put $arg = \langle value_B, value_A, id_A, id_B \rangle K_{ab}$ for the course of this discussion. The term PK refers to the use of public key cryptography, whereas DH refers to the use of the Diffie-Hellman key exchange (Y = Yes, N = No). The last column in the table indicates whether the SKEME mode provides support for PFS.

Table 9.1
The four modes of SKEME

Mode	PK	DH	$value_A$	$value_B$	K_{ab}	K	PFS
Basic	Y	Y	g^{x_a}	g^{x_b}	$h(K_a, K_b)$	$h(g^{x_a x_b})$	Y
Share-only	Y	N	n_a	n_b	$h(K_a, K_b)$	$\langle arg \rangle K_{ab}$	N
Preshared key	N	Y	g^{x_a}	g^{x_b}	pre-shared	$h(g^{x_a x_b})$	Y
Fast rekey	N	N	n_a	n_b	pre-shared	$\langle arg \rangle K_{ab}$	N

Basic Mode

The SKEME basic mode combines public key cryptography with a Diffie-Hellman key exchange. It follows the discussion above and includes all four phases. Consequently, the SKEME protocol in basic mode provides PFS.

Share-Only Mode

The SKEME share-only mode uses public key cryptography but does not perform a Diffie-Hellman key exchange. Consequently, this mode of the SKEME protocol does not provide PFS. The EXCH phase is used to exchange nonces n_a and n_b between A and B. These nonces are randomly and freshly generated by the parties and sent instead of the Diffie-Hellman exponents. Consequently, in the EXCH phase A sends n_a to B and B returns n_b back to A, and in the AUTH phase, A sends $\langle n_b, n_a, id_A, id_B \rangle K_{ab}$ to B and B returns $\langle n_a, n_b, id_B, id_A \rangle K_{ab}$ back to A. In this way, the combination of EXCH and AUTH provides the parties with the assurance that the key K_{ab} they shared through the SHARE phase is now known to both of them, and that the party they talk to is indeed authentic. The nonces n_a and n_b act as challenges to prove to each other the possession of K_{ab}.

One could imagine that the output of the protocol (i.e., the session key K to be shared between A and B would be K_{ab} in this mode). However, since K_{ab} is used in the protocol as the key to authenticate the messages sent in the AUTH phase, it should not be output as the session key. Therefore, instead of outputting $K = K_{ab}$, we define K to be a keyed one-way hash value computed from the message sent from A to B in the AUTH phase, namely $\langle n_b, n_a, id_A, id_B \rangle K_{ab}$, with the same key K_{ab}. Note that in order to find K from this mode of SKEME, an adversary needs to either actively impersonate one of the parties or be able to learn K_{ab} by watching the communications in the protocol. However, the latter requires knowing the private keys of both parties in order to decrypt K_a and K_b.

Preshared Key Mode

In the SKEME preshared key mode, public key cryptography is not used, but a Diffie-Hellman key exchange in performed. Similar to the basic mode, this mode of the SKEME protocol provides PFS, thus ensuring the parties that even a future compromise of their preshared key will not expose all the traffic encrypted with keys derived from the exchanged session keys. In this mode, the protocol assumes that the parties already share a secret key K_{ab}, and that they use this key to derive a new and fresh key. As discussed previously, this shared key could be a manually installed key or come from a KDC. Consequently, the SHARE phase can be skipped and the preshared key used as K_{ab}. The computation of the session key K is identical to that of the basic protocol, namely, $K = h(g^{x_a x_b}(\bmod\ p))$.

Fast Rekey Mode

The fast rekey mode is the fastest mode of the SKEME protocol. It neither uses public key cryptography nor does it perform a Diffie-Hellman key exchange. A and B share a key K_{ab} that they can use to authenticate the key refreshment without going through expensive operations like public key or Diffie-Hellman computations. In fast rekey mode, the SHARE phase is entirely omitted, and the EXCH and AUTH phases are run by exchanging nonces rather than Diffie-Hellman exponents. Afterwards, the computation of the session key K is essentially the same as in share-only mode, namely, $K = \langle arg \rangle K_{ab}$, where $arg = \langle value_B, value_A, id_A, id_B \rangle K_{ab}$ is the value sent in the message from A to B in the AUTH phase. This mode of the SKEME protocol is very closely related to the MKMP previously proposed and submitted for consideration to the IETF IPsec WG.

In conclusion, SKEME has many similarities and some important differences with the STS and Photuris protocols. They are all based on a Diffie-Hellman key exchange that is authenticated with public key cryptography. Photuris does it by first performing a Diffie-Hellman key exchange and then authenticating it through the use of digital signatures. SKEME, in turn, uses public key cryptography to exchange a one-time key and then uses shared-key techniques to authenticate the Diffie-Hellman key exchange. An important advantage of the SKEME approach is that it allows for selective performance of Diffie-Hellman key exchange operations. That is, in SKEME, one can skip the Diffie-Hellman phase and still have a key exchanged between the parties; in Photuris this is not possible. However, because of the many aspects that are common to Photuris and SKEME, the latter was not officially proposed to the IETF IPsec WG to replace Photuris, but rather to be merged with it in oder to broaden and strengthen the functionality of the upcoming IKMP.

Last but not least, SKEME can also be used in conjunction with the SKIP protocol. The latter uses long-term Diffie-Hellman public keys to derive long-term shared keys between parties. These shared keys can then be used in SKEME as K_{ab}. This would provide a combined scheme that provides PFS and a possibility to efficiently rekey the parties involved.

9.4.5 ISAKMP

The *Internet security association key management protocol* (ISAKMP) was mainly designed and proposed by the NSA Office of INFOSEC Computer Science. The protocol is specified in an Internet Draft authored by Douglas Maughan, Mark Schneider, and Jeff Turner from NSA, as well as Mark Schertler from Terisa Systems,

Inc.[15] Work is currently going on to refine the protocol proposal for its elevation to an Internet standards track RFC.

In principle, ISAKMP can be implemented over any Internet or transport layer protocol. Implementations must include support for ISAKMP using UDP on port 500. This port has been officially assigned to ISAKMP by the IANA. In addition to that, implementations may also support ISAKMP over other transport layer protocols or over IP itself.

Unlike the other key management protocols overviewed and discussed in this section, ISAKMP does not bind itself to any specific cryptographic algorithm, key establishment technique, or other security mechanism, but rather describes a protocol utilizing general security concepts necessary for establishing SAs and cryptographic keys. As such, ISAKMP cleanly separates the details of SA management from the details of key exchange. In general, there are many different key exchange techniques and corresponding protocols, each with different security properties, and a common framework is required for agreeing to the format of SA attributes, and for negotiating, establishing, modifying, and deleting SAs accordingly. ISAKMP has been designed to serve as a common framework for the evolving Internet, where numerous security mechanisms and several options for each mechanism may coexist. ISAKMP can be used to establish an SA between negotiating parties on behalf of some other protocol. It consists of two phases:

- During the first protocol phase, a basic set of security attributes may be agreed upon. This basic set provides protection for subsequent ISAKMP exchanges. It also indicates the authentication and key exchange methods that will be used in the second phase. The first phase results in an ISAKMP SA. This initial ISAKMP SA establishment, however, may be skipped if a basic set of security attributes is already in place. In this case, the establishment of the SA can also be done directly.

- During the second protocol phase, the ISAKMP SA is used to have the entities negotiate the security services that will be contained in the SA for the other security protocol or application.

Although the two-phase negotiation causes some overhead compared to other protocols, it also provides additional benefits. For example, one benefit is that once the ISAKMP SA has been negotiated, it can also be used to negotiate SAs for other entities. Another benefit is that the ISAKMP SA can provide additional security

---

[15]draft-ietf-ipsec-isakmp-*.txt

during the second negotiation. For example, the ISAKMP SA may provide identity protection, and therefore a less complicated exchange might be used for the second negotiation. Finally, the ISAKMP SA can also be used during the maintenance of SAs.

ISAKMP provides support for several authentication and authenticated key establishment techniques. It also adapts the use of cookies or ACTs to protect against denial of service attacks. In ISAKMP terminology, a domain of interpretation (DOI) defines payload formats, exchange types, and conventions for naming security-relevant information, such as security policies or cryptographic algorithms and modes. A DOI identifier is used to interpret the payloads of ISAKMP messages. The rules for the Internet IPsec DOI (assigned number 1) are specified in an Internet draft.[16]

An ISAKMP message has a header with a fixed format, followed by a variable number of payloads. The header contains the information required by the protocol to maintain state, process payloads, and possibly prevent denial of service or replay attacks. As such, the header includes 64-bit initiator and responder cookies, a reference for the next payload, an exchange type, and some other fields. The payloads in turn are daisy-chained. They provide modular building blocks for constructing ISAKMP messages. The payload types are fully defined in the ISAKMP specification and not further addressed here. Each payload begins with a generic header, which provides a payload chaining capability and clearly defines the boundaries of the payload.

The ISAKMP supports the creation of exchanges for the establishment of SAs and related keying material. In the current protocol specification, there are five default exchange types defined for ISAKMP. Each exchange type defines the content and ordering of ISAKMP messages during communications between peers. The defined exchange types are not meant to satisfy all DOI and key exchange requirements. If the defined exchange types meet the DOI requirements, then they can be used as specified. But if the defined exchange types do not meet these requirements, then it is up to the DOI to specify a new exchange type and the valid sequences of payloads that make up a successful exchange, and how to build and interpret those payloads. The five default ISAKMP exchange types are defined as follows:

- The ISAKMP *Base Exchange* is designed to allow the authentication and key exchange information to be transmitted together. Combining the authentication and key exchange information into one single message reduces the number of

---

[16]`draft-ietf-ipsec-ipsec-doi-*.txt`

round trips at the expense of not providing identity protection. Identity protection is not provided because identities are exchanged before a shared secret has been established, and therefore encryption of the identities is not possible.

- The ISAKMP *Identity Protection Exchange* is designed to separate the authentication and key exchange information. Separating this information provides protection of the communicating identities at the expense of an additional message flow. For this exchange, the key information is exchanged first. The authentication information is sent next, but is now encrypted and is therefore protected from hostile users.

- The ISAKMP *Authentication-Only Exchange* is designed to allow only authentication information to be transmitted. Obviously, the benefit of this exchange is the ability to perform only authentication without the computational expense of computing keys and shared secrets. This can be used, for example, to have peer entities intermittently reauthenticate to each other during communications.

- The ISAKMP *Aggressive Exchange* is designed to allow the SA, key exchange, and authentication-related payloads to be transmitted all together, attempting to establish all security relevant information in a single exchange and to reduce the number of round trips accordingly. Consequently, this exchange is the most efficient in terms of the number of messages exchanged. But again, it does not protect the secrecy of the identities.

- The ISAKMP *Informational Exchange* is designed as a one-way transmittal of information that can be used for SA management.

Again, we refer to the ISAKMP specification for a formal treatment of the message flows in each of these exchange types.

There are several ISAKMP implementations available on the Internet today. For example, the DoD prototype implementation is freely available from the MIT for distribution within the United States and Canada.[17] Similarly, Cisco Systems has made its ISAKMP daemon software publicly and freely available.

In conclusion, ISAKMP provides a flexible and extensible framework for establishing and managing SAs and cryptographic keys. The framework provided by ISAKMP consists of header and payload definitions, exchange types for guiding message and payload exchanges, and some general processing guidelines. ISAKMP does not define the mechanisms that will be used to establish and manage SAs and

---

[17]http://web.mit.edu/network/isakmp/

cryptographic keys in an authenticated and confidential manner. The definition of mechanisms and their application is the purview of individual DOIs.

9.4.6 OAKLEY

The OAKLEY key determination protocol is another protocol that can be used to establish a shared secret with an assigned identifier and associated authenticated identities for the parties involved. It was originally proposed by Hilarie Orman from the Department of Computer Science of the University of Arizona. The latest version of the protocol specification was released in May 1996 as an Internet draft.[18]

Similar to STS, Photuris, and SKEME, the OAKLEY key determination protocol is based on an authenticated Diffie-Hellman key exchange to achieve PFS for the shared secrets. In addition to that, the OAKLEY protocol also incorporates the cookie exchange mechanism from the Photuris protocol for two purposes: anti-clogging and key naming. The two parties of a protocol execution each contribute one cookie at the initiation of the key establishment, and the pair of cookies then becomes the key identifier, a reusable name for the key material. Similar to SKEME, the OAKLEY protocol has several options to determine keys. In addition to the Diffie-Hellman key exchange, the protocol can also be used to derive a new key from an existing key and to distribute an externally derived key by encrypting it. Also similar to SKEME, the OAKLEY protocol does not require the two parties to compute the shared secret prior to authentication.

The main difference between OAKLEY and its predecessors is due to the fact that the former allows the two parties to select mutually agreeable supporting algorithms for encryption, key exchange, and authentication. For example, the protocol explicitly defines how the two parties can select mathematical structures for performing the Diffie-Hellman key exchange; they can either use standard groups or define their own. Three distinct group representations can be used with OAKLEY. Each group is defined by its group operation and the kind of underlying field used to represent group elements. The three types are

- Modular exponentiation groups (named MODP);

- Elliptic curve groups over the field $GF(2^n)$ (named EC2N);

- Elliptic curve groups over $GF(p)$ (named ECP).

---

[18] draft-ietf-ipsec-oakley-01.txt

The three group types are further described in Appendix A of the OAKLEY protocol specification and not further addressed here. It is assumed that user-defined groups may provide an additional degree of security in the long term.

Another difference between OAKLEY and its predecessors mentioned above is due to the fact that the OAKLEY key determination protocol was designed to be a compatible component of ISAKMP for managing SAs from the very beginning. In this case, ISAKMP and OAKLEY run over UDP using a well-known port. However, OAKLEY could also be used directly over IP or UDP, if suitable protocol or port number assignments were available.

The primary goal of the OAKLEY protocol is the secure establishment of common keying information state in the two parties involved. This state information is a key name, secret keying material, the identification of the two parties, and three algorithms for use during authentication. These algorithms are to be used for encryption, hashing, and authentication. In this context, the term EHAO is used to refer to a list of encryption, hashing, and authentication algorithm choices. Each item is a pair of values: a class name and an algorithm name. Similarly, the term EHAS is used to refer to a set of three items selected from the EHAO list, one from each of the classes for encryption, hashing, and authentication. The OAKLEY main mode exchange has five optional features:

- Stateless cookie exchange;

- PFS for the keying material;

- Secrecy for the identities;

- PFS for identity secrecy;

- Use of signatures (for non-repudiation).

The two parties involved in an execution of the OAKLEY key determination protocol can use all or none of these features. The general outline of processing is that the initiator of the key exchange begins by specifying as much information as he or she wishes in the first message. The responder replies, supplying as much information as he or she wishes. The two parties exchange messages, supplying more information at each step, until their requirements are finally satisfied. The choice of how much information to include in each message depends on which optional features are desirable. For example, if stateless cookies are not required, and identity secrecy and PFS for the keying material are not requirements either, and if non-repudiable signatures are acceptable, then the exchange can be completed in three messages. Additional features may increase the number of round trips needed for the keying material determination.

Similar to the STS and Photuris protocols, the three components of the OAKLEY key determination protocol are as follows:

- Cookie exchange;

- Diffie-Hellman key exchange;

- Authentication.

The cookie exchange can be made optionally stateless. The Diffie-Hellman key exchange is optional, but essential for PFS. Finally, authentication can be performed with privacy for identifiers, privacy for identifiers with PFS, as well as non-repudiation.

The initiator can supply as little information as a bare exchange request, carrying no additional information. On the other hand the initiator can also begin by supplying all of the information necessary for the responder to authenticate the requests and complete the key determination quickly, if the responder chooses to accept this method. If not, the responder can also reply with a minimal amount of information. The OAKLEY protocol specification contains several examples that illustrate the use of the protocol's optional features.

It has already been mentioned that the OAKLEY key determination protocol was designed to be mapped into the ISAKMP message structure. As such, the OAKLEY protocol does not define SA encodings or corresponding message formats. Instead, the resolution of ISAKMP with OAKLEY is addressed in a separate Internet draft.[19] This resolution uses the framework of ISAKMP to support a subset of the OAKLEY key determination protocol modes.

In the past, there were people supporting each of the key management protocols presented in this section, and an even larger number of people who were looking for a single protocol to emerge. Shortly after the June 1996 IETF meeting in Montreal, a working group was created to meet with the principals behind the various protocols and come up with a compromise that all could live with. Unfortunately, the working group failed, and in September 1996, Jeffrey Schiller, the current IETF Security Area Director, posted a document on the Internet to end the controversy. The document stated that the mandatory nature of IPsec means that for its various protocols variants may exist, but one of each class of protocol will need to be

---

[19]draft-ietf-ipsec-isakmp-oakley-*.txt

designated as mandatory to provide guidance to vendors wishing to build IPsec-compliant versions of products. The goal is for two compliant implementations of IPSP to be able to interoperate and communicate securely because they, at a minimum, have the mandate to implement protocols common between them. They may have other protocols, such as other AH and ESP transforms, in common, which they may negotiate the use of instead of the mandatory protocols. Note that a mandatory transform may not always be the ideal approach for a particular network application. For example, the mandatory ESP transform involves the use of DES in CBC mode. This encryption algorithm and mode is commonly regarded as being secure enough for most applications. However, it is also recognized that DES is a slow algorithm and applications requiring high-speed data throughput may elect to use a faster encryption algorithm, such as IDEA, RC2, RC4, or RC5.

Keeping in mind that the primary goal of a mandatory protocol is to provide strong security and interoperability, Schiller has reviewed the two major contenders for the IKMP standard, namely SKIP and ISAKMP/OAKLEY, and concluded in his posting that ISAKMP/OAKLEY should be the mandatory standard and that SKIP would still be able to become an elective Internet standard. The rationale is fairly simple. Given an arbitrarily chosen pair of hosts, it is likelier that an ISAKMP/OAKLEY approach will result in a working SA than SKIP. Furthermore, going back to the original IPsec WG chapter, the ISAKMP/OAKLEY approach more closely follows the goals established in the charter of the IKMP portion of the IPsec work.

According to this strategy, a set of RFCs is being written to further refine the ISAKMP/OAKLEY approach. These RFCs will enter the Internet standards track, ultimately resulting in a protocol that is elective for IPv4 implementations and mandatory for IPv6 implementations. Another set of RFCs is being written to define and further refine the SKIP approach. These RFCs are intended to follow the IETF standards track, ultimately resulting in a protocol that is elective for both IPv4 and IPv6 implementations. In addition, one or more RFCs are being written to describe the application domain for both ISAKMP/OAKLEY and SKIP. It is assumed that there exist applications where the SKIP approach makes more sense than the ISAKMP/OAKLEY approach.

Finally, we point out that most of the key management protocols outlined in this section are based on UDP as a transport layer protocol. This introduces a number of security considerations. Since UDP is unreliable, but a key management protocol must be reliable, the reliability must be built into the key management protocols. While the protocols utilize UDP, they usually don't rely on any UDP information for their processing. Another issue that must be considered in the development of

UDP-based key management protocols is the effect of firewalls. Many firewalls filter out UDP datagrams, making reliance on UDP questionable in certain environments.

9.5   DISCUSSION

In this chapter, we have overviewed IPSP and IKMP, as well as the current status of Internet standardization. Both protocols are mandatory for IPv6 implementations and likely to become widespread during the next few years. According to an IETF IPsec WG implementation survey, there were 29 IPSP implementations available in March 1997.[20] This number has probably increased since the writing of this book. Some of these implementations are freely distributable, whereas others are commercial products. Not all implementations claim conformance with IPsec specifications or interoperability with other implementations.

Not surprisingly, most of the current implementations are based on various flavors of the UNIX operating system. One reason for this is due to the fact that these implementations are deeply entwined in the source code of the corresponding protocol stacks, and that this source code is readily available for UNIX systems. However, if Internet layer security protocols are to be widely deployed, they must be available for MS-DOS and Windows systems, too. An immediate problem that one faces when trying to implement IP layer security for MS-DOS systems is due to the fact that the source code to the most widely deployed TCP/IP implementation, PC/TCP from FTP Software, is not publicly available. In order to overcome this problem, David Wagner and Steven Bellovin have implemented an IPSP module as a device driver, entirely below IP [29].

More recently, a Socket-based key management application programming interface (API) was proposed by the U.S. Naval Research Laboratory (NRL) [30]. The idea is to come up with an environment that allows implementations of key management strategies to exist outside the operating system kernel, where they can be implemented, debugged, and updated in a safe environment. User-level key management programs and the operating system kernel communicate key management information through a socket with the protocol family PF_KEY. The PF_KEY key management socket provides a set of messages that the kernel can use to indicate the need for a new or updated SA, and that user-level key management programs can use to add, remove, and update SAs. Version 2 of the PF_KEY key management API was specified in an Internet draft in March 1997.[21]

---

[20]ftp://research.ftp.com/pub/ipsec/results.htm
[21]draft-mcdonald-pf-key-v2-02.txt

The situation is overviewed in Figure 9.11. On the right side, there is a traditional network programming environment, whereas on the left side there are some additions that are required for the IP security architecture to be implemented. A sample implementation of PF_KEY is available in the NRL IPv6/IPSEC distribution.[22] Note that successful use of user-oriented keying requires a significant level of operating system support.

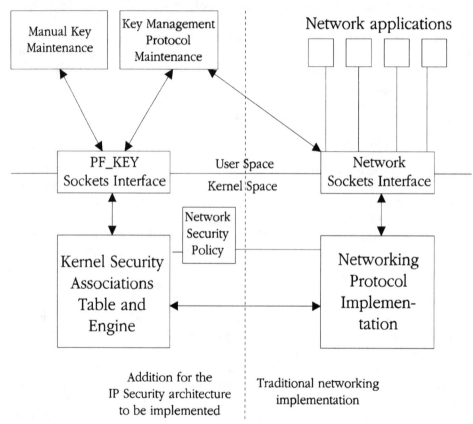

Figure 9.11   A Socket-based key management API (PF_KEY).

There are several scenarios that gain a lot from having IPSP and IKMP implementations readily available:

---

[22]ftp://ftp.c2.org or ftp://ftp.ripe.net

- IPSP could be used to establish a secure tunnel between two distant firewalls, for example between two distant units of the same organization. The IP packet exchanges between the two units would be encapsulated into IPSP packets transmitted from one firewall to the other through the Internet, using either the AH if only authentication is required or the ESP if confidentiality is needed. Several firewall vendors have in fact implemented IPSP and have also established interoperability testing programs with other vendors.

- Another example for IPSP are mobile hosts, which cause increasingly important concerns for security-conscious organizations. Mobile computers are typically plugged into all sorts of remote networks on which the organizations' managers have little control. An obvious way to fend off the specific attacks on mobile computers is to establish a secure tunnel between the mobile computer and the home network's firewall.

The use of IPSP and IKMP enables a company or organization to set up a virtual private network (VPN). In short, a VPN consists of a collection of hosts that have implemented protocols to securely exchange information. Often, these hosts communicate over the Internet or some related public networks. Telecommuting is a practical application thereof. Currently, telecommuters are either dialing into their intranet's modem pools or using local Internet service providers to access intranets remotely through the Internet. Most companies are using one-time passwords or challenge-response mechanisms to protect the users' passwords from being sniffed off the Internet and being reused by intruders. However, all subsequent data traffic is unprotected. The benefits of using a VPN in this situation are many. A company that supports a large number of modems will have to continually update their modems to the latest commonly supported speeds and have to maintain and administer the modems and users. Instead, a company can let those worries fall in the hands of the Internet service providers. Instead of long-distance calls back to the company, employees can call local access numbers established by the Internet service providers, thus saving more expense. However, a VPN can also be created within an intranet. For example, the military may define a highly secure VPN that is realized within its privately owned network or intranet.

S/WAN (secure wide area network) is an initiative led by RSA Data Security, Inc. to promote IPsec-based multivendor VPNs among firewall and TCP/IP vendors. The initiative was introduced for Internet and intranet VPNs in January 1996. At that time, one of the main drawbacks of VPNs was that they worked only between homogeneous firewalls or tunnel servers, due to proprietary implementations. Consequently, S/WAN has tried to make recommendations and additions to the underlying IPSP and IKMP standards. With regard to IPSP, S/WAN proposes the additional use of RC5 at key sizes ranging from 40 bits for international exportability to 128 bits, and with regard to IKMP, both the SKIP and the ISAKMP/OAKLEY approaches are being investigated. Many firewall and TCP/IP software vendors have announced support for S/WAN-compliant VPNs and corresponding products.

There are also some open issues related to Internet layer security. For example, Steven Bellovin has compiled a list of problem areas for IPSP in [31]. The problems that he has found are indeed troubling and may leave us feeling uncomfortable with the current status of IPSP. Many problems stem from the intrinsic properties of the encryption modes used, coupled with the lack of integrity protection in some security transforms and the use of host-oriented keying. In [32], Bellovin has further investigated on the feasibility of so-called probable plaintext and traffic analysis attacks against IPSP.

Another interesting open issue is related to the use of compression in IPSP. Although the initial introduction of the topic was already presented at the 1994 IETF meeting in San Jose, the IETF IPsec WG has been debating the subject of incorporating lossless data compression into IPSP for almost three years now. Meanwhile, several companies have started to implement proprietary methods for compressing IP packets prior to encrypting them. In short, there are two main reasons for putting compression in IPSP:

- First of all, properly encrypted data is no longer compressible. More precisely, when an IP packet is properly encrypted, compression methods used at the network access layer, such as the PPP compression control protocol (CCP) [33], no longer work. If both compression and encryption are required, compression must always be performed first. At the same time that the CCP was defined, two sister protocols, the PPP encryption control protocol (ECP) and the PPP DES encryption protocol (DESE), were also defined [34,35]. In the corresponding protocol specifications, it is clearly mentioned that if the use of compression has been negotiated for a connection, compression must be performed prior to encryption. Unfortunately, ECP and DESE are not widely deployed on the Internet today.

- Secondly, Internet layer compression can reduce AH and ESP processing costs, as well as the likelihood of IP packet fragmentation.

With regard to Internet layer compression, two approaches have been discussed in the IETF: either make compression an optional feature of the IPSP ESP mechanism or create a separate and IPSP independent transform to support compression.

The two approaches are further addressed in a related Internet draft.[23] More recently, it has been proposed to charter an IETF IP Payload Compression Protocol (IPPCP) WG. The output of this WG would consist of a base architectural document that provides the framework for how Internet layer compression will be done, together with one or more documents giving specific compression algorithms and formats. The architectural document will describe how different compression algorithms can be negotiated and supported, but leave the documenting of specific compression algorithms to other documents. A registration mechanism for various compression formats will be specified as part of the base protocol.

In the next chapter we will focus on transport layer security protocols. In this context it is interesting to note that transport layer security protocols have a similar need to address compression. As a matter of fact, we will see that all transport layer security protocols in widespread use today do incorporate compression. Since transport layer security protocols are typically session-oriented, compression state can be maintained from one message to the next, thereby improving compression ratio. This is different for Internet layer security protocols. Since IP is a connectionless and stateless protocol, it is important that each compressed packet be capable of being decompressed independently of any other packet. Consequently, the successful decompression of a packet must not depend on the contents of any other packet(s), nor should it depend on order of receipt of any other packet(s). This makes the task of integrating compression into the Internet layer much more difficult than integrating it into the transport layer.

REFERENCES

[1] R. Nelson, "SDNS Services and Architecture," *Proceedings of National Computer Security Conference*, 1987, pp. 153 – 157.

[2] ISO/IEC 11577, Information technology - Telecommunications and information exchange between systems - Network layer security protocol, Geneva, Switzerland, 1993.

[3] J. Ioannidis, and M. Blaze, "The Architecture and Implementation of Network-Layer Security Under Unix," *Proceedings of the USENIX UNIX Security Symposium IV*, October 1993, pp. 29 – 39.

[4] R.J. Atkinson, "Security Architecture for the Internet Protocol," Request for Comments 1825, August 1995.

[5] R.J. Atkinson, "IP Authentication Header," Request for Comments 1826, August 1995.

---

[23] draft-monsour-compr-ipsec-00.txt

[6] R.J. Atkinson, "IP Encapsulating Security Payload," Request for Comments 1827, August 1995.

[7] P. Metzger, and W. Simpson, "IP Authentication using Keyed MD5," Request for Comments 1828, August 1995.

[8] P. Karn, P. Metzger, and W. Simpson, "The ESP DES-CBC Transform," Request for Comments 1829, August 1995.

[9] R.J. Atkinson, "Towards a More Secure Internet," *IEEE Computer*, Vol. 30, January 1997, pp. 57 – 61.

[10] A. Ballardie, and J. Crowcroft, "Multicast-specific Security Threats and Countermeasures," *Proceedings of Internet Society Symposium on Network and Distributed System Security*, February 1995, pp. 17 – 30.

[11] A. Ballardie, "Scalable Multicast Key Distribution," Request for Comments 1949, May 1996.

[12] R. Oppliger, and A. Albanese, "Distributed registration and key distribution (DiRK)," *Proceedings of IFIP SEC' 96*, May 1996, pp. 199 – 208.

[13] R. Oppliger, and A. Albanese, "Participants Registration, Validation, and Key Distribution for Large-scale Conferencing Systems," *IEEE Communications Magazine*, June 1997, pp. 130 – 135.

[14] L. Gong, "Using One-Way Functions for Authentication," *ACM Computer Communication Review*, Vol. 19, 1989, pp. 8 – 11.

[15] G. Tsudik, "Message Authentication with One-Way Hash Functions," *ACM Computer Communication Review*, Vol. 22, 1992, pp. 29 – 38.

[16] P. Metzger, and W. Simpson, "IP Authentication using Keyed SHA," Request for Comments 1852, September 1995.

[17] B. Preneel, and P. van Oorschot, "Building fast MACs from hash functions," *Proceedings of CRYPTO '95*, August 1996, pp. 1 – 14.

[18] M. Bellare, R. Canetti, and H. Krawczyk, "Keyed Hash Functions an Message Authentication," *Proceedings of CRYPTO '96*, August 1996, pp. 1 – 15.

[19] H. Krawczyk, M. Bellare, and R. Canetti, "HMAC: Keyed-Hashing for Message Authentication," Request for Comments 2104, February 1997.

[20] M. Oehler, and R. Glenn, "HMAC-MD5 IP Authentication with Replay Prevention," Request for Comments 2085, February 1997.

[21] P. Karn, P. Metzger, and W. Simpson, "The ESP Triple DES Transform," Request for Comments 1851, September 1995.

[22] P.C. Cheng, J.A. Garay, A. Herzberg, and H. Krawczyk, "Design and Implementation of Modular Key Management Protocol and IP Secure Tunnel on AIX," *Proceedings of USENIX UNIX Security Symposium*, June 1995.

[23] A. Aziz, and M. Patterson, "Design and Implementation of SKIP," ICG-95-0004 White Paper published by the Internet Commerce Group of Sun Microsystems, Inc. in June 1995, also printed in the *Proceedings of INET '95* under the title "Simple Key Management for Internet Protocols (SKIP)".

[24] R. Oppliger, "Internet Security: Firewalls and Beyond," *Communications of the ACM*, Vol. 40, May 1997, pp. 92 – 102.

[25] G. Caronni, H. Lubich, A. Aziz, T. Markson, and R. Skrenta, "SKIP – Securing the Internet," *Proceedings of WET ICE '96*, June 1996, pp. 62 – 67.

[26] W. Diffie, P.C. van Oorshot, and M.J. Wiener, "Authentication and Authenticated Key Exchanges," *Designs, Codes and Cryptography*, Kluwer Academic Publishers, 1992, pp. 107 – 125.

[27] J. Lowe, "A Grant of Rights to Use a Specific IBM patent with Photuris," Request for Comments 1822, August 1995.

[28] H. Krawczyk, "SKEME: A Versatile Secure Key Exchange Mechanism for Internet," *Proceedings of Internet Society Symposium on Network and Distributed System Security*, February 1996.

[29] D.A. Wagner, and S.M. Bellovin, "A "Bump in the Stack" Encryptor for MS-DOS Systems," *Proceedings of Internet Society Symposium on Network and Distributed System Security*, February 1996.

[30] D.L. McDonald, B.G. Phan, and R.J. Atkinson, "A Socket-Based Key Management API," *Proceedings of INET '96*, June 1996.

[31] S.M. Bellovin, "Problem Areas for the IP Security Protocols," *Proceedings of USENIX UNIX Security Symposium*, July 1996, pp. 205 – 214.

[32] S.M. Bellovin, "Cryptanalysis of the IP Security Protocols," *Proceedings of Internet Society Symposium on Network and Distributed System Security*, February 1997.

[33] D. Rand, "The PPP Compression Control Protocol (CCP)," Request for Comments 1962, June 1996.

[34] G. Meyer, "The PPP Encryption Control Protocol (ECP)," Request for Comments 1968, June 1996.

[35] K. Sklower, and G. Meyer, "The PPP DES Encryption Protocol (DESE)," Request for Comments 1968, June 1996.

Chapter 10

Transport Layer Security Protocols

In this chapter, we focus on the security protocols that have been proposed for the transport layer. After having a brief look at previous work in Section 10.1, we overview and further discuss the secure shell (SSH) in Section 10.2, the secure sockets layer (SSL) in Section 10.3, and the private communication technology (PCT) in Section 10.4. In Section 10.5, we focus on the work that is being done in the IETF transport layer security (TLS) WG to standardize a TLS protocol, and in Section 10.6 we conclude with a brief discussion of transport layer security in general and the various protocol proposals in particular.

10.1 PREVIOUS WORK

Again, the idea of having a standardized transport layer security protocol is not new, and several protocols had been proposed before the IETF TLS WG even started to meet:

- The *Security Protocol 4* (SP4) is a transport layer security protocol that was developed by the NSA and NIST as part of the secure data network system (SDNS) suite of security protocols [1].

- The *Transport Layer Security Protocol* (TLSP) was developed and standardized by the International Organization for Standardization (ISO) [2].

In addition to that, Matt Blaze and Steven Bellovin from AT&T Bell Laboratories have developed an *Encrypted Session Manager* (ESM) software package [3]. As this package resembles the secure shell (SSH) overviewed and discussed in the following section, it is not further addressed in this book.

10.2 SECURE SHELL

The *secure shell* (SSH) is a relatively simple program that can be used to securely log in to a remote machine, to execute commands on that machine, and to move files from one machine to another. SSH provides strong authentication and secure communications over insecure channels. As such, it is intended as a complete replacement for the Berkeley r-tools, such as `rlogin`, `rsh`, `rcp`, and `rdist`. It can also replace `telnet` in many cases. Furthermore, X11 and arbitrary TCP/IP connections can be secured using the integrated port forwarding feature of SSH. There is also support for SOCKS.

SSH was created mostly by one person, Tatu Ylönen from the Helsinki University of Technology, Finland. There are currently two versions of SSH available:

- A public version that has been freely available for various UNIX systems since July 1995. The current SSH version 1.2.17 was officially released in October 1996. Source, documentation, and configuration scripts are publicly available and can be downloaded from the SSH home page on the WWW.[1]

- A commercial version called *F-Secure SSH* that is available for various UNIX systems, as well as for Windows 3.x, Windows 95, Windows NT, OS/2, and MacOS. F-Secure SSH products are jointly developed and sold as part of a marketing and technology alliance between Data Fellows Ltd.[2] and SSH Communications Security Oy.[3] Data Fellows Ltd. is a privately held Finish software development company with subsidiaries in the United States and Estonia, whereas SSH Communications Security Oy is a small startup company founded by Ylönen. The commercial version of SSH is equipped with a number of additional features and utilities. For example, the Encrypting Data Dumper (EDD) can be used to

---

[1] http://www.cs.hut.fi/ssh

[2] http://www.DataFellows.com or http://www.Europe.DataFellows.com

[3] http://www.ssh.fi

transparently encrypt arbitrary data streams (i.e., for backup purposes). Also, professional technical support and maintenance agreements are available only for the commercial version of SSH. F-Secure SSH is used and widely deployed on the Internet today. According to a press release issued in April 1996, F-Secure SSH is being used at thousands of sites in at least 40 countries.

SSH and F-Secure SSH both utilize a generic transport layer security proto-col. When used over TCP/IP, the server normally listens for TCP/IP connections on port 22. This port number has been registered with the IANA and is offi-cially assigned for SSH. In short, the SSH protocol provides support for both host authentication and user authentication, together with data compression and data confidentiality and integrity protection. Disadvantageous is the fact that SSH uses manually distributed and preconfigured public keys instead of a certificate-based key management.

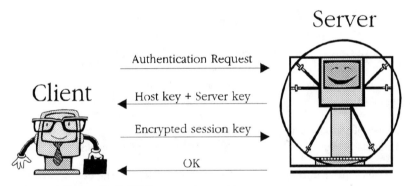

Figure 10.1   A Secure Shell (SSH) protocol execution.

Figure 10.1 illustrates and overviews an SSH protocol execution. The protocol starts with the client sending an authentication request to the server. The server, in turn, sends back to the client its public host key, which is typically a 1,024-bit RSA key, and a public server key, which is typically a 768-bit RSA key that changes every hour by default. The purpose of the host key is to bind the connection to the desired server host, whereas the purpose of the periodically changing server key is to make decrypting recorded traffic impossible even in the case of a host key compromise. The server key must therefore never be saved on disk. The client now compares the received host key against its own database of manually distributed and preconfigured public host keys. The client normally accepts the key of an unknown host and stores it in its database for future use. This makes the use of SSH practical in most environments. However, in high-security environments it is also possible to configure the SSH client to refuse access to any host whose public key is not properly registered in the client database. If the client accepts the host key, it generates a 256-bit random number that serves as the session key. Furthermore, the client chooses an encryption algorithm from those supported by the server, typically Blowfish, DES, or three-key Triple-DES in CBC mode. The client pads the session key with random bytes, double encrypts it with the public host and server RSA keys, and sends the result to the server. The server, in turn, decrypts the RSA double encryption and recovers the session key accordingly. Both parties can now start using the session key and transparently encrypt the connection. The server sends an encrypted confirmation to the client. Receipt of this confirmation tells the client that the server has been able to successfully decrypt the session key, and must therefore hold its private keys. From that moment on, the client assumes the server to be authentic and transport layer encryption and integrity protection to be in proper use.

In certain cases, user authentication may be required as well. The corresponding exchange is initiated by the client who sends an authentication request to the server. The request declares the user name to log in. Depending on the authentication method, the dialogue that takes place between the client and the server may look different. There are two authentication methods currently supported in F-Secure SSH version 1.0:

- In the case of *password authentication*, the user password is transmitted over the communication channel that is transparently encrypted by SSH.

- In the case of *RSA authentication*, the server challenges the client with a random number that is encrypted with the public key of the user. In this case, the server must also have access to a database of manually distributed and preconfigured public keys for registered users. The client can only decrypt the challenge if it knows the private key of the user. It therefore requests a passphrase that is needed to temporarily unlock the user's private key. To authenticate to the server, the client must respond with a correct MD5 hash value of the decrypted challenge and some additional data that binds the result to the current session.

In either case, the server must respond with an authentication success or failure. If client authentication is not required, or if the client has been able to successfully authenticate to the server, it can now request a service. In particular, it can securely log in to a remote system (`slogin`), execute commands (`ssh`), transfer files (`scp`), and so on. Session keys can also be reexchanged dynamically. In addition, there are several tools that the client and server can use for the management of SSH and related configuration files [4].

The SSH transport layer protocol requires manually distributed and preconfigured public keys of hosts and users. In this matter, SSH differs from other transport layer security protocols introduced in this chapter. In particular, we will see that SSL, PCT, and TLSP all support certificate-based key management instead of manual key management. This is advantageous for the wide use and deployment of any transport layer security protocol. However, SSH is intentionally open to any public key infrastructure (PKI) that may be put in place. Each PKI may define its own public key and certificate format.

It is also important to note that the cryptographic technologies that are used by SSH and F-Secure SSH have been developed in Europe and do not fall under the U.S. export controls. The products can be used in every country where encryption is legal, including the United States. Note, however, that SSH cannot be used in countries that either control the use of encryption technology or restrict the import of corresponding products. The licensing and legality issues are a little more complicated due to the use of RSA, IDEA, and some other patented technologies. SSH can be used legally for noncommercial applications, since noncommercial use of RSA and IDEA is usually allowed without a license. In addition to that, F-Secure SSH products are being sold with the licenses required to legally use them.

More recently, an IETF secure shell (SECSH) WG was chartered to update and standardize the SSH transport layer security protocol. In September 1996, the SSH protocol described above was divided into an SSH transport layer protocol and a related SSH authentication protocol layered on top of the SSH transport layer protocol. This distinction is different than with the other transport layer security protocols that typically distinguish between a record and a handshake protocol. Both the SSH transport layer protocol and the SSH authentication protocol are specified in Internet Drafts and overviewed next. The version number that refers to these SSH protocols is 2.0. It is very likely that future implementations of SSH and F-Secure SSH will conform to SSH 2.0.

10.2.1   SSH Transport Layer Protocol

The *SSH transport layer protocol* provides cryptographic host authentication as well as data confidentiality and integrity protection. The protocol does not provide user authentication. As described above, the SSH authentication protocol is layered on top of the SSH transport layer protocol to provide user authentication for services that need it.

The SSH transport layer protocol supports various key exchange, secret and public key, hash and message authentication algorithms that are negotiated during connection establishment. There are mandatory algorithms that all implementations are required to support, and other algorithms that are defined in the protocol specification but are optional. Furthermore, it is expected that in real applications, organizations will also want to use proprietary algorithms. This leads to the problem of how algorithm identifiers are allocated. In principle, anyone can define additional algorithms for SSH by using names in the format `name@domainname`. For example, the Swiss Federal Office of Information Technology and Systems (BFI) can define a new encryption algorithm `newcipher@bfi.admin.ch`, with `newcipher` referring to the name of the encryption algorithm and `bfi.admin.ch` referring to the domain name of the BFI.

When the SSH protocol is used to establish a TCP/IP connection between a client and a server, the two parties first exchange identification strings that contain the SSH protocol and software version numbers in use. Key exchange will begin immediately afterwards. All SSH messages use a specific binary packet protocol that is specified in the Internet Draft mentioned above. When a protocol execution starts, no data compression, encryption, and message authentication are typically in use. During key exchange, however, data compression, encryption, and message authentication algorithms are negotiated, selected, and used for all subsequent messages. The currently defined algorithms for SSH data compression, encryption, message authentication, and key exchange are overviewed in Tables 10.1 to 10.4.

Table 10.1

Data Compression Algorithms Supported by SSH 2.0

Value	Description	Status
none	No compression	Mandatory
zlib	GNU ZLIB compression at level 6	Optional

The GNU ZLIB compression algorithm is specified in RFC 1950. It is a stateful compression algorithm, meaning that compression state and context is initialized and passed from one message to the next with only a partial flush being performed at the end of each message. A partial flush means that all data will be output, but the next message will continue using compression tables from the end of the previous message. Compression is independent in each direction, and different compression algorithms may also be used for each direction.

Table 10.2

Encryption Algorithms Supported by SSH 2.0

Value	Description	Status
none	No encryption	Optional
3des-cbc	Three key Triple-DES in CBC mode	Mandatory
idea-cbc	IDEA in CBC mode	Optional
arcfour	ARCFOUR stream cipher	Optional
blowfish-cbc	Blowfish in CBC mode	Optional

An encryption algorithm and a corresponding cryptographic key are also negotiated and selected during key exchange. When encryption is in effect, certain fields
of each message are encrypted with this algorithm and key. Therefore, all messages
sent in one direction are considered as a single data stream, and the initialization
vectors are passed from the end of one message to the beginning of the next. The
encryption steps in each direction run independently of each other; they typically
use different keys, and different encryption algorithms may also be used in each
direction. Note that three key Triple-DES is the only encryption algorithm that
is mandatory for SSH 2.0. Also note that ARCFOUR is a stream cipher that is
compatible with RC4, developed by Ron Rivest for RSA Data Security, Inc.

Table 10.3

Message Authentication Algorithms Supported by SSH 2.0

Value	Description	Status
none	No MAC	Optional
hmac-md5	HMAC-MD5	Optional
hmac-sha	HMAC-SHA	Optional
md5-8	First 8 bytes of MD5 key + data + key	Optional
sha-8	First 8 bytes of SHA key + data + key	Optional
sha	SHA of key + data + key	Mandatory

Data authenticity and integrity are protected by including with each SSH message a message authentication code (MAC) that is computed from a shared secret,
a 32-bit sequence number, and the actual contents of the message. The sequence
number is never transmitted between the communicating peers, but is included in
MAC computation and verification to ensure that no messages are lost or received
out of order. The sequence number of the first message is set to zero; from there

on the sequence number is incremented by 1 for each packet sent. The MAC is transmitted without encryption as the last part of the SSH message. The length of the MAC depends on the algorithm in use. Again, the message authentication algorithm and key are negotiated during key exchange and may be different for each direction. We have discussed the various message authentication algorithms in Section 9.3, when we talked about the HMAC construction and the possibility of truncating the output of a MAC algorithm. SSH 2.0 makes use of these options. In particular, `hmac-md5` and `hmac-sha` make use of the HMAC construction, and `md5-8` and `sha-8` make use of the possibility of truncating the output of a MAC algorithm to 8 bytes. Even though only the `sha` message authentication algorithm is mandatory for SSH 2.0, it is recommended that implementations may support other algorithms as well.

Table 10.4
Key Exchange Algorithm Supported by SSH 2.0

Value	Description	Status
double-encrypting-sha	Double-encrypting key exchange	Mandatory

Currently, only the double-encrypting key exchange algorithm is used in F-Secure SSH and is defined for SSH 2.0. Remember that the double-encrypting key exchange requires that the host and server keys both support encryption, and that their sizes must be compatible in such a way that the result of encrypting a value with one of them can be encrypted with the other. The smaller of the keys must be able to encrypt at least 48 bytes. With this key exchange algorithm server authentication is implicit, meaning that the client can't be sure about the server's identity until it receives a message from the server that uses proper encryption and message authentication. An attacker could fool the client into using no encryption, and the client might in some cases reveal sensitive data, such as a password, before it notices that the server is not responding properly. For this reason, it is strongly recommended that the client wait for a server response before it starts sending sensitive data.

In short, the message flows of an SSH transport layer protocol execution between a client C and a server S can be summarized as follows:

1 : C	$\longrightarrow$	S	: SSH_MSG_KEXINIT
2 : S	$\longrightarrow$	C	: SSH_MSG_KEXINIT
3 : S	$\longrightarrow$	C	: SSH_MSG_KEXRSA_HOSTKEY
4 : C	$\longrightarrow$	S	: SSH_MSG_KEXRSA_SESSIONKEY
5 : C	$\longrightarrow$	S	: SSH_MSG_NEWKEYS
6 : S	$\longrightarrow$	C	: SSH_MSG_NEWKEYS

In steps 1 and 2, the client and server exchange SSH_MSG_KEXINIT messages that include lists of supported data compression, encryption, message authentication, and key exchange algorithms. For each algorithm type, the first algorithm on the client's list that is also on the the server's list will be selected.

In step 3, the server starts the double-encrypting key exchange by sending an SSH_MSG_KEXRSA_HOSTKEY message to the client. The message includes the public host and server keys. After receiving the SSH_MSG_KEXRSA_HOSTKEY message, the client verifies whether the host key belongs to the intended server. How this verification happens is not specified by SSH. Currently, it may be checked against a database of known name-key mappings. In the future, it will be validated using a PKI. It is now up to the client to generate a 256-bit random session key. In order to make sure that no one has been manipulating the key exchange so far, the client computes an SHA-1 hash value from the concatenated payloads of the client and server SSH_MSG_KEXINIT messages, the server SSH_MSG_KEXRSA_HOSTKEY message, and the session key. This value is called the session identifier and is used to authenticate the key exchange as a whole. The session identifier is computed only once; it is neither changed nor recomputed if keys are reexchanged later.

In step 4, the client concatenates six 0 bytes, the first 10 bytes of the session identifier, and the 32 bytes of the shared secret, double encrypts the resulting 48 bytes with both the public host and server keys (the smaller key is applied first), and sends a corresponding SSH_MSG_KEXRSA_SESSIONKEY message to the server. Upon receiving this message, the server uses its private host and server public keys to decrypt the session key. As a result of the key exchange, the client and server share a 256-bit secret that can now be used to compute session keys.

The key exchange ends by having each side sending an SSH_MSG_NEWKEYS message to the other side in steps 5 and 6. These messages are sent with the old algorithms and keys in use. All messages sent after these messages will use the new algorithms and keys.

Either side may request a key reexchange at any point in time after the initial key exchange by sending a new SSH_MSG_KEXINIT message to the other. When this message is received, the peer entity must respond with an SSH_MSG_KEXINIT message of its own. Key reexchange is performed under whatever encryption was in effect when the exchange was started. Data compression, encryption, and message authentication algorithms and keys are changed when SSH_MSG_NEWKEYS messages are sent after the key exchange. The SSH protocol specification recommends performing a key reexchange after each gigabyte of transferred data or after one hour of connection time, whichever comes sooner.

After having executed the SSH transport layer protocol, the client may request a service on the user's behalf. Each service is identified by a unique service name. Most SSH server implementations have a table of services that are supported, specifying what to do for each of these services. The client requests a service by sending an SSH_SERVICE_REQUEST message to the server. If the server supports the service and permits the client to use it, it responds with a corresponding SSH_SERVICE_ACCEPT message. Once a particular service has been selected, data is transmitted in SSH_STREAM_DATA messages. When the server or client application closes its output, a SSH_STREAM_EOF message is sent to the other side. When either side wants to terminate communications, it sends an SSH_STREAM_CLOSE message to the other side. Upon receiving this message, the other side sends back another SSH_STREAM_CLOSE message.

10.2.2   SSH Authentication Protocol

The *SSH authentication protocol* is designed to run over the SSH transport layer protocol to provide user authentication. The corresponding service name is ssh-userauth. In short, user authentication works by the client first declaring the service name and the user name to access the service. The server, in turn, responds with the set of authentication methods that are acceptable for this service, and the client sends back a corresponding authentication request to the server. The dialogue continues until access has been granted or denied.

Similar to encryption algorithms, some user authentication methods are predefined in the SSH protocol specification and additional methods may be defined by using names in the format name@domainname. This ensures that private extensions can be implemented without breaking compatibility and without requiring a central registry of user authentication method names. Table 10.5 overviews the authentication methods that are predefined in the current SSH authentication protocol specification.

Mainly to declare the service and user name, the client sends an SSH_USERAUTH_START message to the server. The server, in turn, may send back an SSH_USERAUTH_BANNER message that contains a prelogin banner to

Table 10.5
Authentication Methods Supported by SSH

Value	Authentication Method
password	Password authentication
securid	SecurID authentication
skey	S/Key one-time password authentication
opie	OPIE one-time password authentication
publickey	Possession of private key
hostbased	Identity of client host and user
kerberos4	Kerberos V4 authentication
kerberos5	Kerberos V5 authentication
kerberos-afs	AFS Kerberos authentication

be displayed on the client before attempting to authenticate a user. Next, the client sends an SSH_USERAUTH_REQUEST message to the server. This message is authentication-method-specific but uses a generic message format. Only the first few fields are defined; the remaining fields depend on the authentication method in use. There are several user authentication methods that basically work by the client sending some kind of identification and authentication information to the server, and the server directly responding with either success (SSH_USERAUTH_SUCCESS message) or failure (SSH_USERAUTH_FAILURE message). Examples of this type are the password and securid authentication methods. Note that in the case of the password method, the authenticating information is basically a user password. The password is yet sent in the clear, but the entire SSH message (including the password) is encrypted by the SSH transport layer protocol. Another common form of user authentication is one where the server sends a challenge to the client and the client returns an appropriate response. In this case, the server challenges the client with a SSH_USERAUTH_OTP_PROMPT message, and the client responds with a SSH_USERAUTH_OTP_RESPONSE message. Most one-time password methods use this form of user authentication; examples include the skey and opie authentication methods. The publickey and hostbased authentication methods work by having the client send a signature created with a private key. In the case of the publickey authentication method, the private key belongs to the user, whereas in the case of the hostbased authentication method, the private key belongs to the client host and the user is registered on that particular host. Finally, there are several authentication methods, such as the Andrew File System (AFS), that use either Kerberos (V4 and V5) or a Kerberized file system. In this case, the SSH_USERAUTH_REQUEST messages typically include some sort of user credentials or tickets.

The various authentication methods are further described in the SSH authentication protocol specification. Once the server has successfully returned a SSH_USERAUTH_SUCCESS message to the client, any nonauthentication messages sent by the client will be passed directly to the addressed service layered on top of the SSH authentication protocol.

10.3   SECURE SOCKETS LAYER

In Internet application programming, it is common to use a generalized interprocess communications facility (IPC) to work with different transport layer protocols. Two popular IPC interfaces are BSD Sockets and the transport layer interface (TLI), found on System V UNIX derivats. One idea that one may think of first when trying to provide security services for TCP/IP applications in general, and the Internet in particular, is to enhance an IPC interface such as BSD Sockets with the ability to authenticate peer entities, to exchange secret keys, and to use these keys to authenticate and encrypt data streams that are transmitted between the communicating peer entities.

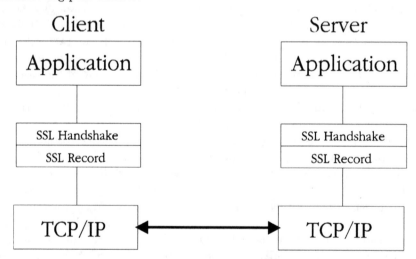

Figure 10.2   The architectural placement of the Secure Sockets Layer (SSL).

Netscape Communications Corporation followed this approach when it specified a *secure sockets layer* (SSL) and a corresponding SSL protocol. Version 1.0 of the SSL protocol was used inside Netscape only. It was not before version 2.0 that the SSL protocol was shipped with the Netscape Navigator versions 1 and 2. As such, SSL 2.0 has become a de facto standard for cryptographic protection of HTTP traffic. But SSL 2.0 has several limitations and restrictions both in cryptographic security and functionality. Consequently, the protocol was upgraded with public review and significant input from industry to SSL 3.0. This newer version of the SSL protocol was officially released in December 1995. The latest Internet Draft specifying SSL 3.0 was issued in November 1996.[4] The following description of SSL is based on this latest protocol specification. Note that most implementations available today conform either to SSL 2.0 or SSL 3.0. Comparably few implementations conform to both versions of the SSL transport layer security protocol.

The architectural placement of SSL is illustrated in Figure 10.2. Note that SSL is layered on top of a reliable transport service, such as that provided by TCP/IP, and that it is conceptually able to provide security services for arbitrary TCP/IP applications. As a matter of fact, one major advantage of transport layer security in general, and SSL in particular, is that it is application-independent, meaning that it can be used to transparently secure any TCP/IP application that may be layered on top of it. In short, the SSL protocol provides TCP/IP connection security that has three basic properties:

- First, the communicating peers can authenticate each other using public key cryptography.

- Second, the confidentiality of the transmitted data is protected, as the connection is transparently encrypted after an initial handshake and session key determination.

- Third, the integrity of the transmitted data is protected, as messages are transparently authenticated and integrity-checked with MACs.

It is important to note that the SSL protocol does not protect against traffic analysis attacks. For example, by examining the unencrypted IP source and destination addresses and TCP port numbers, or examining the volume of network traffic flow, a traffic analyst can eventually determine what parties are interacting, what types of services are being used, or sometimes recover information about business or personal relationships. We have already mentioned previously that users generally consider the threat of traffic analysis to be relatively harmless, and SSL therefore does not attempt to address it either.

---

[4]`draft-ietf-tls-ssl-version3-00.txt`

In order to make use of SSL, the client and server must both know that the other side is using SSL. In general, there are three possibilities to address this issue:

- The first possibility is to use dedicated port numbers reserved by the IANA. In this case, a separate port number must be assigned for every application protocol with SSL support.

- The second possibility is to use the normal port number for every application protocol, and to negotiate security options as part of the application protocol.

- The third possibility is to use a TCP option to negotiate the use of a security protocol, such as SSL, during the normal TCP/IP connection establishment phase.

The application-specific negotiation of security options has the disadvantage of requiring each application protocol to be modified to understand the negotiation process. Also, defining a TCP option would be a fine solution, but has not been seriously discussed so far. In practice, separate port numbers have been reserved and assigned by the IANA for every application protocol with SSL support. The port numbers that have been officially assigned by the IANA are overviewed in Table 10.6.

Table 10.6
Port Numbers Assigned for Application Protocols with SSL Support

Keyword	Port	Description
https	443	HTTP with SSL support
ssmtp	465	SMTP with SSL support
snntp	563	NNTP with SSL support
sldap	636	LDAP with SSL support
spop3	995	POP3 with SSL support

We have introduced HTTP, SMTP, and NNTP in Chapter 2. The lightweight directory access protocol (LDAP) is a streamlined and simplified version of the OSI directory access protocol (DAP) that is used to access X.500 directory services. It is commonly agreed that LDAP will be the short-term solution to provide access to directory services within the Internet, and that LDAP with SSL support will be used to secure this access. Finally the post office protocol (POP) is used by an SMTP user agent to access a message store or mailbox.

Table 10.7

Port Numbers Used for Application Protocols with SSL Support

Keyword	Port	Description
ftp-data	889	FTP data with SSL support
ftps	990	FTP control with SSL support
imaps	991	IMAP4 with SSL support
telnets	992	TELNET with SSL support
ircs	993	IRC with SSL support

IANA registration and assignment should not be pursued until there is consensus that exploiting dedicated port numbers is the architectural direction in which SSL should be going. Unfortunately, this concensus has not been reached so far. Also note that it is not necessary to register port numbers with the IANA in order to use a specific application protocol with SSL support. The port numbers must just be agreed-to within the community of users, either by pre-agreement or by explicit specification within a URL. As a matter of fact, there are several port numbers used for application protocols with SSL support that are not yet assigned officially by the IANA. These port numbers are overviewed in Table 10.7. Note, however, that some of these port numbers will have been assigned officially by the IANA at the time this book is published.

Table 10.8

SSL Session State Elements

Element	Description
Session ID	Identifier chosen by the server to identify an active or resumable session state.
Peer certificate	X.509 version 3 certificate of the peer entity.
Compression method	Algorithm used to compress data prior to encryption.
Cipher spec	Specification of the data encryption and MAC algorithms.
Master secret	48-byte secret shared between the client and server.
Is resumable	Flag that indicates whether the session can be used to initiate new connections.

In general, an SSL session is stateful and it is the responsibility of the SSL handshake protocol to coordinate the session and connection states on both the client and server side. The corresponding session and connection state elements are overviewed in Tables 10.8 and 10.9. Parties may have multiple simultaneous sessions as well as sessions with multiple connections.

Table 10.9
SSL Connection State Elements

Element	Description
Server and client random	Byte sequences that are chosen by the server and client for each connection.
Server write MAC secret	Secret used for MAC operations on data written by the server.
Client write MAC secret	Secret used for MAC operations on data written by the client.
Server write key	Key used for data encryption by the server and decryption by the client.
Client write key	Key used for data encryption by the client and decryption by the server.
Initialization vector	Initiatization state for a block cipher in CBC mode. This field is first initialized by the SSL handshake protocol. Thereafter, the final ciphertext block from each record is preserved for use with the following record.
Sequence number	Each party maintains separate sequence numbers for transmitted and received messages for each connection.

As also illustrated in Figure 10.2, the SSL protocol consists of two subprotocols, namely the SSL record protocol and the SSL handshake protocol. In short, the SSL record protocol provides data authenticity, confidentiality, and integrity services, as well as replay protection over a connection-oriented reliable transport service, such as provided by TCP. Several SSL protocols may be layered above the record protocol. Notably the most important protocol is the SSL handshake protocol, an authentication and key exchange protocol that also negotiates, initializes, and synchronizes security parameters and corresponding state at both endpoints of the connection. After the SSL handshake protocol completes, sensitive application data may be sent via the SSL record protocol according to the negotiated security parameters and state. The SSL record and handshake protocols are overviewed next.

10.3.1   SSL Record Protocol

The *SSL record protocol* receives data from higher layer protocols and deals with data fragmentation, compression, authentication, and encryption accordingly. More precisely, the protocol takes as input a data block of arbitrary size, and produces as output a series of SSL records of maximal $2^{14} - 1 = 16,383$ bytes each.

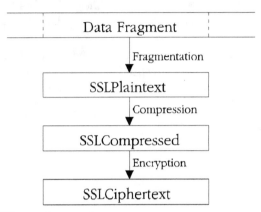

Figure 10.3 The SSL record protocol steps.

The various steps of the SSL record protocol that lead from a raw data fragment to an SSLPlaintext, SSLCompressed, and SSLCiphertext record are illustrated in Figure 10.3. Each SSL record contains the following information:

- Content type;

- Protocol version number;

- Length;

- Data payload (optionally compressed and encrypted);

- Message authentication code (MAC).

The content type defines the higher layer protocol that must be used to subsequently process the SSL record data payload. The protocol version number determines the SSL version number (typically version 3.0). Each SSL record data payload may be compressed and encrypted according to the current compression method and encryption algorithm. At the start of an SSL session, the compression method and encryption algorithm are usually defined as null. They are both set during the SSL handshake protocol execution. Finally, a MAC is appended to the SSL record. The MAC is computed before the data payload is encrypted. The techniques that are used to compute the MAC and to encrypt the data payload are actually defined in the cipher spec of the current session state. By default, the SSL record protocol uses a slightly modified version of the HMAC construction introduced in Section 9.3. In essence, the modification refers to the inclusion of a sequence number in the message before hashing in order to prevent some forms of replay attacks.

In general, several SSL protocols may be layered on top of the SSL record protocol. Each SSL protocol may refer to specific types of messages that are sent using the SSL record protocol. The SSL 3.0 specification defines the following three SSL protocols:

- Alert protocol;

- Handshake protocol;

- ChangeCipherSpec protocol.

The SSL alert protocol is used to transmit alerts by the SSL record protocol. Alerts are a specific type of message that consist of two parts: an alert level and an alert description. The SSL handshake is the main SSL protocol and is overviewed in the following subsection. Finally, the SSL ChangeCipherSpec protocol is used to change between one cipher spec and another. Although the cipher spec is normally changed at the end of an SSL handshake, it can also be changed at any time. In addition to these SSL protocols, the record protocol can also be used to send arbitrary user data.

10.3.2   SSL Handshake Protocol

The *SSL handshake protocol* is the main protocol that is layered on top of the SSL record protocol. Consequently, SSL handshake messages are supplied to the SSL record layer, where they are encapsulated within one or more SSL records, which are processed and transmitted as specified by the compression method and cipher spec of the current session and connection states. The aim of the SSL handshake protocol is to have a client and server establish the protocols that will be used during communications, select the compression method and cipher spec, optionally authenticate each other, and create a master secret from which the various session keys for message authentication and encryption may be derived. The corresponding SSL handshake protocol can be summarized as follows:

1 : C	$\longrightarrow$	S	: CLIENTHELLO
2 : S	$\longrightarrow$	C	: SERVERHELLO
:			: [CERTIFICATE]
:			: [SERVERKEYEXCHANGE]
:			: [CERTIFICATEREQUEST]
:			: SERVERHELLODONE
3 : C	$\longrightarrow$	S	: [CERTIFICATE]
:			: CLIENTKEYEXCHANGE
:			: [CERTIFICATEVERIFY]
:			: CHANGECIPHERSPEC
:			: FINISHED
4 : S	$\longrightarrow$	C	: CHANGECIPHERSPEC
:	•		: FINISHED

Again, the messages that are put in square brackets are optional. An SSL handshake protocol execution usually starts with the client and server sending hello messages to each other. The hello messages are used to exchange security enhancement capabilities. Any time, the server can send a HELLOREQUEST message to the client. It is a simple notification that the client should begin the negotiation process anew by sending a CLIENTHELLO message to the server. If a handshake protocol execution is already underway, the client simply ignores the server's HELLOREQUEST message. Otherwise, a normal SSL handshake protocol execution may start.

When a client wants to connect to a particular server, he or she sends a corresponding CLIENTHELLO message in step 1. The client can also send a CLIENTHELLO message in response to a HELLOREQUEST message or on its own initiative in order to renegotiate the security parameters of an existing connection. The CLIENTHELLO message includes

- The number of the highest SSL version understood by the client (typically 3.0);

- A client-generated random structure that consists of a 32-bit timestamp in standard UNIX format, and a 28-byte value generated by a random number generator;

- A session identity the client wishes to use for this connection;

- A list of cipher suites that the client supports;

- A list of compression methods that the client supports.

Note that the Session Identity field should be empty if no session is currently available or the client wishes to generate new security parameters. In either case, a nonempty session identity value declares a session between the same client and server whose security parameters the client wishes to reuse. The session identity may be from an earlier connection, this connection, or another currently active connection. Also note that the list of supported cipher suites, passed from the client to the server in the CLIENTHELLO message, contains the combinations of cryptographic algorithms supported by the client in order of preference. Each cipher suite defines both a key exchange algorithm and a cipher spec. The server will select a cipher suite or, if no acceptable choices are presented, return an error message and close the connection accordingly. After having sent the CLIENTHELLO message, the client waits for a SERVERHELLO message. Any other handshake message returned by the server except for a HELLOREQUEST message is treated as an error.

In step 2, the server processes the CLIENTHELLO message and responds with either an error message or a SERVERHELLO message. The SERVERHELLO message includes the same fields as the CLIENTHELLO message. In particular, the SERVER-HELLO message includes

- A server version number that contains the lower version of that suggested by the client in the CLIENTHELLO message and the highest supported by the server;

- A server-generated random structure that also consists of a 32-bit timestamp in standard UNIX format, and a 28-byte value generated by a random number generator;

- A session identity corresponding to this connection;

- A cipher suite selected by the server from the list of cipher suites supported by the client;

- A compression method selected by the server from the list of compression algorithms supported by the client.

If the session identity in the CLIENTHELLO message was nonempty, the server looks in its session cache for a match. If a match is found and the server is willing to establish the new connection using the corresponding session state, the server responds with the same value as supplied by the client. This indicates a resumed session and dictates that both parties must proceed directly to the CHANGECI-PHERSPEC and FINISHED messages. Otherwise, this field contains a different value identifying the new session. The server may also return an empty session identity to indicate that the session will not be cached and therefore cannot be resumed later. Also note that in the SERVERHELLO message the server selects a cipher suite and a compression method from the corresponding lists provided by the client in the CLIENTHELLO message. The key exchange, authentication, encryption, and message authentication algorithms are determined by the cipher suite selected by the server and revealed in the SERVERHELLO message. The cipher suites that are currently defined for the SSL protocol are overviewed in Appendix C of the SSL protocol specification and therefore not repeated in this book.

In addition to the SERVERHELLO message, the server may also send other messages to the client. For example, if the server is to be authenticated, it sends a certificate in a corresponding CERTIFICATE message immediately following the SERVERHELLO message. The certificate type must be appropriate for the selected cipher suite's key exchange algorithm, and is generally an X.509 certificate. The same message type will be used later for the client's response to the server's CERTIFICATEREQUEST message. In the case of X.509 certificates, the certificate may actually refer to an entire chain of certificates, ordered with the sender's certificate first followed by any CA certificates proceeding sequentially upward.

Next, the server may send a SERVERKEYEXCHANGE message to the client if it has no certificate, a certificate that can be used only for signing, or uses the FORTEZZA token-based key exchange algorithm (KEA). This message is not used if the server certificate contains Diffie-Hellman parameters. Also, a nonanonymous server can optionally request a certificate in order to authenticate the client. It therefore sends a CERTIFICATEREQUEST message to the client. The message includes a list of the types of certificates requested, sorted in order of the server's preference, as well as a list of distinguished names for acceptable CAs. At the end of step 2, the server sends a SERVERHELLODONE message to the client that indicates the end of the SERVERHELLO and associated messages.

Upon receipt of the SERVERHELLO and associated messages, the client verifies that the server provided a valid certificate, if required, and checks that the security parameters provided in the SERVERHELLO message are acceptable. If the server has requested client authentication, it sends a CERTIFICATE message that includes a certificate for its public key to the server in step 3. Next, the client sends a CLIENTKEYEXCHANGE message, whose format depends on the key exchange algorithm selected by the server:

- If RSA is used for server authentication and key exchange, the client generates a 48-byte premaster secret, encrypts it under the public key from the server's certificate or temporary RSA key from the SERVERKEYEXCHANGE message, and sends the result back to the server in the CLIENTKEYEXCHANGE message. The server, in turn, uses its private key to decrypt the premaster secret.

- If FORTEZZA tokens are used for key exchange, the client derives a token encryption key (TEK) using the KEA. The client's KEA calculation uses the public key from the server certificate along with some private parameters in the client's token. The client sends public parameters needed for the server to also generate the TEK, using its private parameters. It generates a pre-master secret, wraps it using the TEK, and sends the result together with some initialization vectors to the server as part of the CLIENTKEYEXCHANGE message. The server, in turn, can decrypt the premaster secret accordingly.

- If a Diffie-Hellman key exchange is performed, the server and client send their public parameters as part of the SERVERKEYEXCHANGE and CLIENTKEYEX-CHANGE messages to each other. Obviously, this is only required if the Diffie-Hellman public parameters are not included in the server and client certificates. The negotiated Diffie-Hellman key may then serve as a pre-master secret.

For RSA, FORTEZZA, and Diffie-Hellman key exchange, the same algorithms are used to convert the premaster secret into a 48-byte master secret, and to derive session keys for encryption and message authentication accordingly. Nevertheless, some key exchange algorithms, such as FORTEZZA token-based key exchange, may also use their own procedures for generating encryption keys. In this case, the master key is used only to derive keys for message authentication. The procedures to derive master and session keys, as well as initialization vectors, are fully described in the SSL protocol specifications and are not further addressed in this book.

Next, the client may send a CERTIFICATEVERIFY message to the server. This message is used to provide explicit verification of a client certificate. It is only sent following a client certificate that has signing capability (i.e., all certificates except those containing fixed Diffie-Hellman parameters). Finally, the client finishes step 3 by sending a CHANGECIPHERSPEC message and a corresponding FINISHED message to the server. The FINISHED message is always sent immediately after the CHANGECIPHERSPEC message to verify that the key exchange and authentication processes were indeed successful. As a matter of fact, the FINISHED message is always the first message protected with the newly negotiated algorithms and secret keys. No acknowledgment of the FINISHED message is required; parties may begin sending encrypted data immediately after having sent the FINISHED message. The SSL handshake protocol execution finishes up by also having the server send a

CHANGECIPHERSPEC message and a corresponding FINISHED message to the client in step 4.

After the SSL handshake is complete, a secure connection is established between the client and the server. This connection can now be used to send application data that is encapsulated by the SSL record protocol. More precisely, application data may be fragmented, compressed, encrypted, and authenticated according to the SSL record protocol and the session and connection states just established.

When the client and server decide to resume a previously installed session or duplicate an existing session, the SSL handshake protocol can be shortened to six messages. The corresponding message flow can be summarized as follows:

1 : C	$\longrightarrow$	S	:	CLIENTHELLO
2 : S	$\longrightarrow$	C	:	SERVERHELLO
:			:	CHANGECIPHERSPEC
:			:	FINISHED
3 : S	$\longrightarrow$	C	:	CHANGECIPHERSPEC
:			:	FINISHED

In this case, the client sends a CLIENTHELLO message to the server that includes a session identity to be resumed in step 1. The server, in turn, checks its session cache for a match. If a match is found, and the server is willing to re-establish the connection under the specified session state, it returns a SERVERHELLO message with the same session identity in step 2. At this point in time, both the client and server must send CHANGECIPHERSPEC and FINISHED messages to each other in steps 2 and 3. Once the reestablishment is complete, the client and server can begin exchanging application data.

In summary, the SSL protocol can be used to establish secure connections between clients and servers. In particular, it can be used to authenticate a server, and optionally, the client, to perform a key exchange, and to provide message authentication, as well as data confidentiality and integrity services for arbitrary TCP/IP applications. Although it may seem that not providing client authentication goes against the principles that should be espoused by a secure and safe system, an argument can be made that the decision to optionally support it helped SSL gain widespread use. Support for client authentication requires individual public keys and certificates for each client, and since support for SSL must be embedded in the corresponding client software (i.e., a HTTP client and WWW browser), requiring client authentication would involve distributing public keys and certificates to every user on the Internet. In the short term, it was believed to be more crucial that consumers be aware of with whom they are conducting business than to give the merchants the same level of assurance. Furthermore, since the number of Internet servers is much smaller than the number of clients, it is easier and more practical to outfit servers with the necessary public keys and certificates. Meanwhile, support for client-specific public keys and certificates is growing rapidly.

A comprehensive security analysis of SSL 3.0 is given by David Wagner and Bruce Schneier in [5]. Except for some minor flaws and worrisome features that can be easily corrected without overhauling the basic structure of the SSL protocol, they have found no serious vulnerability or security problem in SSL 3.0. They conclude that the SSL protocol provides excellent security against eavesdropping and other passive attacks, and that there are some sophisticated active attacks that implementators should be aware of.

Today, the SSL protocol is by far the most pervasive security protocol for the Internet in general and the WWW in particular. Examples of publicly and freely[5] available SSL implementations are SSLref, developed by Netscape Communications, and SSLeay, developed by Eric Young. SSLeay is very popular today, since it was developed in Australia and therefore does not have to care about U.S. export controls. It is also interesting to know that most of the Swiss banks that offer their services over the Internet have their corresponding home banking software based on SSL. This decision conforms to the strategic view of the European Committee for Banking Standards (ECBS) [6].

Nevertheless, the most widely deployed and heavily used implementations of SSL are usually found in HTTP server and client products. For example, there are several HTTP servers available that support SSL. Typically, these servers are called secure or commerce servers. On the client side, most WWW browsers support SSL today. In particular, the Netscape Navigator and the Microsoft Internet Explorer both support SSL. Most of these products support RC4 for encryption and MD2 and MD5 for hashing.

One problem, however, arises from the fact that users outside the United States and Canada, in general have only international versions of these products available. What this usually means is that the international versions of these products in- corporate weak cryptography. In particular, most international versions of HTTP server and client products support RC4 encryption with an effective key length re- stricted to 40 bits. This is accomplishedby by encrypting only 40 bits of the 128-bit RC4 session key and sending the remaining 88 bits of the key in the clear. It is

---

[5]SSLref is publicly and freely available for noncommercial use. Commercial use requires a license from Netscape Communications.

commonly agreed today that 40-bit keys are far too weak to be used in serious applications. Also, certificate chains containing one or more 512-bit RSA key(s) or signatures may not be appropriate in these environments. Fortunately, there are some products available today that have been developed entirely outside the United States and Canada, and that can be used to provide strong cryptography.

10.4 PRIVATE COMMUNICATION TECHNOLOGY

In September 1995, Microsoft Corporation published an Internet Draft[6] that proposed an updated and slightly enhanced version of SSL 2.0 called *Private Communication Technology* (PCT) version 1.0. Similar to SSL, PCT 1.0 runs on top of a connection-oriented and reliable transport service, such as that provided by TCP/IP, and can be used to secure any TCP/IP application protocol that is layered on top of it. Also similar to SSL, PCT 1.0 is divided into two subprotocols, namely the PCT record protocol and the PCT handshake protocol.

- The *PCT record protocol* is used to encapsulate handshake and application data into PCT records.

- The *PCT handshake protocol* is layered on top of the PCT record protocol. It is used to authenticate the server to the client (and, optionally, vice versa), and to agree on encryption and MAC algorithms and corresponding keys.

According to the protocol specification, the PCT record format is similar and compatible with that of SSL. Not only is the record header format identical in both protocols, but the first handshake message sent in each direction also contains a Version Number field in the same location in both protocols. In PCT handshake protocol messages, the most significant bit of the protocol Version Number field is set to 1. Hence, PCT is compatible with SSL in the sense that PCT handshake messages can be recognized and distinguished from SSL handshake messages by examination of the most significant bit of the Version Number field. Consequently, an Internet server may provide support for both transport layer security protocols and dynamically decide whether a request refers to SSL (the most significant bit of the protocol version number is set to 0) or PCT (the most significant bit of the protocol version number is set to 1). This strategy is being followed by Microsoft's Internet server products.

---

[6]`draft-microsoft-PCT-01.txt`

PCT 1.0 differs from SSL 2.0 mainly in the design of its handshake protocol. In particular, the number of transmissions and the message structure of the PCT handshake protocol are considerably shorter and simpler than the SSL handshake protocol. For example, a resumed session without client authentication requires only one message in each direction, and no other type of PCT handshake requires more than two messages in each direction. Most of the other differences that are mentioned in the PCT protocol specification have become obsolete since the publishing of SSL 3.0.

In general, the PCT handshake protocol is used to negotiate security enhancements for data sent using the PCT record protocol. The security enhancements refer to authentication as well as data confidentiality and integrity services. Similar to SSL, PCT supports RSA-based key exchange, Diffie-Hellman key exchange, and FORTEZZA token-based key exchange.

A PCT handshake protocol execution between a client C and a server S consists of only four messages that can be summarized as follows:

$$
\begin{aligned}
1 &: \mathrm{C} \longrightarrow \mathrm{S} : \mathrm{CLIENT\_HELLO} \\
2 &: \mathrm{S} \longrightarrow \mathrm{C} : \mathrm{SERVER\_HELLO} \\
3 &: \mathrm{C} \longrightarrow \mathrm{S} : \mathrm{CLIENT\_MASTER\_KEY} \\
4 &: \mathrm{S} \longrightarrow \mathrm{C} : \mathrm{SERVER\_VERIFY}
\end{aligned}
$$

The general contents of the messages depend upon two criteria: whether the connection being made is a continuation of a previous session or a new session, and whether the client is to be authenticated or not.

- The first criterion is determined by the client and server together. The CLIENT_HELLO message will have different contents depending on whether a new session is being initiated or an old one is being resumed, and the SERVER_HELLO message will either confirm a requested continuation of an old session or require that a new session be initiated.

- The second criterion is determined by the server, whose SERVER_HELLO message may contain a demand for authentication of the client. If the server does not require client authentication, and the reconnection of an old session is requested by the client and accepted by the server, the CLIENT_MASTER_KEY and SERVER_VERIFY messages are unnecessary and may be omitted accordingly.

When the client first connects to the server it sends a CLIENT_HELLO message in step 1. The message contains a 32-bit random authentication challenge for the server as well as a request for the type and level of cryptographic protection to be used for the session. In particular, the client provides lists of supported encryption and key exchange algorithms, hash functions, and server certificate types, in order of the client's preference. Also, if the client finds a session identity in its cache for the server, it may attempt to resume that session. In this case, the client also supplies the session identity in its CLIENT_HELLO message. The lists of encryption and key exchange algorithms, hash functions, and server certificate types are then only relevant in the case where the server cannot recognize the session identity, and a new session must be initialized accordingly. If the session identity is recognized, the lists will be ignored by the server.

In step 2, the server sends back a SERVER_HELLO message to the client. In the case of a new session, the message contains a server certificate and a randomly chosen connection identity that also doubles as an authentication challenge if the server requires client authentication. The server also selects an encryption and key exchange algorithm, a hash function, and a server certificate type among the choices presented by the client in its CLIENT_HELLO message. If the client is attempting to resume an old session, the SERVER_HELLO message also includes a response to the client's authentication challenge. In this case, the session keys from the resumed session are used to compute a keyed MAC value that serves as response. Optionally, the server can also request client authentication. In this case, lists of corresponding client certificate types and signature algorithms, in order of the server's preference, may be placed in the SERVER_HELLO message as well.

If a new session is being initiated, the client sends a CLIENT_MASTER_KEY message to the server in step 3. The message includes a master key for the session. Similar to SSL, PCT provides support for RSA-based, Diffie-Hellman, and FORTEZZA token-based key exchange:

- If a RSA-based or FORTEZZA token-based key exchange is performed, the master key is encrypted using the public key from the server.

- If a Diffie-Hellman key exchange is performed, the server has provided its public parameter in a Diffie-Hellman certificate as part of the SERVER_HELLO message, and the client provides its public parameter as part of the CLIENT_MASTER_KEY message. Equipped with their corresponding private parameters, both the client and server can compute the master key.

The CLIENT_MASTER_KEY message may also include a client certificate and a response to the server's authentication challenge if client authentication is requested. In this case, the client digitally signs the server's authentication challenge with its private key. To ensure that previous unencrypted handshake messages were not tampered with, the CLIENT_MASTER_KEY message also includes a keyed MAC value for the CLIENT_HELLO and SERVER_HELLO messages.

Finally, the server sends a SERVER_VERIFY message to the client in step 4. The message includes a random session identity and a response to the client's authentication challenge. The various session keys that are used to cryptographically protect the session can now be derived from the master key on either side. Again, we refer to the PCT protocol specification for a comprehensive description of the various session keys derivation algorithms.

The PCT handshake messages are sent in the clear using the PCT record protocol. They consist of one byte message type code, followed by some data. The client and server exchange messages as described above, sending either one or two messages to each another. Once the handshake is complete, the client may send arbitrary application data to the server, and vice versa.

In summary, the PCT protocol is closely related and very similar to the SSL protocol, in particular SSL 2.0. The main difference between the two transport layer security protocols is that the PCT protocol requires only four messages to be sent before a secure TCP/IP connection is established, whereas the SSL protocol requires seven to thirteen messages. Taking this into account, one could argue that PCT is more efficient than SSL. However, it is only fair to mention that the number of messages is a considerably weak argument for efficiency. Further investigations are required in order to decide which of the protocols is in fact more efficient or provides more functionality. In the meantime, it remains unclear what rationale has led to the development of the PCT protocol in the first place. Instead of proposing the PCT protocol, Microsoft could have adapted and helped Netscape to improve and further enhance the SSL protocol. But Microsoft specified and implemented PCT, hoping that its market strength would cause other companies to also adapt it. Unfortunately, Microsoft has remained the only company that supports PCT in its product line.

10.5   TRANSPORT LAYER SECURITY PROTOCOL

In April 1996, the IETF chartered a Transport Layer Security (TLS) WG of the Security and Transport Areas. The objective of the TLS WG is to write Internet standards track RFCs for a TLS protocol (TLSP) using the currently available specifications of SSL (2.0 and 3.0), PCT (1.0), and SSH (2.0) as a basis. Note that at this point in time the SSH has been investigated by the IETF TLS WG, and that it was not until recently that the IETF chartered a SECSH WG to update and standardize the SSH protocol independently of the TLS protocol.

Shortly before the San Jose IETF meeting in December 1996, a first TLS 1.0 document was released as an Internet Draft. The document was essentially the same as the SSL 3.0 specification. According to the IETF TLS WG minutes of the San Jose meeting, it was the explicit strategy of the working group to have the TLS 1.0 specification be based on SSL 3.0, as opposed to SSL 2.0, PCT 1.0, SSH 2.0, or any other transport layer security protocol proposal. The modifications to the SSL 3.0 specification were mostly minor points of clarification that are summarized in another Internet Draft[7]. There were, however, at least three major modifications suggested for SSL 3.0 to be incorporated into TLS 1.0:

- First, the HMAC construction developed in the IETF IPsec WG should be adopted and used in TLS 1.0.

- Second, the FORTEZZA token-based KEA should be removed from TLS 1.0, since it refers to a proprietary and unpublished technology.

- Third, the TLS record protocol and the TLS handshake protocol should be separated out and specified in related documents.

After having adopted these modifications, the resulting TLS protocol was specified in an Internet Draft in March 1997.[8] The differences between TLS 1.0 and SSL 3.0 are not huge, but they are significant enough that TLS 1.0 and SSL 3.0 do not easily interoperate. Nevertheless, TLS 1.0 does incorporate a mechanism by which a TLS implementation can back down to SSL 3.0.

Similar to SSL and PCT, the TLS protocol itself is a layered protocol. On the lower layer, the *TLS record protocol* takes messages to be transmitted, fragments the data into manageable blocks, optionally compresses them, computes and appends a MAC to each block, encrypts the result, and transmits it. The corresponding blocks are called TLSPlaintext, TLSCompressed, and TLSCiphertext. A received TLSCiphertext record, in turn, is decrypted, verified, decompressed, and reassembled before it is delivered to a higher level client. A TLS connection state is the operating environment of the TLS record protocol. It specifies compression, encryption, and message authentication algorithms, and determines parameters for these algorithms, such as encryption and MAC keys and IVs for a connection in both the read and write directions. There are always four connection states outstanding: the current read and write states and the pending read and write states. All records

---

[7]draft-ietf-tls-ssl-mods-00.txt
[8]draft-ietf-tls-protocol-01.txt

are processed under the current read and write states. The security parameters for the pending states can be set by the TLS handshake protocol, and the handshake protocol can selectively make either of the pending states current, in which case the appropriate current state is disposed of and replaced with the pending state; the pending state is then reinitialized to an empty state.

On the higher layer, the *TLS handshake protocol* is used to negotiate a session state that consists of a session identifier, a peer certificate, a compression method, a cipher spec, a master key, and a flag whether the session is resumable and can be used to initiate new connections. These items are used to create security parameters for use by the TLS record protocol when protecting application data. More precisely, the TLS handshake protocol consists of three subprotocols that are clients of the TLS record protocol:

- The *TLS change cipher spec protocol* consists of a single CHANGECIPHERSPEC message that is sent by the client and server during the handshake after the security parameters have been agreed upon, but before the verifying FINISHED message is sent.

- The *TLS alert protocol* is used to send alert messages that convey the severity of a message and a description of the alert. Like other messages, alert messages are compressed, authenticated, and encrypted, as specified by the current connection state.

- Finally, the *TLS handshake protocol* is used to negotiate a session state as described above. When a client and server first start communicating, they agree on a protocol version, select cryptographic algorithms, optionally authenticate each other, and use public key cryptography to generate a master secret and corresponding session keys. The corresponding message flow is essentially the same as the message of the SSL handshake protocol discussed previously.

After a TLS handshake has been performed, the client and server can exchange application data messages. These messages are carried by the TLS record protocol and are fragmented, compressed, authenticated, and encrypted accordingly. The messages are treated as transparent data to the TLS record layer.

TLS 1.0 has been submitted to the IESG for consideration as a proposed standard. However, there are still some proposals to improve and further enhance the TLS protocol. One proposal, for example, is to use Kerberos as additional authentication mechanism. The idea is that Kerberos would be used to replace the RSA and DSS-based key exchange. The premaster secret would then be sent protected with a

Kerberos session key. Another proposal is to fit password-based authentication into TLSP. The reasoning behind this proposal is that passwords are still in widespread use today, as opposed to public key certificates. The result of this effort is a shared key authentication protocol (SKAP).

10.6 DISCUSSION

In this chapter, we have focused on the security protocols that have been proposed for the transport layer. In particular, we have overviewed and discussed the SSH, SSL, PCT, and TLS protocols. It is assumed that the TLS protocol will be the predominant transport layer security protocol on the future Internet, and that support for SSL and PCT will slowly fade away and finally disappear as time goes on. It is, however, not clear what the future of SSH will be. SSH has a large installed base that makes it very unlikely that SSH is going to disappear in the near future. It is thus assumed that SSH and TLS will coexist in the future, with SSH being used in relatively small intranet settings, and TLS being used on the global Internet. There is an interesting possibility of combining the two transport layer security protocols: SSL and TLS connections can be used for the management of SSH public keys. In particular, SSL and TLS connections can be used to secure the upload and download of SSH public keys. A corresponding prototype has been implemented at the Swiss Federal Office of Information Technology and Systems (BFI) for UNIX systems.

At the time of this writing, it is too early to tell what the future will be for transport layer security in general and the TLS protocol in particular. One group of people claims that SSL and TLS are already widely deployed, and that their embedded base will cause the TLS protocol to supersede any other transport layer security protocol. Another school of thought states that TLS provides a convenient short-term solution, since it does not involve the modification of individual application protocols, but that it will also silently drop out once application layer security is implemented and put in place. In the meantime, it is possible and very likely that we will see SSL and TLS, as well as some application layer security protocols, coexist with each used for different purposes.

The reason transport layer security might not be the final solution is that current transport layer security protocols also have disadvantages. For example, they provide support for connection-oriented transport services, such as those provided by TCP/IP, but they usually neither address nor meet the security requirements of connectionless transport services, such as those provided by UDP/IP. As a matter of fact, the question of how to effectively secure UDP-based application protocols at the transport layer has not yet been addressed. Until this happens, one can argue that these application protocols must be secured either at the Internet layer, using IPSP and IKMP, or at the application layer, using an application-specific security enhancement.

Another problem with transport layer security is that it generally does not work with caching and replication with proxy servers. All transport layer security protocols were designed to provide security between the client and server, and to avoid a man-in-the-middle attack. Consequently, these protocols can't be proxied through traditional application gateways because the protocols consider a proxy server to be a middleman. The simplest solution to this problem is to use a packet filter instead of an application gateway. This packet filter can be configured with reserved and trusted ports for the secured services (for example port number 443 for HTTP with SSL or TLS support) allowing all traffic on those ports to pass through unrestricted. A major risk with this solution, however, is that an internal attacker could attempt to use the trusted ports without using SSL or TLS, and there is no general possibility for the firewall to know about that.

For an application gateway to support a transport layer security protocol it must either support SOCKS or use a special tunneling protocol. In the first case, the client is authenticated by SOCKS on the server's behalf, whereas in the second case, the client authenticates directly to the server. In the second case, the application gateway sets up a secure tunnel between the application gateway and the target server, and the client is not authenticated until it is connected to this server through the tunnel. If all that is needed is TCP and UDP restrictions based on client and server IP addresses, SOCKS works fine. However, most proxy servers work at the application level and have the ability to understand header information related to the application protocol as well. Under these circumstances, the use of a special tunneling protocol as mentioned above seems to be advantageous. For example, Netscape has specified an SSL Tunneling CONNECT extension method for HTTP in an Internet Draft, and the Netscape proxy server provides support for both SOCKS and the SSL Tunneling CONNECT extension method accordingly. Another technique, also available on the Netscape proxy server, is its ability to use SSL on behalf of an internal client in the outside world. In this case, the proxy uses SSL to secure communications between itself and the other servers on the Internet, whereas it does not use SSL inside the firewall to communicate with the client. Anyway, a proxy server must just pass SSL directly through without caching.

One problem that usually occurs outside the United States and Canada is that the international versions of HTTP client and server software usually provide support for only 40-bit RC4 encryption. It is, however, commonly agreed that 40-bit keys are far too weak to be used for encryption of sensitive data. Recent results in cryptographic research have shown that 40-bit keys can be easily broken in a couple of hours (compare Section 4.4). For users outside the United States and Canada there are generally two approaches to circumvent weak encryption technology in WWW client software products:

- The first approach is to use client software that has been developed entirely outside the United States and Canada.

- The second approach is to use the international version of a client software, but to also use an HTTP proxy server that provides support for SSL with strong encryption. In this case, weak encryption is used between the client and the proxy server, and strong encryption is used between the proxy server and the target server. The proxy server thus acts as an encryption amplifier between the local client and the remote target server.

The first approach is somewhat difficult, since there are not many software products available that have been developed entirely outside the United States and Canada. Therefore, the second approach seems to be more realistic. In fact, there are some products available that support the second approach. Examples include the SafePassage Web Proxy,[9] the Secure Socket Relay (SSR[10]), and the SecureNet client software that is being used in Switzerland for Internet banking. In addition to that, Baltimore Technologies Ltd. has developed a set of Java applets called WebSecure that provide essentially the same functionality.[11] On the client side, WebSecure works with WWW browsers that support Java 1.0.2 or greater. A similar approach is being followed by the X◇PRESSO software that was developed by a German company named Brokat Systeme.[12]

REFERENCES

[1] R. Nelson, "SDNS Services and Architecture," *Proceedings of National Computer Security Conference*, 1987, pp. 153 – 157.

[2] ISO/IEC 10736, *Information technology - Telecommunications and information exchange between systems - Transport layer security protocol*, Geneva, Switzerland, 1993.

---

[9]http://stronghold.ukweb.com/safepassage/
[10]http://www.medcom.se/ssr/
[11]http://www.baltimore.ie/websecur.htm3summary
[12]http://www.brokat.de

[3] M. Blaze, and S.M. Bellovin, "Session-Layer Encryption," *Proceedings of USENIX UNIX Security Symposium*, June 1995.

[4] F-Secure SSH User's & Administrator's Guide, Data Fellows Ltd., 1996.

[5] D. Wagner, and B. Schneier, "Analysis of the SSL 3.0 protocol," *Proceedings of USENIX Workshop on Electronic Commerce*, December 1996.

[6] European Committee for Banking Standards (ECBS), *Secure Banking over the Internet*, March 1997.

Chapter 11

Application Layer Security Protocols

Providing security at the application layer is often the most intrusive option. It is also the most flexible, because the scope and strength of the protection can be tailored to meet the specific needs of the application. In general, there are two approaches to provide security services at the application layer: either the services are integrated into each application protocol individually, or a generic security system is built that can be used to incorporate the services into arbitrary applications. In this chapter, we are going to overview and discuss both approaches. In Section 11.1, we address security-enhanced application protocols, and in Section 11.2 we focus on generic security systems in terms of authentication and key distribution systems.

11.1 SECURITY-ENHANCED APPLICATION PROTOCOLS

There are several application protocols that have been enhanced to provide integrated security services. In the subsections that follow, we address security enhancements for Telnet, electronic mail, WWW transactions, and some other applications.

11.1.1 Telnet

Referring to the introductory remarks, it is possible to use an authentication and key distribution system to provide security services for a particular application. More precisely, an authentication and key distribution system provides an application programming interface (API) that applications can use to incorporate the security services they require. While something like Kerberos-mediated Telnet encryption [1] might be an ultimate goal, it takes a big effort to deploy. The same is obviously true for any other authentication and key distribution system that one may think of, such as SPX [2].

Instead of waiting until authentication and key distribution systems are used and widely deployed on the Internet, several security-enhanced Telnet software packages have been developed so far. In Chapter 10, we learned about the Secure Shell (SSH) and the application thereof in the `slogin` software. This software can be used as a replacement for `rlogin` and `telnet` programs. Similarly, the Secure Sockets Layer (SSL) and Transport Layer Security (TLS) protocols can be used to establish an authenticated and encrypted TCP/IP connection between a client and a server, and this connection can then be used to carry Telnet traffic. Consequently, Telnet over SSL or TLS provides another approach to secure remote terminal access. Finally, there are several security-enhanced Telnet protocols and corresponding software packages available today. For example, Baltimore Technologies Ltd. has developed an authenticating and encrypting Telnet replacement called S/RLogin.[1] In addition to S/RLogin and other commercial software packages, there are also publicly and freely available software packages available on the Internet. For example, Matt Blaze and Steven Bellovin from AT&T Bell Laboratories have developed a secure Telnet software replacement for 4.4BSD UNIX [3]. The software implements the Diffie-Hellman key exchange with a fixed modulus and a fixed generator. To thwart the man-in-the-middle attack, the software implements the Interlock protocol originally proposed by Ron Rivest and Adi Shamir [4]. In the Interlock protocol, the communicating parties A and B first exchange their public keys. Afterwards, A encrypts a message with B's public key, and sends half of the encrypted message to B. Similarly, B encrypts another message with A's public key, and sends half of the encrypted message to A. After having received B's message, A sends the other half of his encrypted message to B. B puts the two halves of A's message together and decrypts it with his private key. B also sends the other half of his encrypted message to A. Finally, A puts the two halves of B's message together and decrypts it with his private key. The Interlock protocol depends on the fact that half of a message is useless without the other half, and there are a number of ways to achieve this: for example, if the encryption algorithm is a block cipher, half of each block could be sent in each half message. Alternatively, decryption of the message could

---

[1]`http://www.baltimore.ie/srlogin.htm`

be dependent on an initialization vector, which could be sent with the second half of the message. Finally, the first half of the message could also be a one-way hash of the encrypted message and the encrypted message itself could be the second half. In the Interlock protocol, a man in the middle can still substitute his own public keys for A's and B's public keys. However, if he then intercepts the first message sent from A to B after the public key exchange phase, he can't decrypt it with one of his private keys and reencrypt it properly with B's public key. Instead, he must invent a totally new message and send half of it to B. Similarly, when he intercepts half of B's message he has the same problem. He can't decrypt it with one of his private keys and reencrypt it properly with A's public key. Again, he must invent a totally new message and send half of it to A. By the time he intercepts the second halves of the real messages, it is too late for him to change the invented messages. His existence can be detected by either of the two parties.

In addition to the Diffie-Hellman key exchange and Interlock protocols, the secure Telnet software replacement from Blaze and Bellovin also uses Triple-DES for data encryption. Since the software is not widely deployed on the Internet today, two other software packages are described next.

Secure RPC Authentication

The *Secure RPC Authentication* (SRA) software package was developed by David Safford, David Hess, and Douglas Lee Schales at the Texas A&M University (TAMU) [5]. SRA is based on Sun Microsystems' Secure RPC implementation to protect Telnet and FTP connection establishment handshakes against password sniffing attacks. When an SRA-enhanced client connects to an SRA-enhanced Telnet or FTP server, a Diffie-Hellman key exchange is performed to negotiate a session key. This session key is then used to encrypt the user's authentication information, which typically consists of a username and a corresponding password. Unfortunately, the remainder of the Telnet or FTP traffic is left unencrypted. There are two major problems related to the use of SRA:

- First and foremost, the length of the modulus used with Sun Microsystems' implementation of the Secure RPC Diffie-Hellman key exchange is only 192 bits and thus far too small to protect against cryptanalysis. As a matter of fact, we have already mentioned in Chapter 2 that the parameters of the Secure RPC were successfully cryptanalyzed a few years ago.

- Secondly, the Secure RPC and hence also SRA are vulnerable to the man-in-the-middle attack. An attacker can decrypt and reencrypt user identification and authentication information such as a password or an encrypted timestamp.

In addition to that, the SRA software package also contains a DES library that is not exportable from the United States and Canada. Nevertheless, there are some software packages available overseas that combine the SRA basic software with publicly available DES libraries.

More recently, the authors of SRA have started to design and implement NATAS. According to a presentation held by David Safford,[2] the main goals of NATAS are to use the cryptographic library RSAREF from RSA Data Security, Inc. instead of Sun Microsystems' Secure RPC implementation, and to enhance the Diffie-Hellman key exchange with a subsequent authentication step to thwart the man-in-the-middle attack. The resulting NATAS protocol is very similar to the Photuris key management protocol that we discussed in Chapter 9. A NATAS protocol execution between a client C and a server S can be summarized as follows:

$$
\begin{aligned}
1 : C &\longrightarrow S : U, k_U \\
2 : S &\longrightarrow C : k_S \\
3 : C &\longrightarrow S : \{y_c\}k_S \\
4 : S &\longrightarrow C : \{y_s\}k_U \\
5 : C &\longrightarrow S : \{\{y_s\}k_U^{-1}\}k_S \\
6 : S &\longrightarrow C : \{\{y_c\}k_S^{-1}\}k_U
\end{aligned}
$$

In step 1, C sends a username U and this user's public key k_U to S. Optionally, the message may also include a certificate for k_U. In step 2, S returns its public key k_S to C. Again, the message may optionally include a certificate for k_S. Afterwards, C and S perform a Diffie-Hellman key exchange. In step 3, C randomly selects a private Diffie-Hellman parameter x_c, computes the corresponding public parameter $y_c = g^{x_c} (\bmod\ p)$, encrypts y_c with k_S, and sends the resulting ciphertext $\{y_c\}k_S$ to S. Similarly, S selects a private parameter x_s, computes $y_s = g^{x_s} (\bmod\ p)$, encrypts y_s with k_U, and returns $\{y_s\}k_U$ to C in step 4. Obviously, C and S can now agree on a session key K. In fact, C computes $K = y_s^{x_c} = g^{x_s x_c} (\bmod\ p)$ and S computes $K = y_c^{x_s} = g^{x_c x_s} (\bmod\ p)$. Afterwards, they can use K to encrypt subsequent communications. Similar to Photuris key management protocol, a final handshake is used to exchange digital signatures to authenticate the public Diffie-Hellman parameters. In step 5, C sends $\{\{y_s\}k_U^{-1}\}k_S$ to S, and in step 6, S returns

---

[2] ftp://net.tamu.edu/pub/security/TAMU/watson.ps

$\{\{y_c\}k_S^{-1}\}k_U$ to C. In either case, the value that is sent is the other's public Diffie-Hellman parameter digitally signed with one's own private key and encrypted with the other's public key. In the simplest case, RSA is used to digitally sign and encrypt the Diffie-Hellman parameters.

C and S exchange their public keys in the first two steps of the NATAS protocol. So, there must be a way to verify the authenticity and integrity of the public keys. This may be achieved through public key certificates that are included in the messages or retrieved from a corresponding directory service. As well, NATAS is conceptually open to any PKI that may be put in place. For example, it is possible to insist on public keys that are manually distributed and preconfigured. This approach is very similar to SSH. But it is also possible and probably the way to go to accept public key certificates from a secure DNS server or to retrieve them from a directory service. As an intermediate step, the designers of NATAS plan to use authenticated PGP keys instead of X.509 public key certificates.

NATAS-based software is currently being developed for Telnet and FTP. Furthermore, it is intended to develop software that uses NATAS to secure the Internet service daemon `inetd`. In this case, any TCP/IP service that is invoked by `inetd` could make use of the NATAS software to provide basic security services.

Secure Telnet

Secure Telnet (STEL) is another secure Telnet software package for UNIX systems that was developed at the University of Milan in cooperation with the Italian computer emergency response team (CERT) [6]. Again, the purpose of STEL is to provide its users remote terminal access, very similar to `rlogin` and `telnet`. The main differences, however, are that the authentication mechanisms deployed by STEL are much stronger than their `telnet` and `rlogin` counterparts and that all data traffic between the client and server is transparently encrypted. The client software `stel` is intended to be directly run by users, whereas the server software `steld` can be run as a stand-alone daemon by the superuser or automatically be invoked by `inetd`.

Similar to SRA and NATAS, STEL uses a Diffie-Hellman key exchange with a shared prime number p (either 512 or 1,024 bits) and a shared generator $g = 3$ to have a client and a server agree on a common session key. The actual session key is derived from the Diffie-Hellman value by hashing it with MD5. To thwart the man-in-the-middle attack, STEL also implements the Interlock protocol mentioned above. In this matter, STEL differs from the NATAS design. In addition, a variety of authentication methods are currently supported by STEL to provide client authentication. These methods can be listed according to their security, in decreasing order:

- SecurID

- S/Key

- Standard UNIX passwords

In spite of the fact that the first authentication method is considered to be very secure, SecurID tokens are not widely deployed on the Internet today. So using SecurID authentication is not mandatory, and S/Key or standard UNIX password authentication are probably more commonly used today. STEL uses a modification of S/Key to thwart the vulnerability to dictionary attacks. With regard to standard UNIX passwords, it should be noted at this point that the communication channel between the client and server is transparently encrypted and that this encrytion provides a reasonable level of security for the password that is transmitted on the channel. This level of security is very similar to SSL. Remember that SSL is used to set up a secure data channel between a client and a server, and that this channel can then be used to transmit sensitive information, such as credit card information or usernames and corresponding passwords.

After the Diffie-Hellman key exchange and client authentication, all data traffic is transparently encrypted using the specified encryption algorithm keyed with the session key. The default encryption algorithm is DES, since it is fast, but Triple-DES and IDEA are also available. Due to the fact that the STEL software has been developed entirely outside the United States and Canada, there is no problem in distributing the software on a worldwide basis. STEL is publicly available on the Internet in source code.[3]

In summary, it is important to use a secure Telnet software package as a replacement for `rlogin` and `telnet` in a corporate intranet environment. It is even more important to use such a replacement if users regularly connect to intranet hosts from the outside world, such as e.g. the Internet. In the case of `rlogin`, the use of address-based authentication lends itself to IP spoofing attacks. In the case of `telnet`, passwords are transmitted in the clear that are subject to passive eavesdropping and replay attacks. Having agreed on the necessity of a secure Telnet replacement, it is less important which software package is actually being used. All security-enhanced Telnet software packages mentioned above are more alike than

---

[3]`http://idea.sec.dsi.unimi.it/stel.html`

they are different. In fact, they all use a Diffie-Hellman key exchange to negotiate a session key, and this session key is then used to encrypt either only the authentication information or the entire Telnet session. Because remote terminal access involves characters-at-a-time interactions, the CFB and OFB modes of operation are generally used. Error propagation is not an issue, since humans can easily recover from garbage data in an interactive session. In either case, the software packages mentioned above provide sufficient levels of security, even when combined with password-based authentication. Remember that in this case the passwords are transmitted over secure and transparently encrypted data channels. So, anybody eavesdropping on these channels won't be able to extract the passwords in the clear. Keep in mind that with regard to the selection of an appropriate software package, SRA is vulnerable to cryptanalysis and the man-in-the-middle attack. In this case, NATAS should be used instead of SRA as soon as it becomes publicly available.

11.1.2   Electronic Mail

The basis for electronic mail (e-mail) on the Internet is the simple mail transfer protocol (SMTP) specified in RFC 821, the text and ASCII message syntax specified in RFC 822, and the Multipurpose Internet Mail Extensions (MIME) specified in RFC 1521. The major problem addressed by the MIME specification is that e-mail messages typically consist of 7-bit ASCII text, whereas multimedia applications generate data streams that consist of arbitrary binary 8-bit patterns. Consequently, there must be a way to turn these 8-bit patterns into printable characters that can be passed unscathed through various software processes, such as e-mail handlers, and that would otherwise be interpreted as control or illegal characters. One obvious consequence of this encoding (or filtering) step is message expansion. Products that conform to the MIME specification permit sending more than 7-bit ASCII text by providing conventions for making part of a message some kind of 8-bit encoding. More precisely, the MIME specification provides a general structure for the content type of an e-mail message and allows extensions for new content types. For example, MIME can be used to encapsulate electronic data interchange (EDI) objects, as further described in RFC 1767.

Neither SMTP nor the corresponding message syntax provide support for security services. It is, in general, easy to modify a message content or to forge either the sender address or routing information. Also, picking off e-mail messages on public networks such as the Internet has become a documented art. The same hosts and routers that efficiently move e-mail messages along their delivery paths can also be turned against their users to perform massive searching and sorting. A tremendous amount of information about users and organizations can be gathered with traffic analysis, even without a human around. In addition to that, anyone who can intercept an e-mail message can potentially also launch an active attack and tamper with it at will. Even small alterations, such as changing a date or moving a decimal point in a floating point number, can sometimes have disastrous impacts.

It is commonly agreed that widespread use of e-mail messages for commercial applications will require the provision of security services, such as those enumerated in the OSI security architecture. Data confidentiality services are required to ensure that the content of an e-mail message is not revealed to unauthorized parties, whereas data integrity, message authentication, and non-repudiation of origin services are required to provide the assurance that a message has not been tampered with during transmission since it left the sender. It is also commonly agreed that the enabling technique for providing this kind of end-to-end security for e-mail messages is digital enveloping. What this basically means is that the sender of an e-mail message randomly selects a transaction key, encrypts the entire message with this key, and appends the transaction key encrypted with the recipient's public key to the message. The recipient, in turn, uses his private key to decrypt the transaction key, and then uses this transaction key to decrypt the original message. If the message is addressed to several recipients, then the sender must iterate the encryption of the transaction key. More precisely, he must generate an appendix for each recipient. This appendix contains the transaction key encrypted with this recipient's public key. Additionally, the sender can also use his private key to digitally sign the message. In this case, the recipient uses the sender's public key to verify the digital signature.

During the past few years, three primary schemes for e-mail security have emerged on the Internet: privacy enhanced mail (PEM), Pretty Good Privacy (PGP), and secure MIME (S/MIME). These schemes are overviewed and briefly discussed next. Note that all schemes use digital enveloping to provide the security services mentioned above. Also note that the schemes are more alike than they are different, and that the Internet Mail Consortium therefore convened to begin addressing the resolution of their differences early in 1996.

Privacy Enhanced Mail

In 1985, the Internet Architecture Board (IAB) chartered a Privacy Enhanced Mail (PEM) working group (WG) under its IRTF Privacy and Security Research Group (PSRG) to work on a standard protocol for e-mail security. To facilitate introduction and acceptance by the Internet community, the PEM WG decided to opt for integration within the existing SMTP-based e-mail infrastructure rather than building a new infrastructure. It was decided that secure messages would be included as body parts in standard e-mail messages and sent via an SMTP-based message transfer agent (MTA). Consequently, the secure e-mail messages are not necessarily visible to the message transfer system (MTS).

Early in 1993, the PEM WG came up with a series of specifications that the IESG approved as a Proposed Standard for the Internet. The specifications were published in a set of four related PEM RFCs [7 – 10]. A comprehensive summary is given in [11]. Each PEM message provides support for message authentication, data integrity, and non-repudiation of origin services by using a message integrity check (MIC). Additionally, the message may also provide support for data confidentiality services by encrypting the entire message. Consequently, the PEM specification distinguishes the following three types of messages:

- A MIC-CLEAR message contains a MIC and therefore provides support for message authentication, data integrity, and non-repudiation of origin services. It does not, however, provide support for data confidentiality services and transmission encoding. By excluding the encoding step, a MIC-CLEAR message can be received and read by user agents that do not currently support PEM. A PEM-capable user agent can verify the authenticity and integrity of a MIC-CLEAR message, whereas a PEM-oblivious user agent can display the message but not verify its authenticity and integrity. As such, MIC-CLEAR messages are typically used for mailing lists that consist of both PEM capable and PEM oblivious user agents.

- A MIC-ONLY message provides the security services of MIC-CLEAR plus transmission encoding. The encoding step ensures that PEM messages can be passed through various MTS and e-mail gateways without being transformed in such a way as to invalidate the MICs they contain.

- Finally, an ENCRYPTED message provides the security services of MIC-ONLY plus data confidentiality services. Consequently, an ENCRYPTED message provides support for all security services mentioned above. It is digitally enveloped by the sender, as well as decrypted and verified by the recipient.

Note that PEM is not able to provide access control and non-repudiation of receipt services. If required, these services must be provided outside the scope of a PEM-conformant implementation.

Each PEM message consists of two basic elements: a header and a text portion. The header contains specific information that the recipient requires for the interpretation and validation of the message. This includes information about the algorithms used, MIC information, and certificates. The text portion contains the actual message, eventually in encrypted and encoded form. Consequently, PEM message processing consists of four steps that can be summarized as follows:

- In the first step, the canonicalization step, the sender converts the e-mail message to a standard format. In this way, the message can be received and interpreted by the receiver even though the sending user agent and receiving user agent may be based on different operating systems.

- In the second step, the digital signature step, the sending user agent computes and digitally signs a MIC to avoid attacks against the authenticity and integrity of the message. MD2 or MD5 and RSA are used for these purposes. In order to allow the receiving user agent to verify the digital signature, the sending user agent must also include an X.509 certificate for its own public key into the message.

- In the third step, the encryption step, the sending user agent may optionally encrypt the message with DES in CBC mode. Prior to encrypting the message, however, the sender must obtain a valid certificate for each receiver of the message. The sender then digitally envelopes the message with the public key(s) of the receiver(s).

- In the fourth step, the transmission encoding step, the sender may optionally convert the message into a text using a 6-bit alphabet. This encoding is compatible with the SMTP canonicalization format.

Obviously, MIC-CLEAR messages execute steps 1 and 2; MIC-ONLY messages, steps 1, 2, and 4; and ENCRYPTED messages, all steps 1 through 4.

If a user agent receives a PEM message, it first checks the message type. According to this message type, the PEM message processing steps are then reversed. For a MIC-CLEAR or MIC-ONLY message, the authenticity and integrity of the message is checked by verifying the MIC. In the case of a MIC-ONLY message, the transmission encoding step must be reversed before verifying the MIC. For an ENCRYPTED message, the confidentiality of the message can be revealed by decrypting it with the transaction key that a legitimate recipient can obtain with his or her private key. Again, the transmission encoding step must be reversed before decrypting the digital envelope.

Although the PEM specification is intended to be compatible with a broad range of key management strategies, including those based on both symmetric and asymmetric cryptography, a certificate-based key management was specified first. Both the structure of PEM certificates and the certificate management comply to the ITU-T recommendation X.509. To enable worldwide use of PEM, a certification hierarchy was formally approved. The PEM certification hierarchy is illustrated in Figure 11.1. It consists of the following three levels:

- On the top level, the certification hierarchy is headed by an *Internet Policy Registration Authority* (IPRA). The IPRA defines the directions for all underlying domains and serves as root CA for the Internet community. The IPRA acts under the auspices of the Internet Society (ISOC).

- In the IPRA domain, *Policy Certification Authorities* (PCAs) can be set up. PCAs are parties that inform their target group by means on an informational RFC how individual users and organizations may be registered and certified.

- One or more *Certification Authorities* (CAs) can then be set up under the responsibility of a particular PCA.

Conceptually, the IPRA issues certificates to the PCAs, and the PCAs issue certificates to the CAs. Finally, the CAs issue certificates to individual users and organizations. Note that the PEM certification hierarchy is strictly hierarchical, meaning that there is no possibility or support for cross certificates.

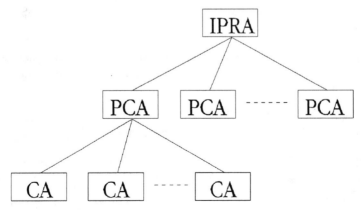

Figure 11.1   The PEM certification hierarchy.

Since 1993, several PEM implementations have been developed for the Internet community. For example, Trusted Information Systems, Inc. (TIS) and RSA Data Security, Inc. have jointly developed and made publicly available in source code a UNIX-based implementation of PEM, called TIS/PEM.[4] Due to U.S. export controls, TIS/PEM and other PEM implementations cannot be used outside the United States and Canada. Consequently, several European research and development projects have focused on implementing the PEM specification, too. Examples include the COSINE P8 and the PASSWORD projects [12,13], as well as the COST-PEM system [14].

Unfortunately, PEM never really took off, and there are several reasons for that [15]. Probably the most important reason is related to the fact that PEM requires an existing and fully operable certification hierarchy and PKI as described above. This requirement has not been fulfilled so far. Also, the range of supported cryptographic algorithms is limited. For example, encryption is based on DES, which is assumed not to provide sufficient levels of security today. Finally, PEM is also confined to a textual environment and does not provide support for binary attachments and MIME types.

Mainly with regard to the last point, a PEM extension has been proposed to combine PEM with MIME [16]. The extension has been named *MIME Object Security Services* (MOSS). It is specified in a pair of related RFCs [17,18]. The security services that MOSS provides, as well as the cryptographic algorithms that are used to provide those services, are essentially the same as with PEM. However, there are some differences between the PEM and MOSS specifications. Let's briefly overview the most important ones:

- PEM users are required to have X.509 certificates, whereas MOSS users must only have a public key pair.

- Contrary to PEM, MOSS broadens the allowable name forms that users may choose to identify their public keys, including arbitrary strings, e-mail addresses, and distinguished names.

- As discussed above, PEM restricts its use to the textual mail environment. For obvious reasons, this restriction no longer exists for MOSS.

- PEM requires that data encryption be applied only to message bodies that have been digitally signed. By providing for each of the security services separately

---

[4]The RSA cryptographic functions are excluded from the source code distribution. They are provided as an object library.

within MOSS, they may be applied in any order according to the needs of the requesting application.

Although MOSS has been submitted to the IETF for possible standardization, it has not achieved substantial momentum so far. Also, the prevalence and anticipated growth of PGP and S/MIME usage makes the future of MOSS unclear at the moment. For these reasons, we are not going to delve into the technical details of the MOSS specification in this book. Note, however, that TIS has again developed and made publicly available a reference implementation for MOSS, called TIS/MOSS.

Pretty Good Privacy

Unlike PEM and MOSS, the term *Pretty Good Privacy* (PGP) does not refer to a standard specification, but rather to a software package that is widely used on the Internet to secure textual e-mail messages [19,20].[5] The original PGP software was developed by Phil Zimmermann in 1991. Mainly because of patent claims and U.S. export controls, the worldwide distribution of the PGP software over the Internet has raised a lot of legal questions that have all been resolved [21]. Today, the PGP software is publicly and freely available for noncommercial use, but must be licensed for commercial use. The Massachusetts Institute of Technology (MIT) serves as software distribution center for the noncommercial version of the PGP software.[6] More recently, Phil Zimmermann founded a company called Pretty Good Privacy, Inc.[7] to further promote the commercial version of the PGP software. Currently, the software is available in a beta version 5 for Windows 95 and Windows NT version 4.

Similar to the PEM specification, PGP provides support for data confidentiality services, as well as message authentication, data integrity, and non-repudiation of origin services by means of encryption and digital envelopes. But unlike the PEM specification, PGP uses IDEA (instead of DES) for data encryption. Since IDEA uses 128-bit keys (instead of 56-bit DES keys), PGP is considered to be cryptographically stronger and harder to break than any product that conforms to the PEM specification. With regard to digital signatures, PGP uses MD5 and RSA; it is thus comparable to the PEM specification. PGP supports three security levels that vary in the length of the corresponding RSA keys:

---

[5]RIPEM is another publicly and freely available software package that is used on the Internet to secure textual e-mail messages. It was developed by Mark Riordan and later enhanced by Jeff Thompson. RIPEM is not addressed in this book, since it is steadily replaced by PGP.

[6]htpp://web.mit.edu/network/pgp.html

[7]http://www.pgp.com

- 512-bit RSA keys for low-commercial-grade security;

- 768-bit RSA keys for high-commercial-grade security;

- 1,024-bit RSA keys for "military" grade security.

Due to recent improvements in factoring large integers, it is strongly recommended to use 1,024-bit RSA keys today.

PGP has certain unique attributes. First of all, PGP cannot only be used to secure e-mail messages, but also to encrypt local files with IDEA. The second attribute relates to digital signatures. Usually, digital signatures are appended to the messages they sign, but PGP also allows the digital signatures to be detached and transmitted separately from the corresponding messages. There are certain advantages in providing detached digital signatures. For example, the digital signatures can be recorded and archived separately. Another attribute of PGP is that it compresses messages using the commonly available ZIP 2.0 program. Compression generally reduces the size of messages and removes redundancies in plaintext messages accordingly. As a result, compression makes cryptanalysis more difficult.

Probably the biggest and most obvious difference between PEM and PGP is related to the fact that PEM depends on the existence of a fully operable certification hierarchy that serves as PKI, whereas PGP relies on the notion of trust among users. Note that trust is a social concept, and that people usually trust their friends. For example, if A and B have a friend C in common, then B will accept A's public key if C has issued a digitally signed certificate for it. It is also possible that A has certificates from several friends. In this case, B accepts A's public key if at least one of these friends is also a friend of B. The notion of transitive trust is used and implemented by the PGP software, generating a so-called "web of trust." A PGP user can pick up an arbitrary public key in his or her public key ring and assign a specific level of trust to it. He or she can also collect certificates for that particular key that have been issued by some other PGP users. In addition, the user also has a secret key ring that essentially comprises the user's private key encrypted with a secret key derived from a user passphrase.

There are several advantages and disadvantages related to the PGP approach. For example, a web of trust makes it relatively simple for a user to obtain and verify a public key certificate. In a hierarchical model, users must usually share a common hierarchy in order to communicate with each other. This is obviously not the case in the PGP model. Nevertheless, a disadvantage of the PGP model is due to the fact that a user cannot necessarily verify the identity of any other user (if they have no friend in common). In PGP, there may be several isolated user groups that share their trust within the group, but not with others. Another more important disadvantage is certificate revocation, which is difficult if not impossible in a web of trust.

Due to its pragmatic approach to certification, the PGP software is in widespread use today. This is especially true in intranet environments, where a centralized PGP public key server may be established. For example, it is possible to use an authentication and key distribution system to secure a corporate PGP public key server. As a matter of fact, Jeff Schiller and Derek Atkins from the MIT have come up with a design that combines the Kerberos authentication system with PGP messaging [22]. In addition to that, several add-on products have been developed that enhance the security of commercial applications with PGP messaging. Examples include SecGUI from iXOS Software for SAP, as well as CryptoEx from Glück & Kanja for Microsoft Exchange.[8] More recently, work has also begun to standardize the basic PGP message exchange formats [23] and the use of PGP to secure MIME messages [24].

Secure MIME

Besides PEM/MOSS and PGP, *secure MIME* (S/MIME) has emerged as a third approach for secure e-mail. Similar to PEM and MOSS, S/MIME refers to a specification rather than a software package, and similar to MOSS, S/MIME was also designed to add security to e-mail messages in MIME format. The S/MIME specification was developed by an industry working group led by RSA Data Security, Inc. [25]. The first specification was released for public scrutiny in July 1995, with announced support from many e-mail product vendors. For example, the Netscape Communicator version 4 comes with an SMTP user agent that provides support for S/MIME messaging. Currently, the S/MIME specification consists of two Internet Drafts: one specifying the S/MIME message format[9] and the other the S/MIME certificate handling. It is intended to submit the S/MIME specification to the IETF for possible consideration as an Internet standards track protocol as soon as interoperability tests are complete. In fact, the S/MIME community places great importance on interoperability. The vendors participate in an S/MIME compliance testing program. These tests are conducted over the Internet, and put the applications through a test suite that includes online certification, digitally signed and digitally enveloped message creation, as well as verification and decryption of received messages. As vendors successfully complete the tests, the results are reported

---

[8]http://www.glueckkanja.de/de/home/default.asp
[9]draft-dusse-mime-masg-spec-*.txt

and recorded by the S/MIME Interoperability Center of RSA Data Security, Inc.

Similar to the PEM specification, the certification hierarchy for S/MIME is based on the ITU-T recommendation X.509. In order to avoid the need for a global certification hierarchy, however, the guidelines for CAs and certification hierarchies are more flexible in S/MIME than they are in PEM. Some consideration was given to the setup for small workgroups that don't need to be part of a global certification hierarchy. VeriSign has set up a certification hierarchy specifically to support the S/MIME effort.

The cryptographic algorithms that are defined in the S/MIME specification to digitally sign messages are MD2, MD5, and RSA. In addition to that, DES, Triple-DES, and RC2 in CBC mode may be used for message encryption. The use of RC2 with variable key sizes is important since it allows software companies to ship products that include cryptography overseas. Note that S/MIME clients can use strong cryptography domestically and interoperate with international versions using a smaller key size, typically 40 bits today.

S/MIME relies on the Public Key Cryptography Standards (PKCSs) to ensure cryptographic compatibility and interoperability across vendors. In short, the PKCSs refer to a set of standards that address the implementation of public key cryptography. It has been defined since 1991 by a consortium of computer vendors, including DEC, Apple, Lotus, and Sun Microsystems, together with RSA Data Security, Inc. and the MIT. Most notable in S/MIME are PKCS #7 and #10.

The PKCS #7 specifies a cryptographic message syntax standard and defines bit encodings of digital signatures and digital envelopes accordingly [26]. PKCS #7 is defined in terms of the Abstract Syntax Notation 1 (ASN.1) and is concretely represented using the Basic Encoding Rules (BER). A PKCS #7 message refers to a sequence of typed content types. There are currently six recursively composable content types defined in the PKCS #7:

- Data;

- SignedData;

- EnvelopedData;

- SignedAndEnvelopedData;

- DigestedData;

- EncryptedData.

The names of the PKCS #7 content types are self-explanatory and need no further explanation. In addition to S/MIME, PKCS #7 is also being used in a number of other standards and applications. For example, Mastercard and Visa use it as the basis for the secure electronic transaction (SET) specification that can be used to secure credit card payments over the Internet. We will focus on the SET specification in Chapter 12. To support PKCS #7, S/MIME defines a new content type application `application/x-pkcs7-mime` that specifies that a MIME body part has been cryptographically enhanced according to PKCS #7.

In addition to that, the PKCS #10 specifies a message syntax for certification requests, and the S/MIME specification also comprises a MIME type `application/x-pkcs10` that can be used to submit certification requests according to PKCS #10 [27].

The acid test of any standard is market acceptance. As of this writing, several U.S. vendors are readying to market SMTP clients and corresponding user agents that provide support for S/MIME. Also, some vendors have announced plans for making S/MIME-compatible versions of their products available to the public domain. For example, a future version of the RIPEM software package will implement S/MIME.[10] In addition to that, RSA Data Security, Inc. provides two toolkits for developers looking to build S/MIME functionality into their products: S/MAIL and TIPEM. One can reasonably expect that S/MIME will be the dominant standard for secure e-mail in the near future, and that users will be able to choose from a variety of interoperable software packages that all provide support for S/MIME. In addition to that, it is also possible and very likely that S/MIME will extend beyond traditional e-mail applications and make its way into Web browsers, intranet groupware products, and electronic data interchange (EDI) software. As a matter of fact, some EDI companies have already announced support for secure e-mail using the S/MIME specification. However, the use and deployment of S/MIME is still restricted to the United States, and no European or Asian implementations of S/MIME are currently available on the global marketplace.

11.1.3 WWW Transactions

The continuing growth and popularity of the Internet is mainly driven by the World Wide Web (WWW) and the hypertext transfer protocol (HTTP) that is primarily used on the WWW. Similar to the Internet as a whole, the WWW was also designed for complete openness rather than security. It was believed that all information provided by HTTP servers would be public in nature and not require any form of

---

[10]`http://www.cs.indiana.edu/ripem/dir.html`

user authentication and authorization. This situation has changed fundamentally. Today, it is very often necessary to restrict access to specific information pages on the WWW, or to protect the confidentiality and integrity of data that is transmitted between HTTP clients and servers. It may even be desirable to provide some sort of non-repudiation services for WWW transactions.

Some of the security requirements for WWW applications and transactions have already been addressed in the past. For example, most HTTP servers provide support for address-based and password-based authentication and authorization. The problems related to these mechanisms are obvious: IP addresses can be spoofed easily, and passwords transmitted in the clear can be eavesdropped and used for replay attacks. In this respect, the security of HTTP does not differ from any other TCP/IP application protocol. To do it better requires the use of cryptographic techniques. For example, one proposal is to replace the basic password-based authentication scheme with something called digest authentication [28]. In short, digest authentication is very similar to the challenge-response authentication protocol (CHAP) for serial line access to TCP/IP networks. In either case, the verifier challenges the claimant with a random number that serves as a nonce, and the claimant must respond with a proper keyed one-way hash value of that nonce and some other information in order to authenticate. While digest authentication is probably a good way to start; it is definitely not the ultimate solution for WWW applications and transaction security.

Today, general security requirements and specific protocol enhancements for HTTP are investigated by the IETF Web Transaction Security (WTS) WG [29]. A lot of public research is going on to design and implement new security techniques and corresponding mechanisms for WWW transactions [30,31]. For example, the design of the SSL, PCT, and TLS protocols is mainly driven by the need to secure HTTP traffic. We have already discussed these transport layer security protocols in Chapter 10. In addition, there is some work going on to develop a means of using the generic security service application programming interface (GSS-API) to secure WWW transactions. This work is in progress and has been described in a corresponding Internet Draft.[11] For the WWW integration of the GSS-API, a new HTTP URL protocol designator has been defined, called `gss-http`. This protocol designator indicates that the associated HTTP traffic must be protected using GSS-API security mechanisms. Today, it looks like the GSS-API approach to secure WWW transaction is not going to make it. This is equally true for another approach that was independently proposed by Judson Weeks, Adam Cain, and Brian

---

[11]`draft-ietf-wts-gssapi-*.txt`

Sanderson in late 1995 [32]. The proposal was to make use of the general-purpose common client interface (CCI) to enhance the security of WWW transactions with PGP messaging. The CCI was an early attempt at extending the functionality of WWW browsers. Now largely abandoned, CCI was an experimental protocol that allowed some versions of the NCSA Mosaic WWW browser to be controlled by an HTTP server. Today, many of the more useful functions of CCI are also present in the Java and JavaScript languages. The PGP-CCI application was basically a link between a WWW browser and the functionality provided by the PGP software. The application may be implemented as a graphical user interface (GUI) shell to a command line interface (CLI) for PGP, or as a complete application built using the PGP source code or the upcoming PGP API.

Instead of further describing the GSS-API and PGP-CCI approaches to secure WWW transaction, we are going to address two other proposals next: the secure hypertext transfer protocol (S-HTTP) and the security extension architecture (SEA) that follows and further extends the basic principles of S-HTTP.

Secure HTTP

The *secure hypertext transfer protocol* (S-HTTP) was developed and originally proposed by Eric Rescorla and Allan Schiffman from the Enterprise Integration Technologies (EIT) Corporation on behalf of the CommerceNet consortium. Launched in 1994 as a nonprofit organization, CommerceNet is dedicated to advancing electronic commerce on the Internet. Its nearly 250 member companies and organizations seek solutions to technology issues, sponsor industry pilots, and foster market and business development.[12] S-HTTP supports WWW transaction security by incorporating cryptographic enhancements to HTTP traffic at the application layer. S-HTTP version 1.0 was publicly released in June 1994 and distributed by the CommerceNet consortium. Since 1995, the S-HTTP specification has been developed and further refined under the auspices of the IETF WTS WG. In March 1997, the S-HTTP specification was upgraded to version 1.3 and specified in a corresponding Internet-Draft.[13]

In its current form, the S-HTTP defines an extension of HTTP that can be used to provide end-to-end security services for WWW transactions. The protocol emphasizes flexibility in choice of key management mechanisms, security policies, and cryptographic algorithms by supporting option negotiation between an S-HTTP-capable client and an S-HTTP-capable server. For example, S-HTTP does not

---

[12]http://www.commerce.net
[13]draft-ietf-wts-shttp-04.txt

require the use of client certificates. If a client has a certificate, then it is used. If, however, a client does not have a certificate, then other security techniques are employed. This is important because it means that spontaneous WWW transactions can occur even without requiring users to have public key certificates. S-HTTP can also be used with manually distributed and configured shared secret keys or Kerberos tickets instead of public key certificates. While S-HTTP is able to take advantage of a PKI, its deployment does not require it. Also, S-HTTP provides full flexibility of cryptographic algorithms, modes, and parameters.

The current S-HTTP specification suggests support for the cryptographic techniques and algorithms summarized in Table 11.1. In this table, 3DES refers to Triple-DES and DESX refers to a proprietary DES version from RSA Data Security, Inc.

Table 11.1
Cryptographic Techniques and Algorithms Supported by S-HTTP

Cryptographic Technique	Algorithms
One-way hash functions	MD2
	MD5
	SHA-1
Encryption algorithms	DES-CBC
	3DES-CBC (with 2 or 3 keys)
	DESX-CBC
	IDEA-CFB
	RC2-CBC
	RC4
	CDMF-CBC
Digital signature algorithms	RSA
	DSS

S-HTTP supports interoperation among a variety of implementations and is compatible with HTTP. What this basically means is that an S-HTTP-capable client can communicate with an S-HTTP-oblivious server and vice versa, although such communications would not make use of the S-HTTP security features.

Syntactically, S-HTTP messages are similar to HTTP messages. They consist of a request or status line followed by a series of header lines and a body that may contain an encapsulated content.

• The request and status lines of S-HTTP are similar to their HTTP counterparts. In order to differentiate S-HTTP messages from HTTP messages and allow for

Table 11.2
S-HTTP and Encapsulated HTTP Headers

Header Type	Header
S-HTTP headers	Content-Privacy-Domain
	Content-Transfer-Encoding
	Content-Type
	Prearranged-Key-Info
	MAC-Info
HTTP Non-negotiation headers	Key-Assign
	Encryption-Identity
	Certificate-Info
	Nonce
	Nonce-Echo
HTTP negotiation headers	SHTTP-Privacy-Domains
	SHTTP-Certificate-Types
	SHTTP-Key Exchange-Algorithms
	SHTTP-Signature-Algorithms
	SHTTP-Message-Digest-Algorithms
	SHTTP-Symmetric-Content-Algorithms
	SHTTP-Symmetric-Header-Algorithms
	SHTTP-Privacy-Enhancements
	Yor-Key-Pattern

special processing, the request and status lines should use the special protocol designator `Secure-HTTP/1.3`. Consequently, S-HTTP and HTTP processing can be intermixed on the same TCP port (e.g., port 80). If a future version of HTTP subsumed S-HTTP, an explicit distinction between this version of HTTP and S-HTTP would be unnecessary.

- The S-HTTP specification defines a set of new RFC 822-style header lines that can go in the header of an S-HTTP message. The possible S-HTTP headers are overviewed in Table 11.2 (together with the encapsulated HTTP headers). Most of the S-HTTP headers are optional. Only two of them are required: the `Content-Privacy-Domain` that defines a cryptographic message format, such as PKCS #7 or MOSS,[14] and the `Content-Type` that defines the actual MIME type of the encapsulated data, such as e.g. `application/http` in the case of HTTP.

---

[14]In earlier versions of the S-HTTP specification, PEM was used instead of MOSS, and PGP was mentioned as an additional cryptographic message format. In S-HTTP version 1.3, however, PKCS #7 and MOSS are the only two possible values.

- The encapsulated content of an S-HTTP message is largely dependent upon the values of the `Content-Privacy-Domain` and eventually the `Content-Transfer-Encoding` fields. Refer to the S-HTTP specification for a comprehensive summary of the various possibilities. Anyway, the encapsulated content of an S-HTTP message may start with an arbitrary number of HTTP nonnegotiation headers and HTTP negotiation headers as illustrated in Table 11.2.

Once the message content has been decapsulated, it should either be an S-HTTP message, an HTTP message, or simple data.

S-HTTP provides message content protection on three orthogonal axes: digital signature, authentication, and encryption. Any message may be digitally signed, authenticated or encrypted, or any combination of these (including no protection).

- If the digital signature enhancement is applied, an appropriate certificate (or certificate chain) may either be attached to the message or the sender may expect the recipient to obtain the corresponding certificate (chain) independently.

- If the message authentication enhancement is applied, a MAC is computed as a keyed one-way hash value over the document using a shared secret key. Again, this key could potentially have been arranged in a number of ways, including manual distribution and configuration or Kerberos tickets. The provision of message authentication as a separate security mechanism is motivated by the fact that the process of digitally signing a transaction should be explicit and conscious for the user, whereas many authentication needs can be met with a somehow lighter-weight mechanism, such as that provided by a keyed one-way hash function.

- In support of data encryption, S-HTTP defines two key distribution mechanisms. The first mechanism requires public key certificates to perform an in-band key exchange. In this case, the sender passes the transaction key encrypted under the receiver's public key. The second mechanism does not require public key certificates. In this case, the transaction is encrypted with an externally arranged key and corresponding key information is specified on one of the specific S-HTTP header lines. Alternatively, transaction keys may also be extracted from Kerberos tickets.

Table 11.3
S-HTTP Anchor Attributes

Anchor Attribute	Description
DN	Contains the distinguished name (DN) of the principal for whom the request should be encrypted when dereferencing the anchor's URL
NONCE	Contains a nonce that must be returned in a separate header line when the anchor is dereferenced
CRYPTOPTS	Contains the cryptographic option information

To identify the use of S-HTTP, a new URL protocol designator shttp has been defined. Use of this protocol designator as part of an anchor URL implies that the target server is S-HTTP-capable, and that a dereference of this URL should be enveloped accordingly. For this enveloping, three new anchor attributes are currently defined for S-HTTP. These attributes are summarized in Table 11.3. Binding cryptographic options to anchors using HTML extensions is the topic of a companion Internet draft[15] and is not treated here. An S-HTTP-oblivious client should not be willing to dereference a URL with an unknown protocol designator. Otherwise, sensitive information could be accidentally sent in the clear by careless users of these clients.

In summary, S-HTTP is very flexible in terms of the security mechanisms and cryptographic algorithms it supports. While its flexibility bodes well for interoperability, critics claim it makes it too difficult to develop a working implementation of S-HTTP. In fact, they point to the lack of widely available reference implementations of S-HTTP. Also, there is considerable confusion in the literature about what exactly distinguishes SSL from S-HTTP. Following the general structure of this book, one reasonable answer is that SSL refers to a transport layer security protocol, whereas S-HTTP refers to an application layer security protocol. More precisely, SSL establishes a secure TCP/IP connection between a client and a server, and this secure TCP/IP connection is used for HTTP traffic. Contrary to this approach, the S-HTTP uses normal TCP/IP connections to transmit data. Security services are negotiated through additional headers and the attributes attached to specific documents. Given the fact that S-HTTP works at the application layer and SSL works at the transport layer, it may be conceivable to devise a combined approach and to stack S-HTTP over SSL.

---

[15]draft-ietf-wts-shmtl-*.txt

Initially, there seemed to be a divergence of support for S-HTTP and SSL, with most vendors aligning themselves with one standard or the other. Since then, we have seen some unification of support for both security protocols. For example, to facilitate the use of security services for WWW applications and transactions, most WWW server manufacturers have announced support for both S-HTTP and SSL. For example, Terisa Systems, a company jointly founded by EIT and RSA Data Security, Inc., has released a WWW server toolkit that allows developers to incorporate both S-HTTP and SSL into their Web applications. More recently, however, the widespread use of SSL has started to supersede the use of S-HTTP.

Security Extension Architecture

The World Wide Web Consortium (W3C) is currently working on a *security extension architecture* (SEA) for HTTP that is based on the design principles of both the S-HTTP and the protocol extension protocol (PEP). In short, PEP allows an HTTP client and server to ask one another what extension modules they currently support, negotiate parameters for these extension modules, and ask the other end to commence using an extension if possible. This work is being folded into the specifications of HTTP 1.2 through the IETF standards process.

The SEA for HTTP was first published in January 1996. The corresponding specifications are still very immature and subject to ongoing changes. In short, the SEA specifies three different protocol extension classes for HTTP: Signature, Key-Exchange, and Encryption. With these extensions, the SEA is able to provide similar security services for HTTP as for S-HTTP. Also similar to S-HTTP is the fact that vendors as well as users are reacting cautiously with regard to SEA. At the time of this writing, there is a lot of interest in transport layer security to protect WWW transactions.

11.1.4   Other Applications

Note that the security-enhanced application protocols mentioned in the previous subsections are just examples. In principle, any application protocol can be enhanced to provide additional security services. For example, the version 2 of the simple network management protocol (SNMP) was already enhanced to provide message authentication services in 1992 [33]. SNMP is used to remotely control bridges, routers, and other (inter)networking devices. The need for authentication of SNMP requests is obvious. In fact, when an SNMPv2 message is sent, the originator generates a keyed one-way hash value that serves as a MAC. The receiver of the message, in turn, uses a shared secret key to verify the authenticity of the message.

Other examplary applications that are often enhanced with security features are (distributed) file systems. Note that security professionals may feel well protected with strong encryption mechanisms, such as those provided by IPSP/IKMP or SSL. But what good is transferring encrypted data over a network connection if the data are stored unencrypted on local machines that may get compromised. Thus, instead of having each application handle encryption and decryption, it is also possible to enhance a file system so that files are automatically encrypted after they leave applications but before they are sent to the file system. This approach has several advantages with regard to transparency and efficiency. For example, Matt Blaze from AT&T Bell Laboratories has developed a cryptographic file system (CFS) for the UNIX operating system [34,35].

Another example of a security-enhanced distributed file system is the Andrew File System (AFS) that was originally developed at Carnegie-Mellon University and is now marketed, maintained, and extended by Transarc Corporation [36,37].[16] In principle, AFS refers to a Kerberized file system. As such, it uses Kerberos for authentication, and optionally encryption, and is designed to work across wide area networks. Consequently, AFS provides a considerably higher level of security than does the Network File System (NFS) more commonly used today. NFS is shipped as part of the operating system with most versions of UNIX, while AFS is a commercial third-party product. Because Kerberos and AFS require significant technical expertise to set up and maintain, AFS is not widely used outside of a relatively small number of sites. If wide area network file systems must be secured, it may be worth investigating AFS. There have been security problems with some earlier versions of AFS, but those have been fixed [38].

11.2   AUTHENTICATION AND KEY DISTRIBUTION SYSTEMS

During the past few years, a considerable amount of work has been spent to develop authentication and key distribution systems that can be used by arbitrary applications to incorporate security services. Examples include the following authentication and key distribution systems:

- Kerberos, originally developed at the MIT;

- Network Security Program (NetSP), developed by IBM;

---

[16]http://www.transarc.com/

- SPX, developed by DEC;

- The Exponential Security System (TESS), developed at the University of Karlsruhe.

In addition, there are several extensions to the basic Kerberos authentication system, such as those provided by Yaksha, SESAME (a Secure European System for Applications in a Multivendor Environment), and the Distributed Computing Environment (DCE) developed by the Open Group.[17] In this section we are not going to describe and discuss the authentication and key distribution systems mentioned above. Instead we refer to [39] and the companion book, *Authentication Systems for Secure Networks* also published by Artech House [40]. We have discussed the close relationship between *Authentication Systems for Secure Networks* and *Internet and Intranet Security* in the Preface, so we are not going to repeat this discussion at this point. Remember that *Authentication Systems for Secure Networks* provides a comprehensive overview and comparison of the authentication and key distribution systems that are currently available.

Although the idea of building an authentication and key distribution system that may serve several applications is promising, the proliferation of these systems has turned out to be rather slow. One reason for that is because the specification of the generic security services application programming interface (GSS-API) has come rather late. As a matter of fact, the use of the GSS-API for Kerberos V5 has not been specified until recently [41]. Also, more work is need to standardize and eventually simplify the GSS-API, such as demonstrated by GSS-API version 2 or the Simple Public-Key GSS-API Mechanism [42,43]. As well, Kerberos is not the best currently available authentication and key distribution system, especially for use in large administration domains. Taking this into account, it is rather astonishing that Microsoft has announced support for the Kerberos authentication system in its upcoming version 5 of Windows NT.

REFERENCES

[1] D. Borman, "Telnet authentication: Kerberos Version 4," Request for Comments 1411, January 1993.

[2] K. Alagappan, "Telnet authentication: SPX," Request for Comments 1412, January 1993.

---

[17]The Open Group was formed in early 1996 by the consolidation of two open systems consortia, namely the Open Software Foundation (OSF) and the X/Open Company Ltd. The Open Group includes a large number of computer vendors, including e.g. IBM, DEC, and Microsoft.

[3] M. Blaze, and S.M. Bellovin, "Session-Layer Encryption," *Proceedings of USENIX UNIX Security Symposium*, June 1995.

[4] R.L. Rivest, and A. Shamir, "How to Expose an Eavesdropper." *Communications of the ACM*, Vol. 27, No. 4, 1984, pp. 393 – 395.

[5] D.R. Safford, D.K. Hess, and D.L. Schales, "Secure RPC authentication (SRA) for TELNET and FTP," *Proceedings of USENIX UNIX Security Symposium*, October 1993, pp. 63 – 67.

[6] D. Vincenzetti, S. Taino, and F. Bolognesi, "STEL: Secure Telnet," *Proceedings of USENIX UNIX Security Symposium*, June 1995.

[7] J. Linn, "Privacy Enhancement for Internet Electronic Mail: Part I — Message Encryption and Authentication Procedures," Request for Comments 1421, February 1993.

[8] S.T. Kent, "Privacy Enhancement for Internet Electronic Mail: Part II — Certificate-Based Key Management," Request for Comments 1422, February 1993.

[9] D. Balenson, "Privacy Enhancement for Internet Electronic Mail: Part III — Algorithms, Modes, and Identifiers," Request for Comments 1423, February 1993.

[10] B. Kaliski, "Privacy Enhancement for Internet Electronic Mail: Part IV — Key Certification and Related Services," Request for Comments 1424, February 1993.

[11] S.T. Kent, "Internet Privacy Enhanced Mail." *Communications of the ACM*, 36(8), August 1993, pp. 48 – 60.

[12] M. Purser, "COSINE Sub-project P8: security services." *Computer Networks and ISDN Systems*, 25 (1992), pp. 476 – 482.

[13] P. Kirstein, Piloting Authentication and Security Services within OSI Applications for RTD Information (PASSWORD). *Computer Networks and ISDN Systems*, 25 (1992), pp. 483 – 489.

[14] S. Muftic, N. Kapidzic, and A. Davidson, "The Structure and Functioning of the COST Privacy Enhanced Mail (PEM) System," *Proceedings of IFIP SEC' 94*, May 1994.

[15] R. Braden, D. Clark, S. Crocker, and C. Huitema, "Report of the IAB Workshop on Security in the Internet Architecture (February 8 – 10, 1994)," Request for Comments 1636, June 1994.

[16] J. Galvin, and M.S. Feldman, "MIME object security services: Issues in a multi-user environment," *Proceedings of USENIX UNIX Security V Symposium*, June 1995.

[17] J. Galvin, S. Murphy, S. Crocker, and N. Freed, "Security Multiparts for MIME: Multipart/Signed and Multipart/Encrypted," Request for Comments 1847, October 1995.

[18] S. Crocker, N. Freed, J. Galvin, and S. Murphy, "MIME Object Security Services," Request for Comments 1848, October 1995.

[19] P.R. Zimmermann, *The Official PGP User's Guide*, The MIT Press, Cambridge, MA, 1995.

[20] P.R. Zimmermann, *PGP Source Code and Internals*, The MIT Press, Cambridge, MA, 1995.

[21] S. Garfinkel, *PGP: Pretty Good Privacy*, O'Reilly & Associates, Sebastopol, CA, 1995.

[22] J.I. Schiller, and D.A. Atkins, "Scaling the Web of Trust: Combining Kerberos and PGP to Provide Large Scale Authentication," *Proceedings of USENIX Technical Conference on UNIX and Advanced Computing Systems*, January 1995, pp. 83 – 94.

[23] D. Atkins, W. Stallings, and P. Zimmermann, "PGP Message Exchange Formats," Request for Comments 1991, August 1996.

[24] M. Elkins, "MIME Security with Pretty Good Privacy (PGP)," Request for Comments 2015, October 1996.

[25] RSA Data Security, Inc., *S/MIME Implementation Guide*, Interoperability Profile, Version 1, August 1995.

[26] RSA Laboratories, *PKCS #7: Cryptographic Message Syntax Standard*, Version 1.5, November 1993.

[27] RSA Laboratories, *PKCS #10: Certification Request Syntax Standard*, Version 1.0, November 1993.

[28] J. Franks, P. Hallam-Baker, J. Hostetler, P. Leach, A. Luotonen, E. Sink, and L. Stewart, "An Extension to HTTP: Digest Access Authentication," Request for Comments 2069, January 1997.

[29] G. Bossert, S. Cooper, and W. Drummond, "Considerations for Web Transaction Security," Request for Comments 2084, January 1997.

[30] P. Lipp, and V. Hassler, "Security Concepts for the WWW," *Proceedings of Communications and Multimedia Security Conference*, September 1996, pp. 84 – 95.

[31] S. Garfinkel, and E.H. Spafford, *Web Security & Commerce*, O'Reilly & Associates, Sebastopol, CA, 1997.

[32] J.D. Weeks, A. Cain, and B. Sanderson, "CCI-Based Web Security - A Design Using PGP," *Proceedings of 4th International World Wide Web Conference*, December 1995, pp. 381 – 395.

[33] J. Galvin, K. McCloghrie, and J. Davin, "SNMP Security Protocols," Request for Comments 1352, July 1992.

[34] M. Blaze, "A Cryptographic File System for UNIX," *Proceedings of ACM Conference on Computer and Communications Security*, November 1993, pp. 9 – 16.

[35] M. Blaze, "Key Management in an Encrypting File System," *Proceedings of USENIX Summer Conference*, June 1994, pp. 27 – 35.

[36] J.H. Howard, "An overview of the Andrew File System," *Proceedings of USENIX Conference,* 1988, pp. 23 – 26.

[37] M.L. Kazar, "Synchronization and Caching Issues in the Andrew File System," *Proceedings of USENIX Conference,* 1988, pp. 27 – 36.

[38] P. Honeyman, L.B. Huston, and M.T. Stolarchuk, "Hijacking AFS," *Proceedings of USENIX Conference,* 1992, pp. 175 – 182.

[39] R. Oppliger, "Authentication and key distribution in computer networks and distributed systems," *Proceedings of Communications and Multimedia Security Conference,* September 1995, pp. 148 – 159.

[40] R. Oppliger, *Authentication Systems for Secure Networks,* Artech House, Norwood, MA, 1996.

[41] J. Linn, "The Kerberos Version 5 GSS-API Mechanism," Request for Comments 1964, June 1996.

[42] J. Linn, "Generic Security Services Application Program Interface, Version 2," Request for Comments 2078, January 1997.

[43] C. Adams, "The Simple Public-Key GSS-API Mechanism," Request for Comments 2025, October 1996.

Chapter 12

Conclusions

In this part of the book we have overviewed and discussed several cryptographic protocols developed and proposed to provide communication security services for the Internet and corporate intranets. While most of these protocols are similar in terms of security services they provide as well as cryptographic algorithms and techniques they use, they vary fundamentally in the manner in which they provide the security services and their placement within the TCP/IP communications protocol stack. In particular, we have seen protocols for the Internet, transport, and application layer.

So far, the question of which layer is best suited to provide security services has not been addressed. This simple question has turned out to be rather difficult to answer. Remember that the OSI security architecture has not been specific about this question either and has proposed several possibilities for proper placement within the OSI reference model and its layered protocol stack instead. In general, there are arguments to provide security services either at the lower or higher layers:

- The proponents of placing security lower in the protocol stack argue that lower-layer security can be implemented transparently to users and application programs, effectively killing many birds with a single stone.

279

- Contrary to the above, proponents of placing security higher in the protocol stack argue that lower-layer security attempts to do too many things simultaneously and that only protocols which work at the application layer or above can actually meet application-specific security requirements and provide corresponding services.

Unfortunately, both arguments are somehow true, so there is no generally agreed upon best layer to provide security services. The best layer actually depends on the security services required and the application environment in which the services must be deployed [1,2].

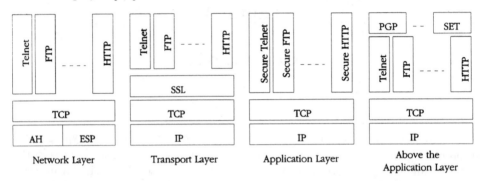

Figure 12.1   Relationships between security protocol proposals and the TCP/IP stack.

The aim of this chapter is to overview and briefly discuss the advantages and disadvantages of the various possibilities. Figure 12.1 illustrates the relationship between several security protocols and the TCP/IP communications protocol stack. More precisely, it illustrates the placement of security protocols and mechanisms that operate at the network (or Internet) layer, at the transport layer, at the application layer, and above the application layer. In this book, we have not explicitly distinguished between the situation in which security services are provided at the application layer and the situation in which the services are provided above the application layer. In the first case, the application protocols must be modified to incorporate security features, whereas in the second case the message syntax and semantics must be modified accordingly. Because there are many authors who (over)emphazise this distinction, it is also included in Figure 12.1.

If security services are provided at the network or Internet layer, the basic IP software module must be replaced or enhanced with modules that additionally implement security mechanisms, such as the authentication header (AH) and encapsulated security payload (ESP) mechanisms that we introduced and fully discussed in

Chapter 9. This replacement is illustrated on the leftmost drawing of Figure 12.1. There are many advantages and disadvantages related to Internet layer security. One of the major advantages is that security services provided at the Internet layer are standard network services any application can make use of in a transparent way. What this essentially means is that the development of secure applications is simplified substantially, and it is now possible to secure applications simply by upgrading the TCP/IP software modules. But Internet layer security has also some disadvantages. Most obviously, it requires the use and deployment of new TCP/IP software modules. This may pose an availability problem for less widely used operating systems, and may also be a costly process. Another disadvantage is that the Internet layer, in general, can't discriminate between IP packets that belong to different associations and corresponding application processes. Hence, it is constrained to use the same cryptographic keys and access policies to all IP packets destined to a particular host. This may not provide the function desired, and may also be costly in performance. Conceptually, this disadvantage could be circumvented with user-oriented or session-unique keying. But user-oriented and session-unique keying have turned out to be rather difficult to implement, use, and deploy. Therefore, it is not likely that we will see user-oriented and session-unique keying being used and widely deployed on the Internet.

In Chapter 2, we saw that several interfaces have been developed for programming at the transport layer, with Berkeley sockets and TLI being the two most commonly used examples. As we have also described and discussed in Chapter 10, the idea of providing security services at the transport layer is to enhance the network programming interface with security features, and to enable application programs to selectively make use of these features. Consequently, modifications are required for both the network programming interface and the corresponding TCP/IP application programs. However, the modifications are comparably small. In Figure 12.1, the use of transport layer security is illustrated on the second drawing from the left, where an intermediate secure sockets layer (SSL) layer is placed between the transport and application layer. Again, there are advantages and disadvantages related to transport layer security. One major advantage, for example, is that transport layer security operates on an end-to-end basis, meaning that secure communication channels can be established between application processes, and these channels can then be used to transmit authenticated and confidential data. Another advantage is that users should neither know about transport layer security techniques nor be aware of their use. Note, however, that it is generally a good idea to inform the users about transport layer security techniques being used. A good example is the little key in the lower left corner of the Netscape Navigator user interface. Using normal TCP/IP connections for HTTP traffic, the key is broken in two pieces. Only if SSL is used to authenticate the server and encrypt the communication channel between the client and server is the key drawn in a single piece. But transport layer security also has some disadvantages. Most obviously, modifications are required for both the network programming interface and the corresponding TCP/IP application programs. More importantly, the use of digital signatures is currently restricted to authentication and key exchange, and there is no possibility of providing non-repudiation services. Also, there is currently no possibility of protecting UDP traffic at the transport layer. Similar to Internet layer security protocols, transport layer security protocols can be used to build virtual private networks on public networks.

Figure 12.2   An analogy for the transportation of valuable goods.

If security services are provided at the application layer, no modifications are required for the TCP/IP software module and the network programming interface. All modifications are restricted to the application layer. What this basically means is that the application protocols must be modified to provide security services, and that the programs that implement these protocols must be modified accordingly. Consequently, application layer security is handled entirely at the application layer. This is advantageous since it does not require modifications to the underlying network infrastructure. The disadvantages of this approach are related to the fact that it is sometimes not possible or too expensive to modify application protocols and implementations thereof. Finally, it is also possible to provide security services above the application layer. What this basically means is that application data is prepared in such a way that it can be transmitted transparently with existing application protocol implementations, and is also able to provide the security services required. In Figure 12.1, the possibilities for providing security services at or above the application layer are illustrated on the two rightmost drawings. In the first case, the TCP/IP applications are replaced with secure counterparts, whereas in the second case, secure applications are layered on top of the TCP/IP applications.

An analogy can help us better understand the possibilities we have to place security services in a communications protocol stack. Referring to Figure 12.2, let's assume that we have some valuable goods to transport from location A to location B. If we use a railway system to transport the goods, we have the choice of either securing the railway system as a whole and transporting the goods as they are, or securing the goods and transporting them on the railway system as it is. In this analogy, the first choice refers to network or Internet layer security, whereas the second choice refers to application layer security. In this analogy, there is also a third possibility, namely to secure parts of the railway system and to transport the valuable goods on the secured parts and the less-valuable goods on the non-secured parts of the railway system. This approach actually refers to transport layer security.

In practice, it is assumed that future solutions will provide communication security services at various layers. This must not be a bad thing, and it may even be desirable to have multiple and complementary architectural approaches to security. It is possible and very likely that each approach will find its niche. For example, IPSP/IKMP is appropriate to build secure tunnels and virtual private networks (VPNs), whereas SSL and TLS are more appropriate for end-to-end applications, especially in the field of electronic commerce. Finally, the use of application layer security is the only way to go if the network infrastructure itself can't be modified.

In summary, the question of which layer(s) is (are) best suited to provide communication security services is not an "either or" decision, but rather an "and" decision, actually traversing and encompassing multiple layers. For example, bulk data cryptographic transformations, such as message authentication, integrity checking, and data encryption, are well suited to be performed at the network or Internet layer, which is usually tightly coupled with the operating system kernel and thus allows for efficient employment and scheduling of potentially available dedicated hardware, random number generators, and other components. At the same time, security policies that may be defined for a site or corporate intranet may be enforced without individual users being able to circumvent them. This has to be supplemented by an application programming interface (API) and other utilities residing in application space. The API and the utilities are to provide applications with information about the level of authenticity a connection actually has, and what algorithms for data encryption and authentication should be used. Finally, the concept of user involvement in the provision of security services is very important, but has not been sufficiently addressed in the past. Currently, each application takes care of its cryptographic keys individually, but this is certainly not the way to go for future applications. From the user's point of view, it would be convenient to have some sort of a key agent that securely stores his or her cryptographic keys and provides the applications with the keys required in order to act on the user's behalf. With regard to digital signature keys, the concept of user involvement is even more important since the application and use of these keys may create liability.

REFERENCES

[1] A. Bhimani, "Securing The Commercial Internet," *Communications of the ACM*, Vol. 39, No. 6, June 1996, pp. 29 – 35.

[2] R. Oppliger, "Internet and Intranet Security," *Computer Security Journal*, Vol. XIII, No. 2, Fall 1997.

Part IV

DISCUSSION

Chapter 13

Electronic Commerce

In previous parts of this book, we addressed techniques that can be used to provide Internet and intranet security. While most of these techniques are interesting mainly from a theoretical point of view, they need a more practical reason to be deployed on the Internet. In this chapter we focus on electronic commerce that may provide such a reason. A brief introduction is given in Section 13.1, and electronic payment systems are further addressed in Section 13.2.

13.1 INTRODUCTION

The aim of electronic commerce (e-commerce) is to use an open and public network, such as the Internet, to market goods and services without having to be physically present at the point of sale [1,2]. In e-commerce, the Internet may serve several purposes, including marketing, services, and sales.

- Internet marketing includes advertising as well as providing information about an organization and its current offerings [3]. Compared to advertising with print media, advertising on the Internet is attractive given its low cost and easy access to many people.

- There are many forms of services that can be provided over the Internet. Many of these services are just electronic counterparts of the services we know and are familiar with today. Examples include online shopping, telebanking, or online casinos [4]. Other services are inherently new and must be explored with regard to user acceptance first. For example, Federal Express and United Parcel Service provide customer access to their databases in order to check the current status of postal deliveries. This service is inherently new and has no contemporary counterpart. We expect many such services to evolve on the future Internet marketplace.

- Finally, the Internet can also be used for sales. Material goods may be delivered with conventional postal services, whereas nonmaterial goods may be delivered directly over the Internet. In either case, the payment may be handled over the Internet. Note that more and more goods that have been offered in material form, are being offered in nonmaterial form today. Examples include all forms of print media, such as newspapers, magazines, and journals. With the wide proliferation of high-speed networks, it may even become feasible to deliver voice and video recordings in nonmaterial form. Also note that the Internet is still seldom used for sales. An Internet storefront simply enhances the sales at the real-world retail outlet. It may take a couple of years for merchants to determine the optimal ways to sell effectively online, as well as to find and maintain corresponding customers. Retailers still need to demonstrate the advantages of virtual malls, such as timeliness, convenience, ease of use, and potentially lower prices.

In general, there are many reasons why a business would like to establish a presence on the Internet or WWW. Probably the first and foremost reason is access to a potentially very large audience. Globalization is somehow a related issue. Through the Internet, a business can reach customers in almost every country of the world. Establishing a presence on the Internet is particularly cheap compared to the alternative of opening physical shops and advertising in various countries. Another important reason is potential savings in sales costs. Note that it costs a business a considerable amount of money to establish a physical shop in a mall, as well as to pay bills, salaries, and commission fees to the corresponding sales staff. Many of these expenses can be reduced by establishing a presence on the Internet or WWW. These savings can in turn help reduce the costs of goods or services and make them more competitive as a whole. Finally, businesses can also provide instant updates to their goods or services. Note that a business can easily insert an update that reaches online customers almost instantly. The availability of such a rapid update mechanism is particularly interesting for selling goods or services that expire in a relatively short amount of time. For example, online updates are attractive to sell vacant seats on airline flights as well as tickets for evening theater shows and plays. Another example where online updates are particularly interesting is the distribution of antivirus software.

In addition, there are benefits from the customer's point of view. Perhaps the most important benefit is the potential savings in time. By logging on to the Internet and accessing information pages on the WWW, customers can browse through shops and merchandise from their home at any time. Alternatively, in the real world a customer usually spends hours on a shopping trip, including travel to and from the shopping mall. A related benefit is convenient access to a wide variety of shops and merchandise. For example, a physical shopping mall may provide clothing and some other merchandise, but it may not include a car dealership, an airline ticket office, or an Asian food store. Consequently, a customer must travel to several places if he or she has specific needs. This is obviously not the case in a shopping trip on the Internet or WWW. A customer may also like to shop in a virtual mall simply to compare instantly the quality and price of a product from different shops. This may help make shopping decisions easier and faster.

In Part 3 of this book, we introduced and discussed technologies that can be used to provide communication security on the Internet. It is, however, important to note that secure communications do not satisfy all security needs for e-commerce. For example, a customer willing to purchase goods or services from an Internet merchant must still trust the Web server's administrator with his credit card information, even if the communication channel is encrypted. Note that communication security, in general, protects only the communication channels; it does not protect against disreputable or careless people who may induce naive customers into entering a transaction with them. In a sense, this is similar to the mode of business conducted over the public switched telephone network (PSTN). It is common practice today to order goods or services over the PSTN with credit card information, such as the credit card brand, the card number, and the expiration date. More precisely, a customer phones the merchant, orders some items, and gives out his credit card information to accomplish the purchase. The merchant, in turn, verifies the credit card information with the corresponding credit card company. If the credit card is valid, the merchant delivers the items and has the credit card account of the customer charged for the corresponding amount of money. The customer gives out his credit card information because he feels secure that nobody is eavesdropping on the PSTN line, and because he trusts the merchant to use the information only in reference to the business being conducted and for nothing else. One thing that is very seldom taken into account is that credit card information is stored locally at the merchant's site for later reuse or marketing purposes. Let's assume the very likely scenario in which a customer who has used his credit card to buy something in the past and who wants to buy some additional items, is kindly asked at the checkout counter of a shop whether he wants to charge the same credit card as the previous time. It is very obvious in this case that the customer's credit card information has been stored at the merchant' site, and that the customer has implicitly trusted the merchant to protect the credit card information against misuse and other security-related threats. This level of trust may not always be justified.

Following this line of argument, the credit card number problem that has driven the Internet security discussion in the recent past is not particularly an Internet security problem; it is rather a problem of how we (carelessly) use credit card information in daily life. The credit card information that is generally used to order goods or services today should simply not be sufficient to place such an order. In addition to the credit card information, a customer should also be able to provide some additional information that would be used to strongly authenticate him and to prove his identity and creditworthiness accordingly. It is also important to note that electronic credit card payments are not the only possible form of payment over the Internet; we will overview and briefly discuss some valuable alternatives in the following section.

13.2   ELECTRONIC PAYMENT SYSTEMS

Typically, a customer or user interacts with an e-commerce merchant or vendor through an HTTP client or WWW browser software. Therefore, the graphical user interface (GUI) of this software should closely emulate a real shopping environment. When a user decides to go shopping online, he or she usually accesses the home page of a familiar shopping mall and selects a merchant or vendor from this mall to purchase goods or services. The shopping mall connects to the selected merchant, and the merchant presents a corresponding home page to the user. The home page may include information about the goods or services that can be purchased from that particular site. The user selects the desired items, interacts with the merchant, and makes the necessary payments. Accordingly, the merchant accesses his bank for proper authorization of the payments. If the payments are authorized, the merchant informs the user that the payments are accepted and the transaction may be completed. At some later point in time, the merchant's bank obtains the payments from the customer's bank, and the customer is informed about the money transfer accordingly.

E-commerce in general and over the Internet in particular depends on the availability and wide deployment of electronic payment systems. These systems may involve several parties and payment methods. In this section, we overview and briefly discuss some approaches for making electronic payments and supporting e-commerce accordingly. In particular, we focus on electronic cash, electronic checks, credit card payments, and micropayments. A more comprehensive overview is given in [5]. Note that there are also some other forms of payment that are not addressed in this book. Examples include money orders, bank checks, debit card payments, purchase orders, and traveler's checks. In addition, there are also some electronic payment systems that don't make use of cryptography at all. Probably the best known example of this kind is the system of the First Virtual Holdings, Inc. [6].[1] In this system, a user registers with First Virtual by providing his or her identification and credit card information. First Virtual then assigns the user a unique First Virtual identification number. When the user wants to make a payment, she sends her First Virtual identification number to the corresponding merchant. The merchant, in turn, verifies the identification number with the First Virtual clearing house and First Virtual confirms the payment with the customer. Upon receiving confirmation, the money is transferred offline. First Virtual uses e-mail messages to place and confirm payment orders, whereas the transfer of money is handled offline through private networks.

At the core of an electronic payment system is one (or several) payment protocol(s). Payment protocols are general in nature and must not depend on the actual transport media in use. As a matter of fact, a payment protocol may be implemented within WWW browsers using HTTP, e-mail agents using SMTP, or some other program using a specific application protocol. In either case, it must be ensured that the data involved in an electronic payment protocol execution is secure, even if the medium is not. In the event that the insecure medium is attacked, nothing more than a useless stream of data must be obtained.

It is possible and very likely that we will see many electronic payment systems coexist in the future. Consequently, there must be a negotiation layer on top of the corresponding systems. In December 1995, the WWW consortium (W3C) and the CommerceNet consortium cosponsored the Joint Electronic Payment Initiative (JEPI[2]) to bring the key industry players together to ensure that multiple payment schemes, protocols, and transport mechanisms will work together and interoperate over the Internet. In short, JEPI is intended to enable automated payment

---

[1]http://www.fv.com
[2]hhtp://www.w3.org/pub/WWW/Payments/jepi.html

negotiation, where computers perform negotiations and users make final decisions. Technically, JEPI hinges around creating specifications for a pair of negotiation protocols:

- A general purpose negotiation protocol based on the protocol extension protocol (PEP). As mentioned in Chapter 11, PEP extends HTTP so that it can dynamically deploy applications that require more functionalities than those provided by HTTP.

- A specific extension module called the universal payment preamble (UPP) that is layered on top of PEP. UPP lets customers use a multipayment wallet and easily move from payment to payment. UPP negotiations occur via exchange of PEP headers before or during shopping. They can be used to negotiate over the payment method, protocol, and some other parameters, such as the credit card brand in the case of a credit card payment.

The JEPI phase one was completed in April 1997 with an implementation that comprises two payment schemes. In the second phase of the JEPI project, it is intended to encompass a larger number of payment schemes, incorporate personal security tokens, and establish common application programming interfaces (APIs). It is also intended to get involvement by a larger number of European and Japanese companies as well as more serious interaction with the financial services industry.

13.2.1   Electronic Cash

Digital or *electronic cash* (e-cash) provides an electronic analog for physical cash. A bank issues e-cash, and customers may use the e-cash to purchase goods or services from merchants that accept this form of electronic payment. In general, there are three parties involved in an e-cash system:

- An e-cash issuing bank;

- A customer;

- A merchant.

The customer and merchant may also have accounts with some other banks. In this case, these banks are referred to as the customer's bank or merchant's bank, respectively. Given this cast, an e-cash transaction may take place in three distinct and independent phases:

- In the first phase, the customer obtains e-cash. Therefore, he requests that his bank transfer some money from his account to the e-cash issuing bank. Following this transfer, the issuing bank sends a corresponding amount of e-cash to the customer, and the customer stores the e-cash locally on his hard disk or smartcard.

- In the second phase, the customer uses the e-cash to make some purchases. In particular, he selects goods or services and transfers the corresponding amount of e-cash to the merchant. The merchant, in turn, provides the goods or services to the customer.

- In the third phase, the merchant redeems the e-cash she has just obtained from the customer. She therefore transfers the e-cash to the issuing bank. Alternatively, the merchant may also transfer the e-cash to her bank, and the merchant's bank in turn may redeem the money from the e-cash issuing bank. In this case, the issuing bank transfers money to the merchant's bank for crediting the merchant's account.

It is commonly agreed that e-cash should satisfy some general properties. For example, e-cash should be independent in the sense that its existence must not depend on a particular system platform or location. Probably one of the distinguishing features of real cash is its anonymity, meaning that cash must not provide information that can be used to trace previous owners. One can reasonably argue that e-cash must provide this form of anonymity as well. Consequently, e-cash must be transferable from one person to another, and this should occur without leaving any trace of who has been in possession of the e-cash in the past. In this case, however, it must be ensured that each owner can spend the e-cash only once and that double spending is detectable accordingly. Also, e-cash should be available in several denominations and be divisible in a way similar to real cash. Finally, e-cash should be available in such a way so it can be securely stored on a hard disk or smart card. Not all e-cash systems that have been proposed in the past satisfy all of these properties. For example, the anonymity property is still very controversial today, since it leads to the undesired possibility of illegal money washing, or hiding of black market and blackmail money. This has led to the development of fairly anonymous e-cash systems, in which the customer's anonymity may be revealed under certain conditions.

David Chaum developed a mechanism to blind RSA signatures and issue anonymous e-cash in 1982 [7 – 9]. Let d be the private and (n, e) the public RSA key of an e-cash issuing bank (for one particular digital coin size, such as one dollar). In this case, n is the modulus and e and d are the exponents that correspond to each other; that is, for all x holds, $x^{de} \equiv x^{ed} \equiv x \pmod{n}$. The customer generates a serial number m for a digital coin and a random number r that serves the role of a blinding factor. He then computes $x = mr^e \pmod{n}$ and sends x to the e-cash issuing bank. Note that the bank cannot recognize m or r from x. The bank digitally signs x by calculating $y = x^d \pmod{n}$ and sends y back to the customer. At the same time, the bank also charges the customer's account with the corresponding amount of money (one dollar in this case). Obviously, this happens in the same way as if the customer would personally withdraw money from his banking account. The customer then divides y by r. This yields the bank's digital signature z of the digital coin's serial number m:

$$
\begin{aligned}
z &= y/r \\
&\equiv x^d/r \\
&\equiv (m(r^e))^d/r \\
&\equiv (m^d r^{ed})/r \\
&\equiv (m^d r)/r \\
&\equiv m^d \pmod{n}
\end{aligned}
$$

Now the customer can use the digital coin (m, z) to buy goods or services from a merchant that accepts e-cash. The merchant, in turn, can verify the coin by verifying the bank's signature z with the corresponding public key (n, e).

Chaum has founded DigiCash, Inc.[3] to market the anonymous e-cash scheme overviewed above under the name Ecash. In October 1995, the Mark Twain Bank of St. Louis, Missouri, was the first bank to offer Ecash services over the Internet. Meanwhile, several banks have followed the Mark Twain Bank. In Germany, for example, the Deutsche Bank is exploring the use of Ecash as well.

In the Ecash system, digital coins are stored locally on the customer' system. One possibility is to encrypt the digital coins with a password-derived secret key; another possibility is to use smart cards. In either case, the customer must transfer the digital coins over the Internet to the merchant. Before accepting a coin, the merchant must examine its authenticity and integrity with the corresponding public key of the issuing bank, and verify online with this bank whether the coin has already been used. A coin can only be used once, in that the bank takes note of all the serial numbers and would recognize and refuse a coin that is used a second time.

---

[3] http://www.digicash.com

In addition to Ecash, the idea of anonymous e-cash has also been explored in a project named Conditional Access for Europe (CAFE[4]). The assumption of this project is that online examinations of digital coins are not always possible, and that offline systems provide a somewhat better approach for widespread use of e-cash over the Internet. However, one problem that immediately arises in an offline system is the double-spending problem. How can one avoid that a digital coin is not used twice? Note that there is no possibility for the merchant to verify the coin with the issuing bank in the offline model. In general, there are two approaches to address this problem:

- The first approach is to use some sophisticated mathematics to ensure that the identity of the owner of a digital coin that has been spent twice can be revealed. In this case, the owner of a coin provides a part of his identification characteristics during the payment process, which alone gives no further information about his identity. Only in combination with another part of his identification characteristics can the identity of the owner be revealed [10].

- The second approach is to use dedicated hardware devices that store the coins and make sure that digital coins are spent only once. These hardware devices are sometimes also called electronic wallets or observers.

The CAFE project follows the second approach with specifically designed electronic wallets. Another offline anonymous e-cash system with hardware support is Mondex.[5] Mondex is mainly deployed within the United Kingdom. NetCash is a research prototype of an e-cash system that provides what one can call weak anonymity. Weak anonymity means that if a customer gives NetCash to a merchant, there is no way for the merchant, on her own, to determine the identity of the customer (unless the customer divulges it through other means). However, if the merchant should collude with the accounting server(s), they may together discover the identity of the customer. The NetCash system was developed at the Information Sciences Institute of the University of Southern California [11]. NetCash uses the NetCheque system overviewed in the following subsection to clear payments between currency servers. Finally, CyberCash is an example of an e-cash system that doesn't care about customer anonymity at all.

---

[4]http://www.cwi.nl/cwi/projects/cafe.html
[5]http://www.mondex.com

13.2.2   Electronic Checks

Since the use of checks is widely deployed in the real world (at least in the United States), electronic checks may provide an interesting payment scheme for e-commerce as well. In short, the customer issues an electronic check to the merchant, and the merchant deposits the check in the bank to redeem the money. Consequently, a system for electronic checks includes the following parties:

- A customer and a customer's bank;

- A merchant and a merchant's bank;

- A clearing house to process checks among different banks.

In such a system, an electronic check transaction consists of several basic steps that can be executed in three distinct phases:

- In the first phase, the customer purchases some goods or services and sends a corresponding electronic check to the merchant. The merchant, in turn, validates the check with her bank for proper payment authorization. If the check is valid, the merchant accomplishes the transaction with the customer.

- In the second phase, the merchant forwards the electronic check to her bank for deposit. This action takes place at the discretion of the merchant.

- In the third phase, the merchant's bank forwards the electronic check to the clearing house for cashing it. The clearing house, in turn, cooperates with the customer's bank, clears the check, and transfers the money to the merchant's bank, which updates the merchant's account accordingly. The customer's bank also updates the customer with the withdrawal information.

From a technical point of view, electronic checks are fairly simple. An electronic check may simply consist of a document that is digitally signed with the customer's private key. The receiver (the merchant or the merchant's bank) can use the customer's public key to verify the digital signature accordingly. Compared with paper checks and some other forms of real-world payments, electronic checks provide several advantages. For example, electronic checks can be issued without needing to fill out, mail, or deliver checks. It also saves time in processing the checks. With paper checks, the merchant typically collects all the checks and deposits them at the merchant's bank. With electronic checks, the merchant can instantly forward checks to the bank and get them credited to her account. As such, electronic checks can greatly reduce the time from the moment a customer writes a check to the time when the merchant receives the deposit. In addition to that, electronic check systems can be designed in such a way that the merchant gets proper authorization from the customer's bank before accepting a check. This is very similar to the cashier's check approach.

Examples of electronic check systems are PayNow from CyberCash, Inc. and NetCheque developed at the Information Sciences Institute of the University of Southern California [11].[6] NetCheque is implemented using features of the Kerberos authentication system [12]. Roughly speaking, a NetCheque check (or a NetCheque in short) is represented by a Kerberos ticket that allows an authorized bearer to withdraw funds from the NetCheque issuer's account and prevents an unauthorized bearer from depositing a NetCheque not issued to him. To make use of the NetCheque system, a user must have registered with a NetCheque accounting server and obtained the corresponding software.

13.2.3 Credit Card Payments

In the recent past, electronic credit card payment systems have become the payment systems of choice for Internet users and customers. There are several security requirements that these systems must address. For example, a mechanism must be provided to authenticate the various parties involved, such as customers, merchants, and participating banks. Another mechanism must be provided to protect the credit card and payment information during transmission over the Internet. Finally, a process must be instituted to resolve credit card payment disputes between the parties involved. Several electronic credit card payment schemes have been designed to address these requirements. Most of these schemes have additional advantages. For example, in some schemes the credit card information can be prevented from disclosure to the merchant. This characteristic does not exist in the traditional credit card systems. Consequently, an electronic credit card payment scheme may provide a higher level of security than a traditional credit card payment scheme. Also, an electronic credit card payment scheme can be designed to obtain almost instant payments to the merchants from credit card sales. For traditional credit card schemes, it takes a significant amount of time for the merchant to deliver the credit card receipts to the bank, and for the bank to settle the payments. Figure 13.1 overviews the parties involved in a secure electronic credit card payment scheme. There are five parties involved:

---

[6]http://gost.isi.edu/info/NetCheque/

- A credit card holder;

- A merchant;

- A merchant's bank;

- A certificate management center (CMC);

- A credit card issuing bank.

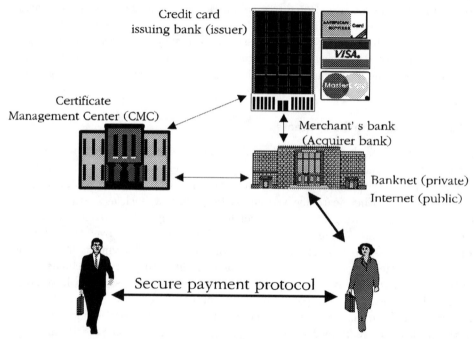

Figure 13.1   The parties involved in a secure electronic credit card payment scheme.

The credit card holder uses his credit card to purchase goods or services from the merchant. The merchant, in turn, interacts with her bank, called the merchant's bank. This bank is sometimes also referred to as the acquirer or acquirer bank. In an electronic credit card payment scheme, the acquirer typically refers to a financial institution that has an account with a merchant and processes credit card authorizations and corresponding payments. In this setting, a payment gateway is a device operated by the acquirer to handle merchant payment messages. A very important party for any secure electronic credit card payment scheme is the certificate management center (CMC) that provides public key infrastructure (PKI) services and issues public key certificates to the parties involved. In addition to that, there are usually two networks involved in an electronic credit card payment scheme: a public network (typically the Internet) and a private network owned and operated by the banking community (therefore called Banknet). The basic assumption is that communications over the Banknet are sufficiently secure (since the Banknet is a private network that can be secured accordingly), whereas communications over the Internet are inherently insecure and must be cryptographically protected. Consequently, an electronic credit card payment protocol mainly focuses on the communications that takes place over the Internet and does not address communications that takes place over the Banknet.

In general, an electronic credit card payment transaction consists of several steps that may be executed in three distinct phases:

- In the first phase, the customer browses through the merchant's offerings and purchases some goods or services. He offers a credit card payment, and the merchant may access the acquirer to obtain a credit authorization for the customer and the amount of money of the purchase. In general, this authorization is requested only if the amount of money exceeds a certain threshold value. In this case, the acquirer completes the authorization and informs the merchant whether to proceed with the purchase or not. Finally, the merchant informs the customer whether the transaction has been settled.

- In the second phase, the merchant accesses the acquirer and provides a collection of receipts of various electronic credit card purchases. The acquirer accesses the credit card issuer to obtain the money for the purchases on the merchant's behalf.

- In the third phase, the credit card issuer updates the credit card holder about the amount of money transferred to other parties as a result of his purchases. The customer may receive the amount updates once a month through postal or secure electronic mail.

In the recent past, several electronic credit card payment schemes have been designed and proposed. Some exemplary schemes are overviewed next.

iKP Protocols

The IBM Research Division has designed a scheme and a corresponding family of protocols to securely transfer electronic payments over the Internet [13]. The most significant feature of this scheme is that it provides complete cryptographic protection of data, including an audit trail to resolve disputes. In this scheme, three parties are directly involved in an electronic payment transaction:

- A customer;

- A merchant;

- An acquirer gateway.

Similar to the payment gateway mentioned above, the acquirer gateway is actually a front end that interfaces for the merchant's bank. The customer makes the payment and the merchant receives the payment. The acquirer gateway interfaces with the existing payment infrastructure and authorizes the transaction by using the existing infrastructure.

The term iKP stands for Internet keyed payments protocol or i-key-protocol, where $i = 1, 2$, or 3. The value of i determines the number of parties that hold a public key pair and a corresponding public key certificate. So, 1KP is the simplest protocol where only the acquirer gateway possesses a public key. For 2KP, the acquirer gateway as well as the merchant possess a public key. Finally, the 3KP protocols require each of the three parties involved in a transaction to possess a public key. The 3KP protocol offers the highest level of security in the iKP protocol family.

- In the *1KP*, the customer and the merchant are not required to possess a public key pair. However, they must be capable of verifying the authenticity of messages originated by an acquirer gateway. Therefore, they must be provided with the public key of the CA that issues certificates for acquirer gateways. So, when a customer or merchant receives a certificate from an acquirer gateway, he can use the CA's public key to verify the certificate's authenticity. Since there are not too many acquirer gateways, a credit card company can typically issue the certificates required by itself. Customers are authenticated by their credit card number and possibly a personal identification number (PIN). Although this scheme is simple, it does not provide non-repudiation services for messages sent either by the customer or the merchant. Consequently, the 1KP does not provide the basic means that are required in order to resolve disputes relating to the authenticity of the payment messages.

- In the *2KP*, the merchant as well as the acquirer gateway possess a public key pair. Consequently, this protocol provides non-repudiation services for the messages sent by the merchant or acquirer gateway.

- Finally, in the *3KP*, all parties possess a public key pair. Consequently, this protocol provides non-repudiation services for the messages sent by the customer, merchant, or acquirer. This protocol requires a PKI to exist and be fully operable.

A consortium chaired by MasterCard has embedded and expanded the iKP protocols into an application context with key management and a more concrete clearing process, which is specified by the name *secure electronic payment protocol* (SEPP). Apart from IBM and MasterCard, some other companies also participated in the SEPP development, including Netscape Communications, GTE, and Cyber-Cash. At the very same time, another consortium chaired by Visa was working with Microsoft and some other companies on the design of a similar technology called *secure transaction technology* (STT). Consequently, there were two consortia and corresponding technologies competing for the same market share.

In February 1996, it was announced that MasterCard and Visa, together with the other companies mentioned above, as well as some new partners (including SAIC, Terisa, and VeriSign) had agreed to jointly develop an open standard for secure credit card payment transactions over the Internet. This standard was named *secure electronic transaction* (SET). Today, it seems possible and very likely that the SET specification will become the standard for secure electronic credit card payment transactions over the Internet.

SET Protocols

A first preliminary version of the SET specification was published in February 1996, and a second version in June 1996. This second preliminary version was extensively used in field trials and had big impacts on the specification of SET version 1.0 that was officially released on May 31, 1997.[7] Today, the SET specification consists of three parts (or books as they are called in the SET terminology):

- Book 1: *Business Description*

- Book 2: *Programmers Guide*

---

[7]The SET specification is publicly and freely available from many Internet sites, including Visa at URL http://www.visa.com and MasterCard at URL http://www.mastercard.com.

- Book 3: *Formal Protocol Definition*

The SET specification version 1.0 is used for general availability and provides one of the most comprehensive descriptions of the various aspects of securing electronic credit card payment transactions over the Internet. Nevertheless, the specification will likely require changes in the future to meet specific market demands.

Similar to the iKP protocols, SET addresses the interactions between credit card holders, merchants, and acquirer banks (or acquirer gateways, respectively). Referring to the iKP terminology, the SET protocol refers to a 3KP, meaning that all parties possess a public key pair and a corresponding public key certificate. More precisely, most parties possess two public key pairs:

- A public key pair for key exchange;

- A public key pair for digital signatures.

The credit card holder and the merchant obtain their public key certificates when they register prior to transacting business. In either case, the SET protocols require the existence of a fully operable X.509 certification hierarchy. In addition to that, the protocols also address certificate revocation by either revoking credit cards or using X.509 certificate revocation lists (CRLs).

It is commonly agreed that an electronic credit card payment transaction protocol should provide the merchant only with the order information, such as the purchased items and their respective sale prices, and the acquirer only with the credit card information. In particular, the merchant should not require access to the customer's credit card information as long as the acquirer authorizes the payment transaction. Similarly, there is no general need for the acquirer to know the details of the purchased items, except in the case of some very expensive goods such as luxury cars and houses. In such a case, the acquirer may want to make very sure that the customer is able to refund the payment. This separation of available information is achieved by a simple and effective cryptographic mechanism known as a dual signature. In essence, two parts of a message are dually signed by hashing them separately, concatenating the two hash values, and digitally signing the result. One recipient gets the plaintext of the first part of the message and the hash value of the second, and the other recipient gets the hash value of the first part of the message and the plaintext of the second part. In this way, each recipient can verify the authenticity and integrity of the complete message, but can only read the plaintext of the part of the message specifically intended for him or her. The other part remains as a hash value, which conceals its actual content.

Let's assume that a credit card holder has selected some items to purchase and wants to initiate a corresponding credit card payment to the merchant. Therefore, the credit card holder constructs two sets of information:

- The order information (OI);

- The payment instructions (PI).

In short, the OI includes some information related to the items purchased, such as the goods or services and their sale prices, whereas the PI includes some information related to the credit card payment, such as the credit card number and the expiration data.

The credit card holder then generates two random session keys. He digitally envelopes the OI with the first session key and the merchant's public key exchange key, and the PI with the second session key and the acquirer's public key exchange key. In addition, he computes $h(OI)$ and $h(PI)$, and uses his private signature key to generate a dual signature for the concatenation of the two hash values $(h(OI), h(PI))$. Next, the credit card holder sends the digitally enveloped OI and PI, $h(OI)$ and $h(PI)$, as well as the dual signature to the merchant. The merchant is able to decrypt one of the digital envelopes with her private key exchange key, and retrieve the OI accordingly. She forwards the digitally enveloped PI, $h(OI)$, $h(PI)$, and the dual signature to the acquirer. The acquirer, in turn, is able to decrypt the digital envelope with his private key exchange key, and retrieve the PI accordingly. He checks with the issuer whether the payment is authorized. This communications may take place over the Banknet and doesn't need any further protection. In either case, the acquirer returns the issuer's decision about the payment authorization to the merchant, and the merchant informs the credit card holder whether she's going to accept the credit card payment.

Finally, we want to reemphasize that due to the use of dual signatures, a merchant does not learn the credit card information of her customers. For all practical purposes this is very important, since it relieves the customers from having to care about host and site security issues at the merchant' side.

13.2.4 Micropayments

An important factor in the evaluation of a payment system is the cost of the overhead involved in collecting payments compared to the actual amount of the payments. Apart from the overhead costs incurred in the extra transactions required to implement a payment scheme, there is also another set of costs that banks may charge for their services. These bank services or transaction fees may be charged when an account or credit card is accessed and may contribute a large component to the overall cost involved in implementing payment schemes. In micropayment systems, where the total payments typically do not exceed a few cents, the cost of the overhead transactions should at most be only a fraction of a cent. The design of efficient micropayment systems is still a research-grade problem. The basic idea is to replace the use of public key cryptography with keyed one-way hash functions. The main advantage of this replacement is efficiency, whereas the main disadvantage is the inability to provide non-repudiation services at all. Note that keyed one-way hash functions do not allow to compute and verify digital signatures that are essential to provide non-repudiation services. However, since micropayments typically do not exceed a few cents, the merchant may carry the risk that a customer later denies a payment.

Today available micropayment systems include Millicent from DEC [14], PayWord and MicroMint from Ron Rivest and Adi Shamir [15], CyberCoin from CyberCash, and NetBill from the Carnegie Mellon University [16,17].[8] More recently, CyberCash, Inc. has acquired the rights to use the NetBill technology from Carnegie Mellon University.

Finally, there are also some banking and other regulations pertaining to handling electronic payments. For example, who has the right to issue e-cash? Can every bank issue its own money? If so, how is fraud prevented, and who's in charge of monitoring the banking operations to protect the customers? These concerns are beyond the scope of this book. Nevertheless, they should be addressed before electronic payment systems are actually used and widely deployed on the Internet. Several parties have become active in this field, including the Group of Ten (G-10) working party on electronic money [18].

REFERENCES

[1] V. Ahuja, *Secure Commerce on the Internet*, Academic Press, Inc., Orlando, FL, 1997.

[2] P. Loshin, *Electronic Commerce: On-line Ordering and Digital Money*, Charles River Media, Inc., 1995.

[3] M. Mathiesen, *Marketing on the Internet*, Maximum Press, 1995.

[4] R. Oppliger, and J.L. Nottaris, "Online Casinos," *Proceedings of KiVS '97*, February 1997, pp. 2 – 16.

---

[8]http://www.netbill.com

[5] D. O'Mahony, M. Peirce, and H. Tewari, *Electronic Payment Systems*, Artech House, Norwood, MA, 1997.

[6] N.S. Borenstein et al., "Perils and Pitfalls of Practical Cybercommerce," *Communications of the ACM*, Vol. 39, No. 6, June 1996, pp. 36 – 44.

[7] D. Chaum, "Blind Signatures for Untraceable Payments," *Proceedings of CRYPTO '82*, August 1982, pp. 199 – 203.

[8] D. Chaum, "Security without Identification: Transaction Systems to Make Big Brother Obsolete," *Communications of the ACM*, Vol. 28, No. 10, October 1985, pp. 1030 – 1044.

[9] D. Chaum, "Achieving Electronic Privacy," *Scientific American*, August 1992, pp. 96 – 101.

[10] D. Chaum, A. Fiat, and M. Naor, "Untraceable Electronic Cash," *Proceedings of CRYPTO '88*, August 1988, pp. 319 – 327.

[11] G. Medvinsky, and B.C. Neuman, "NetCash: A Design for Practical Electronic Currency on the Internet," *Proceedings of ACM Conference on Computer and Communications Security*, November 1993.

[12] R. Oppliger, *Authentication Systems for Secure Networks*, Artech House, Norwood, MA, 1996.

[13] M. Bellare, J.A. Garay, R. Hauser, A. Herzberg, H. Krawczyk, M. Steiner, G. Tsudik, and M. Wiener, "iKP — A Family of Secure Electronic Payment Protocols," *Proceedings of USENIX Workshop on Electronic Commerce*, June 1995.

[14] S. Glassman, M. Manasse, M. Abadi, P. Gauthier, and P. Sobalvarro, "The Millicent Protocol for inexpensive electronic commerce," *Proceedings of 4th International World Wide Web Conference*, December 1995.

[15] R.L. Rivest, and A. Shamir, "PayWord and MicroMint," *RSA Laboratories' CryptoBytes*, Vol. 2, No. 1, Spring 1996, pp. 7 – 11.

[16] B. Cox, J.D. Tygar, and M. Sirbu, "NetBill Security and Transaction Protocol," *Proceedings of USENIX Workshop on Electronic Commerce*.

[17] M. Sirbu, and J.D. Tygar, "NetBill: An Internet Commerce System Optimized for Network Delivered Services," *IEEE Personal Communications*, August 1995, pp. 6 – 11.

[18] Group of Ten, *Electronic Money: Consumer protection, law enforcement, supervisory and cross border issues*, Report of the G-10 working party on electronic money, April 1997.

Chapter 14

Security Tools

In this chapter, we briefly overview some tools that administrators can use to enhance the security of hosts and networks they are responsible for. After a short introduction in Section 14.1, we focus on some example host security tools in Section 14.2 and some complementary network security tools in Section 14.3. But again, this chapter provides only a brief overview and is not intended to be comprehensive. There are many good books, mainly on UNIX and TCP/IP security, that fully cover the topic.

14.1 INTRODUCTION

The Internet security industry is growing very rapidly to embrace the issues of testing hosts and networks for known bugs and security holes. As of this writing, there is a plethora of security tools and corresponding software packages available in the marketplace. Some of these tools are provided by operating system vendors, either as part of the base operating systems or as add-ons that can be purchased separately. Examples include the Automated Security Enhancement Tool (ASET) from Sun Microsystems, as well as OpenV*Secure, OpenV*SecureMax, and OpenV*Gatekeeper from OpenVision [1]. Other tools are provided by independent developers. Many of

307

these tools are publicly available on the Internet and can be downloaded and used for free. Examples include most of the tools that are addressed in the remaining part of this chapter.

In addition to these security tools, some vendors also offer penetration testing services to help organizations determine their own vulnerabilities. These services include testing a target network for known vulnerabilities and reporting the results to the organization that runs the network. Many security consulting companies have hired former hackers to work in their penetration testing teams.

In the sections that follow, we briefly overview some host and network security tools. In short, a host security tool tries to find vulnerabilities on specific hosts, whereas a network security tool actively probes the hosts on a network to determine their relative security levels. A good analogy is to think of a host security tool as a detective you may hire to tell you if your house is secure or not, whereas a network security tool is a detective that not only tells you the security status of your house but of the neighborhood as well. The descriptions that follow are rather short in favor of the referenced material. Most of the tools are further described in [1,2]. Every organization should specify as part of its security policy what security tools should be used on a regular basis.

Most security tools in use today are aimed at the UNIX operating system, and that there is a need to address similar tools for other operating systems, most urgently for Windows NT. Security is not an absolute property, and that no system or network administrator should become complacent simply because she feels her system or network is secure. Real security comes from being vigilant and understanding real and potential vulnerabilities and threats, as well as how to monitor and combat them. Security management is an ongoing activity that does not fit into a conventional project cycle.

14.2   HOST SECURITY TOOLS

The host security tools that are briefly overviewed in this section are COPS, Tiger, the TCP Wrapper, and Tripwire. There are many other host security tools described in [2].

14.2.1   COPS

The Computerized Oracle and Password System (COPS) is a publicly and freely available host security tool for UNIX systems that was developed by Dan Farmer and Gene Spafford shortly after the Internet Worm incident back in 1988 [3].[1] The tool has been around for quite a long time and is heavily used to check the security of Internet hosts today.

COPS has a very simple architecture. Following the spirit of the UNIX operating system, the tool is mostly a collection of about a dozen stand-alone programs that each attempt to tackle a different problem area associated with securing a UNIX system. A shell script called `cops` simply invokes all (or parts) of these stand-alone programs to produce a coherent security report. Problem areas checked by COPS range from ordinary checks on file, directory, and device permissions and modes to the more esoteric areas of analyzing the contents of password and `cron` files, as well as `setuid` and `setgid` scripts.

14.2.2   Tiger

Together with the Drawbridge packet filter and the Secure RPC Authentication (SRA) Telnet replacement, the Tiger host security tool was developed by David Safford, David Hess, and Douglas Lee Schales as part of the Texas A&M University (TAMU) security package [4]. Similar to the architecture of COPS, the Tiger tool contains a set of scripts that can be used to scan a UNIX system against a database of known vulnerabilities and security problems. The tool is publicly and freely available on the Internet today.[2]

14.2.3   TCP Wrapper

The TCP Wrapper is a publicly and freely available security and access control tool for UNIX systems[3] that was developed by Wietse Venema at Eindhoven University in the Netherlands [5].[4] Instead of being started by a user to do its job, the TCP Wrapper constantly runs behind the scenes monitoring possible security breaches. It provides security in the form of logging incoming connections, even down to rejecting unwanted connections.

The TCP Wrapper consists of a collection of tiny daemon wrapper programs that take the place of the original daemon programs. With the TCP Wrapper, network administrators can easily monitor and filter incoming requests for various services that are invoked by `inetd`. They can also configure the TCP Wrapper

---

[1]ftp://ftp.cert.org/pub/tools/cops/cops.tar.Z

[2]ftp://net.tamu.edu/pub/security/TAMU/

[3]The current version 7.0 of the TCP Wrapper works with both Berkeley sockets and the Transport Layer Interface (TLI) found on UNIX System V systems.

[4]ftp://ftp.win.tue.nl/pub/security/tcp_wrappers.7.tar.Z

to deny an incoming connection based on the client's IP address or host name. The access control files to configure are /etc/hosts.allow (to allow access) and /etc/hosts.deny (to deny access).

Note that the use of the TCP Wrapper is restricted to services that are invoked through inetd, and that several companion programs can be used for other services as well. For example, a program called Potmapper can be used for RPC-based services invoked via the Portmapper service. Another example is the Securelib replacement shared library for SunOS that provides a similar functionality for services that are not invoked by inetd. Again, most of these software packages are publicly and freely available on the Internet.

14.2.4   Tripwire

In addition to the host security tools mentioned above, it is strongly recommended to use an integrity checker on a regular basis. In short, an integrity checker is a tool that can be used to determine whether stored data have been changed since their last check. To provide this functionality, the integrity checker is used to compute a checksum for each data file when the system is assumed to be correct. Later on, the checksums can be recomputed to detect file modifications.

Tripwire is the most widely used integrity checker. The tool was developed by Gene Kim and Gene Spafford at Purdue University. Again, it is publicly and freely available on the Internet for noncommercial use.[5]

14.3   NETWORK SECURITY TOOLS

Probably the best way to control network security is to periodically run security breach tests on a network, analyze the results, and take appropriate steps. However, this is not an easy task since there is no single automated method to perform security breach tests. Most network administrators have a few tricks committed to memory that they use to test network security. If such an administrator leaves an organization, so goes the bag of tricks. This is where network security tools come into play. The tools that are briefly overviewed in this section are SATAN, Pingware, the Internet Scanner, and RealSecure.

---

[5]ftp://coast.cs.purdue.edu/pub/COAST/Tripwire

14.3.1 SATAN

The Security Administrator Tool for Analyzing Networks (SATAN) is a publicly and freely available network security tool that was developed by Dan Farmer and Wietse Venema.[6] The current version of SATAN is 1.1.1 [6].

SATAN helps system and network administrators recognize and identify network-related security problems and report these problems without actually exploiting them. The tool can be used to remotely probe networks and collect information on the security holes. It also provides a description about the vulnerability and suggests approaches to actually address them. SATAN provides a flexible approach for testing by aiming the test on a single host, multiple hosts on a network, or hosts connected to the target host. The testing can expand to target various levels of hosts attached to the target host system.

There are two immediate reasons why SATAN has become the network security tool of choice for most network administrators:

- First, SATAN was designed to have a very simple and intuitive user interface. Since it is hard to create a good user interface from scratch, SATAN was designed around the use of a WWW browser to serve as a user interface. Consequently, SATAN formats its findings in hypertext markup language (HTML).

- Second, it is easy to modify, configure, and extend SATAN for specific use. All of SATAN's probes are defined in simple files that reside in a certain directory. SATAN knows how to run these probes on remote systems by using a set of rules. Extending SATAN thus boils down to creating customized probes and rules and updating the SATAN configuration file so that the new rules are tested on subsequent hosts as well. In practice, SATAN's testing capabilities can be expanded simply by adding customized PERL scripts.

SATAN is without any doubt a very useful network security tool. But, as with any other tool, the danger of abuse always exists. Therefore, the computer industry, or more specifically the network industry, was opposed to the public release of SATAN. Their rationale was that with SATAN, intruders would have yet another tool in their arsenal to break into networks. Fortunately, this has not proven to be the case. Since its public release in April 1995, SATAN has not contributed to more serious intruder break-ins. Also, the public release of SATAN has signaled a niche market for products that detect network probes like the ones generated by SATAN. Examples of such products are Gabriel and Courtney.

---

[6]http://www.fish.com

14.3.2   Pingware

Pingware is a commercial network security tool that was developed and is marketed by Bell Communications Research (Bellcore).[7] With regard to its functionality, Pingware is very similar to SATAN.

14.3.3   Internet Scanner

The Internet Scanner is yet another network security tool that was developed by Christopher William Klaus and is being marketed by Internet Security Systems, Inc. Again, the functionality of the Internet Scanner is very similar to the functionality of SATAN. The Internet Scanner runs on UNIX systems and probes each device on a particular network segment for more than 120 potential vulnerabilities.

14.3.4   RealSecure

In addition to network security tools as described above, there may also be a need for a real-time attack recognition and response system. Typically implemented in software, an attack recognition and response system continually monitors data traffic on a network, looking for known patterns of attack. When it detects an unauthorized activity, it responds automatically with predetermined actions. It may report the attack, log the event, or terminate the unauthorized activity. Typically, attack recognition and response systems operate in concert with other security mechanisms and tools.

RealSecure is a real-time attack recognition and response system that was developed and is being marketed by Internet Security Systems, Inc.

REFERENCES

[1] U.O. Pabrai, and V.K. Gurbani, *Internet & TCP/IP Network Security: Securing Protocols and Applications*, McGraw-Hill, New York, NY, 1996.

[2] S. Garfinkel, and E.H. Spafford, *Practical UNIX and Internet Security*, 2nd Edition, O'Reilly & Associates, Sebastopol, CA, 1996.

[3] D. Farmer, and E.H. Spafford, "The COPS Security Checker System," *Proceedings of USENIX Conference*, 1990, pp. 165 – 170.

[4] D.R. Safford, D.K. Hess, and D.L. Schales, "The TAMU Security Package: An ongoing response to Internet intruders in an academic environment," *Proceedings of USENIX UNIX Security Symposium*, October 1993, pp. 91 – 118.

---

[7]http://www.bellcore.com/SECURITY/pingware.html

[5] W. Venema, "TCP Wrapper: Network Monitoring, Access Control and Booby Traps," *Proceedings of USENIX UNIX Security Symposium*, September 1992, pp. 85 – 92.

[6] M. Freiss, *SATAN: Sicherheitsmängel erkennen und beheben*, O'Reilly/International Thomson Verlag, Bonn, Germany, 1997.

Chapter 15

Epilog

Every new technology offers new possibilities and related risks. This is especially true for something as potentially universal as the Internet and the national or global information infrastructure (GII) that may arise from it. Note that the GII is not a single system that will be switched on at some specified date in the future. The GII, at least in its initial shape, is here today in the form of the Internet. Like many other infrastructures, it consists of a wide range of components, including computer and communication equipments, software and applications, information resources, as well as people who develop and eventually make use of it. The Internet perceives some important roles with regard to the evolution of the GII:

- First, the Internet is a working example of an effective global network.

- Second, the technology that is currently used on the Internet may serve as a possible model for future networks.

- Third, and perhaps most important, the Internet may also serve as a living laboratory for the development and experimentation of new technologies, applications, and concepts of information sharing that will be useful if not necessary in the future.

It is generally assumed today that the creation of the GII will transform our world into a global information society, and that this transformation will be coupled with strong requirements related to safety and security [1].

The Internet is often referred to as an information superhighway. Consequently, we can use the highway analogy to better understand the various problems related to the Internet. Referring to this analogy, a communication problem is something like a pothole, a bridge failure, or a closed road. A protocol problem is something like a wrongly marked exit sign or a failure of slower traffic to stay in the proper lane. A network administration problem is something like a lack of emergency vehicle access or notification and response procedures for accidents. Finally, a host problem is something like a store proprietor along the highway leaving the doors open and the store unoccupied. The problem is not the proximity of the highway, but the carelessness of the corresponding store proprietor.

Taking this analogy one step further, it is also intersting to have a look at the way we (try to) achieve safety and security on the existing highway system. In particular, we use and deploy several technical and organizational measures to achieve safe and secure traffic:

- On the technical side, we try to build highways in a way that minimizes the risks of careless drivers being able to cause serious accidents. We also require drivers to have a license and cars to have passed a vehicle authorization test.

- On the organizational side, we have educational programs, traffic laws, and police to enforce these laws.

A similar portfolio of technical and organizational measures can be compiled to provide safety and security on an information superhighway in general, and the Internet in particular. As a matter of fact, several measures are currently under consideration for being deployed on the Internet. For example, it is always a good idea to design and develop communication protocols that minimize risks. There are also many people who demand of Internet users some basic education with regard to the proper use of the Internet. Finally, there are people who think that it is a good idea to require Internet hosts to meet some baseline security requirements. For example, the U.S. government has launched a program called "C2 by 92." This program requires the use of computer systems that are evaluated and certified at least by the C2-level of the Trusted Computer System Evaluation Criteria (TCSEC) defined in the Orange Book. The discussion is even more esoteric with regard to organizational measures. There are many educational programs for teaching proper use of the Internet. However, there are neither Internet laws nor a police force to enforce these laws. Nevertheless, there are many discussions going on that address the introduction of a multinational Internet police. It is, however, not clear at the moment what laws this Internet police would have to enforce. One of the main problems related to Internet jurisdiction is its international nature. There is no national law applicable to the Internet as a whole. Something like the international maritime law could be required for the Internet as well. This law, however, still remains to be defined.

REFERENCES

[1] *Global Information Infrastructure (GII)*, "Industry Recommendations to the G-7 Meeting in Brussels," February 25-26, 1995.

Glossary

Access The ability of a principal to use resources of an information system.

Access control The prevention of unauthorized access to resources including the prevention of their use in an unauthorized manner.

Access control list A list of principals, together with their access rights, that are authorized to have access to a resource.

Access right The right to access to a resource.

Accounting The process of measuring resource usage of a principal.

Accountability The property that ensures that the actions of a principal may be traced uniquely to this particular principal.

Application gateway An internetworking device that interconnects one network to another for a specific application. An application gateway can either work at the application or transport layer. If the gateway works at the application layer, it is usually called an application-level gateway or proxy server. If the gateway works at the transport layer, it is usually called a circuit-level gateway.

ARPANET Predecessor network of the Internet.

Attack An exploitation of a vulnerability by an intruder.

Audit trail Evidence, in documentary or other form, that enables a review of the functioning of elements of an information system.

Authentication The process of verifying the claimed identity of a principal.

Authentication context Information conveyed during a particular instance of an authentication process.

Authentication exchange A sequence of one or more messages sent for authentication.

Authentication information Information used for authentication.

Authorization The process of assigning rights, which includes the granting of access based on specific access rights.

Authorization policy A set of rules, part of an access control policy by which access by subjects to objects is granted or denied. An authorization policy may be defined in terms of access control lists, capabilities, or attributes assigned to subjects, objects, or both.

Availability The property that ensures that a resource is accessible and usable upon demand by an authorized principal.

Baseline controls Control procedures that constitute minimum good practice levels of protection.

Bastion host A computer system that is part of a firewall configuration and hosts one (or several) application gateway(s). A bastion host must be highly secure in order to resist direct attacks from the Internet.

Blowfish Secret key cryptosystem.

Bridge Internetworking device that operates at the data link layer in the OSI reference model.

Capability Data record that can serve as an identifier for a resource such that possession confers access rights for that particular resource.

Certificate Data record that provides the public key of a principal, together with some other information related to the name of the principal and the certification authority that has issued the certificate. The certificate is rendered unforgeable by appending a digital signature from a certification authority.

Certification authority Trusted third party that creates, assigns, and distributes public key certificates.

Certification path A sequence of public key certificates starting with a certificate issued by one principal's certification authority and ending with a certificate for another principal, where each certificate in the path contains the public key to check the following certificate.

Certification revocation Announcement that a private key has or may have fallen into the wrong hands and that the certificate that belongs to the corresponding public key should no longer be used.

Channel Information transfer path.

Ciphertext Data produced through the use of encipherment. The semantic content of the resulting data is not available. Encryption transforms plaintext into ciphertext.

Claimant An entity that is or represents a principal for the purposes of authentication. A claimant includes the functions necessary for engaging in authentication exchanges on behalf of a principal.

Client A process that requests and eventually obtains a network service. A client is usually acting on a specific user's behalf.

Communication compromise Result of the subversion of a communication line within a computer network or distributed system.

Communication security Field that aims to protect data that encodes information during its transmission in a computer network or distributed system.

Computer network Interconnected collection of autonomous computer systems.

Computer security Field that aims to preserve computing resources against unauthorized use and abuse, as well as to protect data that encodes information from accidental or deliberate damage, disclosure, and modification.

Confidentiality The property that ensures that confidential information is not made available or disclosed to unauthorized parties.

Cookie Anticlogging token that is used to to provide a weak form of source address identification for the parties involved in a protocol run.

COPS Host security tool.

Countermeasure A feature or function that reduces or eliminates one (or several) vulnerability(ies).

Credentials Data record that is needed to establish the claimed identity of a principal.

Cross-certifying CA Certification authority (CA) that is trusted to issue certificates for arbitrary principals and other CAs over which it may not have immediate jurisdiction.

Cryptanalysis The discipline that embodies the analysis of a cryptographic system and its inputs and outputs to derive confidential variables or sensitive data including the cleartext.

Cryptography The discipline that embodies principles, means, and the methods for the transformation of data in order to hide its information content, and prevent its undetected modification or unauthorized use. The choice of cryptographic mechanisms determines the methods used in encipherment and decipherment.

Cryptology Science of secure communications.

Daemon Program that runs in the background to perform a specific network service. Unlike other programs that execute and exit, a daemon performs its work and waits for more.

Decipherment The opposite of encipherment.

Denial of service The prevention of authorized access to resources or the delaying of time-critical operations.

DES Secret key cryptosystem (data encryption standard).

Digital signature Data appended to or a cryptographic transformation of a data unit that allows a recipient of the data unit to prove the source and integrity of the data unit and to protect against forgery, for example by the recipient (ISO terminology).

Distributed system Computer network in which the existence of multiple autonomous computer systems is transparent, and thus not necessarily visible to the user.

Dual-homed host Host with two network interfaces. Usually, the routing function is disabled on a dual-homed host.

Electronic commerce The use an open and public network, such as the Internet, to market goods and services without having to be physically present at the point of sale. The Internet may serve several purposes, including marketing, services, and sales.

Encipherment The cryptographic transformation of data to produce ciphertext.

Firewall A blockade between a privately owned and protected network (that is assumed to be secure and trusted) and another network, typically a public network or the Internet (that is assumed to be nonsecure and untrusted). The purpose of a firewall is to prevent unwanted and unauthorized communications into or out of the protected network.

Gateway Internetworking device that operates at any layer higher than the network layer in the OSI reference model. Typically, a gateway operates at the application layer.

Host Addressable entity within a computer network or distributed system. The entity is typically addressed either by its name or its network layer address.

Host compromise Result of the subversion of an individual host within a computer network or distributed system.

IDEA Secret key cryptosystem (international data encryption algorithm).

Information Knowledge communicated or received concerning a particular fact or circumstance in general, and data that can be coded for processing by a computer or similar device in computer science.

Information technology Technology that deals with information.

Initiator Principal acting in an active role, for example, requesting access.

Integrity The property that ensures that data is not altered undetected.

Integrity checker Security tool that tries to determine whether data on a particular host have changed illegitimately.

Internet Internet(work) based on the TCP/IP communications protocol suite.

Internet Scanner Network security tool.

Internet Society International nonprofit membership organization formed in 1992 to promote the use of the Internet for research and scholarly communication and collaboration.

Intranet Corporate or enterprise network that is based on the TCP/IP communications protocol suite.

ISO The International Organization for Standardization (ISO) is a nongovernmental, worldwide federation of national standards bodies established in 1947. The mission of the ISO is to promote the development of standardization and related activities in the world with a view to facilitating the international exchange of goods and services, and to developing cooperation in the spheres of intellectual, scientific, technological, and economic activity.

ITU The International Telecommunications Union (ITU) is an international organization within which governments and the private sector coordinate global telecommunications networks and services. ITU activities include the coordination, development, regulation, and standardization of telecommunications.

Kerberos An authentication and key distribution system developed at the MIT.

Key A sequence of symbols that controls the operations of encipherment and decipherment.

Key management The generation, storage, distribution, deletion, archiving, and application of keys in accordance with a specific security policy.

Key pair A set of a public and private key that belong together.

Label Security-relevant information associated with an object.

Limitation Feature that is not as general as possible.

Link Physical connection between two routers.

Man-in-the-middle attack Attack that includes interception, insertion, deletion, and modification of messages, reflecting messages back to the sender, replaying old messages, and redirecting messages.

Masquerade The unauthorized pretense by a principal to be a different principal.

Multihomed host Host with multiple network interfaces. Similar to the dual-homed host, the routing function is usually disabled on a multihomed host.

NetSP An authentication and key distribution system developed by IBM (Network Security Program).

Network security policy Document that describes an organization's network security concerns and specifies the way network security should be achieved in that organizational environment.

Nonce Fresh and unpredictable random number.

Non-repudiation The property that enables the receiver of a message to prove that the sender did in fact send the message even though the sender might later desire to deny ever having sent it.

One-way function Function that is easy to compute but hard to invert. More precisely, a function $f : X \longrightarrow Y$ is one-way if $f(x)$ is easy to compute for all $x \in X$, but it is computationally infeasible when given $y \in f(X) = Y$ to find an $x \in X$ such that $f(x) = y$.

One-way hash function One-way function $f : X \longrightarrow Y$ for which $\mid Y \mid \ll \mid X \mid$.

Open system System that conforms to open system standards.

Open system standard Standard that specifies an open system, and that allows manufacturers to build corresponding products.

OSI-RM Preeminent model for structuring and understanding communication functions in computer networks and distributed systems. The reference model for open systems interconnection (OSI-RM) was originally proposed by the ISO/IEC JTC1 in 1978.

Packet filter A multiported internetworking device that applies a set of rules to each incoming IP packet in order to decide whether it will be forwarded or dropped. IP packets are filtered based on information that is usually found in packet headers.

Password Confidential authentication information, usually composed of a string of characters.

Password guessing The process of correctly guessing the password of a legitimate user.

Pingware Network security tool.

Plaintext The input of an encryption function or the output of a decryption function. Decryption transforms ciphertext into plaintext.

Principal Human or system entity that is registered in and authenticatable to a computer network or distributed system.

Principal identifer Identifer used to uniquely identify a principal.

Private key Cryptographic key used in public key cryptography to sign and/or decrypt messages.

Process Instantiation of a program running on a particular host.

Protocol Specification of the format and the relative timing of a finite sequence of messages.

Protocol stack Selection of protocols from a protocol suite to support a particular application or class of applications.

Protocol suite Set of protocols that fit a particular network model.

Proxy server Application-specific software that runs on an application-level gateway to deal with external servers on behalf of internal clients.

Public key The key used in an asymmetric cryptosystem that is publicly available.

RC2, RC4, and RC5 Secret key cryptosystems (Rivest ciphers).

RealSecure Network security tool that represents a real-time attack recognition and response system.

Repeater Internetworking device that operates at the physical layer in the OSI reference model.

Replay attack An attack that comprises the recording and replaying of previously sent messages or parts thereof. Any constant authentication information, such as a password, a one-way hash of a password, or electronically transmitted biometric data, can be recorded and replayed.

Repudiation Denial by a principal of having participated in all or part of communications.

Router Internetworking device that operates at the network layer in the OSI reference model and the Internet layer in the Internet model.

RSA Public key cryptosystem invented by Rivest, Shamir, and Adleman.

SATAN Network security tool.

Screening router Router with packet filtering capabilities.

Secret key The key used in a symmetric cryptosystem that is shared between the communicating parties.

Secure Shell Program that can be used to securely log into a remote machine, to execute commands on that machine, or to move files from one machine to another. SSH provides some strong authentication and secure communications over insecure channels.

Secure Sockets Layer Intermediate layer between the transport and application layer that can be used to provide security support for arbitrary TCP/IP applications.

Security architecture A high-level description of the structure of a system, with security functions assigned to components within this structure.

Security association Agreement between two or more entities on the security services that will be used, and how they will be used, to communicate between themselves. A security association entity could be a host, a user, an application, or a process. A security association attribute could be a type of encryption algorithm, or a length of a key.

Security attribute A piece of security-related information that is associated to a principal in a distributed system.

Security audit An independent review and examination of system records and activities in order to test for adequacy of system controls, to ensure compliance with established policy and operational procedures, to detect breaches in security, and to recommend any indicated changes in control, policy, and procedures.

Security audit message A message generated following the occurrence of an auditable security-related event.

Security audit trail Data collected and potentially used to facilitate a security audit.

Security domain A set of machines under common administrative control, with a common security policy and security level.

Self-certified public key Public key that is certified with its corresponding private key. Root certification authorities are using self-certified public key most of the time.

Server Process that provides a network service.

Service Coherent set of abstract functionality.

Session hijacking Attack in which a connection is taken over after a legitimate user has authenticated himself or herself.

Session key A temporary key shared between two or more principals, with a limited lifetime.

SESAME An authentication and key distribution system developed as part of a European research and development project.

Software patent Patent applied to a computer program.

SPX An authentication and key distribution system designed and prototyped by DEC.

Standard A documented agreement containing technical specifications or other precise criteria to be used consistently as rules, guidelines, or definitions of characteristics to ensure that materials, products, processes, and services are fit for their purpose.

S/WAN Initiative led by RSA Data Security, Inc. to promote IPsec-based multivendor virtual private networks (VPNs) among firewall and TCP/IP vendors.

TCP/IP Entire suite of data communications protocols. The suite gets its name from two of its most important protocols, namely the transmission control protocol (TCP) and the Internet protocol (IP).

TCP Wrapper Host security tool.

TESS A toolbox set system of different but cooperating cryptographic mechanisms and functions based on the primitive of discrete exponentiation.

Threat Circumstance, condition, or event with the potential to either violate the security of a system or to cause harm to system resources.

Tiger Host security tool.

Traffic analysis The inference of information from observation of external traffic characteristics (presence, absence, amount, direction, and frequency of data traffic).

Traffic padding The generation of spurious instances of communications, spurious data units, or spurious data within data units.

Transform Specification of the details of how to apply a specific algorithm to data.

Tripwire Host security tool that represents an integrity checker.

Trusted third party A security authority or its agent, trusted by other entities with respect to security-related activities.

Tunneling Technique of encapsulating a data unit from one protocol in another, and using the facilities of the second protocol to traverse parts of the network.

User Principal who is accountable and ultimately responsible for his or her activities within a computer network or distributed system.

Verifier A principal seeking to authenticate a claimant.

Virtual private network Network that consists of a collection of hosts that have implemented protocols to securely exchange information.

Vulnerability A weakness that could be exploited by an intruder to violate a system or the information it contains.

Abbreviations and Acronyms

ACL	access control list
ACT	anti-clogging token
AES	advanced encryption standard
AFS	Andrew file system
AFT	authenticated firewall traversal
AH	authentication header
ANSI	American National Standards Institute
API	application programming interface
ARPA	Advanced Research Projects Agency
AS	authentication server
	applicability statement
ASET	Automated Security Enhancement Tool
ASN.1	abstract syntax notation 1
ATM	asynchronous transfer mode
BAN	Burrows, Abadi, and Needham
BBN	Bolt Beranek and Newman, Inc.
BCP	Best Current Practice
Bellcore	Bell Communications Research
BER	basic encoding rules
BFI	Swiss Federal Agency of Information Technology and Systems

BIND	Berkeley Internet name daemon
CA	certification authority
CAT	common authentication technology
CBC	cipher block chaining
CC	common criteria
CCI	common client interface
CCITT	Consultative Committee on International Telegraphy and Telephony (now ITU-T)
CCP	compression control protocol
CD	compact disk
	committee draft
CDP	certificate discovery protocol
CEC	Commission of the European Communities
CERT	computer emergency response team
CERT/CC	CERT coordination center
CFB	cipher feedback
CHAP	challenge-response authentication protocol
CKDS	conference key distribution system
CLI	command line interface
CLNP	connectionless network protocol
CMC	certificate management center
CMIP	common management information protocol
COPS	computerized oracle and password system
CRC	cyclic redundancy checksum
CSI	Computer Security Institute
CV	control value
DAC	discretionnary access control
DAP	directory access protocol
DARPA	Defense Advanced Research Projects Agency
DCA	Defense Communications Agency
DCE	distributed computing environment
DEC	Digital Equipment Corporation
DES	data encryption standard
DFA	differential fault analysis
DIS	draft international standard
DISA	Defense Information Systems Agency

DIT	directory information tree
DMZ	demilitarized zone
DN	distinguished name
DNS	domain name system
DNSsec	domain name system security
DoC	U.S. Department of Commerce
DoD	U.S. Department of Defense
DoS	U.S. Department of State
DOI	domain of interpretation
DOS	disk operating system
DSA	digital signature algorithm
DSS	digital signature standard
E-cash	electronic cash
ECB	electronic code book
ECBS	European Committee for Banking Standards
E-commerce	electronic commerce
ECP	encryption control protocol
EDI	electronic data interchange
EFT	electronic funds transfer
EGP	exterior gateway protocol
EIT	Enterprise Integration Technologies
E-mail	electronic mail
ESM	encrypted session manager
ESP	encapsulating security payload
ETS	Eurpean trusted third party services
EU	European Union
FAQ	frequently asked questions
FDDI	fiber distributed data interface
FIPS	Federal Information Processing Standard
FNC	Federal Networking Council
FTP	file transfer protocol
FWTK	firewall toolkit
GII	global information infrastructure
GIK	group interchange key
GISA	German Information Security Agency

GKMP	group key management protocol
GNY	Gong, Needham, and Yahalom
GOSIP	government OSI profile
GSS-API	generic security service API
GUI	graphical user interface
HP	Hewlett-Packard
HTML	hypertext markup language
HTTP	hypertext transfer protocol
IAB	Internet Architecture Board
IAM	Institute for Computer Science and Applied Mathematics
IANA	Internet Assigned Numbers Authority
IBM	International Business Machines Corporation
ICMP	Internet control message protocol
ICSI	International Computer Science Institute
IDEA	international data encryption algorithm
IDS	interdomain service
IEC	International Electrotechnical Committee
IEEE	Institute of Electrical and Electronic Engineers
IESG	Internet Engineering Steering Group
IETF	Internet Engineering Task Force
IGP	interior gateway protocol
IKMP	Internet key management protocol
iKP	Internet keyed payments protocol
IMAP	Internet message access protocol
IP	Internet protocol
IPC	interprocess communications facility
IPng	IP next generation
IPPCP	IP payload compression protocol
IPRA	Internet policy registration authority
IPsec	IP security
IPSP	IP security protocol
IPST	IP secure tunnel protocol
IRSG	Internet Research Steering Group
IRTF	Internet Research Task Force
IS	international standard
ISO	International Organization for Standardization

ISOC	Internet Society
ISODE	ISO development environment
IT	information technology
ITSEC	information technology security evaluation criteria
ITU-T	International Telecommunication Union — Telecommunication Standardization Sector
IV	initialization vector
JEPI	joint electronic payment initiative
JTC1	Joint Technical Committee 1
kbps	kilobit per second
KDC	key distribution center
KDS	key distribution server
KEA	key exchange algorithm
KEK	key encryption key
KTC	key translation center
LAN	local area network
LDAP	lightweight directory access protocol
LLC	logical link control
MAC	message authentication code
MAN	metropolitan area network
MBone	multicast backbone
MD	message digest
MDC	modification detection code
MHS	message handling system
MIB	management information base
MIC	message integrity check
MIME	multipurpose Internet mail extensions
MIT	Massachusetts Institute of Technology
MKMP	modular key management protocol
MLS	multilevel security
MOSS	MIME object security services
MTA	message transfer agent
MTS	message transfer system

NAS	network access server
NASA	National Aeronautics and Space Agency
NBS	National Bureau of Standards
NCP	network control protocol
NCSA	National Computer Security Association
NetSP	network security program
NII	national information infrastructure
NIST	National Institute of Standards and Technology
NLSP	network layer security protocol
NMS	network management station
NNTP	network news transfer protocol
NRL	U.S. Naval Research Laboratory
NSA	National Security Agency
NSF	National Science Foundation
NSP	network security policy
NTP	network time protocol

OECD	Organization for Economic Cooperation and Development
OFB	output feedback
OPIE	one-time passwords in everything
OSF	Open Software Foundation
OSI	open systems interconnection
OSI-RM	OSI reference model

PAP	password authentication protocol
PARC	Palo Alto Research Center
PC	personal computer
PCA	policy certification authority
PCT	private communication technology
PEM	privacy enhanced mail
PEP	protocol extension protocol
PFS	perfect forward secrecy
PGP	pretty good privacy
PIN	personal identification number
PKCS	public key cryptography standard
PKI	public key infrastructure
PKP	Public Key Partners
POP	post office protocol

PPP	point-to-point protocol
PSRG	Privacy and Security Research Group
PSTN	public switched telephone network
RACF	resource access control facility
RADIUS	remote authentication dial-in user service
RFC	Request For Comment
RIP	routing information protocol
ROM	read only memory
RPC	remote procedure call
RSA	Rivest, Shamir, and Adleman
RSVP	resource reservation protocol
SA	security association
SAID	secure association identifier
SATAN	security adiministrator tool for analyzing networks
SDNS	secure data network system
SDSI	simple distributed security infrastructure
SEA	security extension architecture
SEAL	screening external access link
SECSH	Secure Shell
SEPP	secure electronic payment protocol
SESAME	secure European system for applications in a multi-vendor environment
SET	secure electronic transaction
SHA	secure hash algorithm
SHS	secure hash standard
S-HTTP	secure HTTP
SKAP	shared key authentication protocol
SKIP	simple key-management for Internet protocols
SLIP	serial line IP
S/MIME	Secure MIME
SMS	service management system
SMTP	simple mail transfer protocol
SNMP	simple network management protocol
SOG-IS	senior officials group on information security
SP3	security protocol 3
SP4	security protocol 4

SPI	security parameters index
SPKI	simple public key infrastructure
SRA	secure RPC authentication
SRI	Stanford Research Institute
SSH	secure shell
	site security handbook
SSL	secure sockets layer
SSR	secure socket relay
ST	stream protocol
STD	Internet standard
STEL	secure telnet
STS	station-to-station
STT	secure transaction technology
S/WAN	secure wide area network
TACAS	terminal access controller access system
TAMU	Texas A&M University
TAN	transaction authentication number
TCB	trusted computing base
TCP	transport control protocol
TCSEC	trusted computer system evaluation criteria
TEK	token enryption key
TESS	the exponential security system
TFTP	trivial FTP
TIS	Trusted Information Systems, Inc.
TLI	transport layer interface
TLS	transport layer security
TLSP	transport layer security protocol
TOS	type of service
TS	technical specification
TTL	time to live
TTP	trusted third party
UC	University of California
UCB	University of California at Berkeley
UID	user identification
U.K.	United Kingdom
UPP	universal payment preamble

URL	uniform resource locator
U.S.	United States
UUCP	UNIX-UNIX copy protocol
VPN	virtual private network
WAIS	wide area information services
WG	working group
WWW	World Wide Web
W3C	World Wide Web Consortium

About the Author

Rolf Oppliger received his M.Sc. and Ph.D. degrees, both in computer science, from the University of Berne, Switzerland, in 1991 and 1993, respectively. After having spent one year as a postdoctoral researcher at the International Computer Science Institute (ICSI) in Berkeley, California, he joined the IT Security Group of the Swiss Federal Agency of Information Technology and Systems (BFI/SI) in September 1995.[1] Besides his professional activities at BFI/SI, he has also continued his research and teaching activities at the Universities of Berne, Lübeck, Essen, and Zürich. Since 1992, he has published several scientific papers, articles, and books mainly on security-related topics. He's an active member of the Swiss Informaticians Society (SI) and its Working Group on Security, the Association for Computing Machinery (ACM) and its Special Interest Group on Security, Audit & Control (SIGSAC), as well as the IEEE Computer Society and several of its Technical Committees. He also serves as vice-chair of IFIP TC 11/WG 4 on Network Security.

---

[1]Similar to the National Institute of Standards and Technology (NIST) in the U.S., BFI/SI has the responsibility – through standards, guidance, and technology transfer – for helping government agencies protect their information resources and applications against malicious attacks and misuse.

Index

The Artech House Computer Science Library

Software Verification and Validation: A Practitioner's Guide, Steven R. Rakitin

Successful C for Commercial UNIX Developers, Mohamed Osman

Survival in the Software Jungle, Mark Norris

UNIX Internetworking, Second Edition, Uday O. Pabrai

Wireless LAN Systems, A. Santamaría and F. J. López-Hernández

Wireless: The Revolution in Personal Telecommunications, Ira Brodsky

X Window System User's Guide, Uday O. Pabrai

For further information on these and other Artech House titles, including previously considered out-of-print books now available through our In-Print-Forever™ (IPF™) program, contact:

Artech House
685 Canton Street
Norwood, MA 02062
781-769-9750
Fax: 781-769-6334
Telex: 951-659
email: artech@artech-house.com

Artech House
Portland House, Stag Place
London SW1E 5XA England
+44 (0) 171-973-8077
Fax: +44 (0)171-630-0166
Telex: 951-659
email: artech-uk@artech-house.com

Find us on the World Wide Web at:
www.artech-house.com